Sensational Flesh

Boricua Pop: Puerto Ricans and the Latinization of American Culture
Frances Négron-Muntaner

Manning the Race: Reforming Black Men in the Jim Crow Era
Marlon Ross

In a Queer Time and Place: Transgender Bodies, Subcultural Lives
Judith Halberstam

Why I Hate Abercrombie and Fitch:
Essays on Race and Sexuality in the U.S.
Dwight A. McBride

God Hates Fags: The Rhetorics of Religious Violence
Michael Cobb

Once You Go Black: Choice, Desire, and the Black American Intellectual
Robert Reid-Pharr

The Latino Body:
Crisis Identities in American Literary and Cultural Memory
Lázaro Lima

Arranging Grief:
Sacred Time and the Body in Nineteenth-Century America
Dana Luciano

Cruising Utopia: The Then and There of Queer Futurity
José Esteban Muñoz

Another Country: Queer Anti-Urbanism
Scott Herring

Extravagant Abjection: Blackness, Power, and Sexuality in the
African American Literary Imagination
Darieck Scott

Relocations: Queer Suburban Imaginaries
Karen Tongson

Beyond the Nation: Diasporic Filipino Literature and Queer Reading
Martin Joseph Ponce

Single: Arguments for the Uncoupled
Michael Cobb

Brown Boys and Rice Queens: Spellbinding Performance in the Asias
Eng-Beng Lim

Transforming Citizenships: Transgender Articulations of the Law
Isaac West

*The Delectable Negro: Human Consumption
and Homoeroticism within US Slave Culture*
Vincent Woodard, Edited by Justin A. Joyce and Dwight A. McBride

Sexual Futures, Queer Gestures and Other Latina Longings
Juana María Rodríguez

Sensational Flesh: Race, Power, and Masochism
Amber Jamilla Musser

Sensational Flesh

Race, Power, and Masochism

Amber Jamilla Musser

NEW YORK UNIVERSITY PRESS
New York and London

NEW YORK UNIVERSITY PRESS
New York and London
www.nyupress.org

References to Internet websites (URLs) were accurate at the time of writing.
Neither the author nor New York University Press is responsible for URLs that
may have expired or changed since the manuscript was prepared.

Library of Congress Cataloging-in-Publication Data

Musser, Amber Jamilla.
Sensational flesh : race, power, and masochism / Amber Jamilla Musser.
pages cm. — (Sexual cultures)
Includes bibliographical references and index.
ISBN 978-1-4798-9181-8 (cl : alk. paper)
ISBN 978-1-4798-3249-1 (pb : alk. paper)
1. Sadomasochism 2. Sexual dominance and submission. 3. Queer theory. 4. Race.
I. Title.
HQ79.M877 2014
306.77'5—dc23

2013049749

New York University Press books are printed on acid-free paper, and their binding materials
are chosen for strength and durability. We strive to use environmentally responsible suppliers
and materials to the greatest extent possible in publishing our books.

Manufactured in the United States of America

10 9 8 7 6 5 4 3 2 1

Also available as an ebook

A book in the American Literatures Initiative (ALI), a collaborative
publishing project of NYU Press, Fordham University Press, Rutgers
University Press, Temple University Press, and the University of Virginia
Press. The Initiative is supported by The Andrew W. Mellon Foundation. For
more information, please visit www.americanliteratures.org.

THE
AMERICAN
LITERATURES
INITIATIVE

For my parents, who bought me my first leather skirt

Contents

Acknowledgments

THIS BOOK HAS had many incarnations and benefited from input of many kinds, from many people along the way. It began as a stubbornly fascinating idea that I discussed over many cups of tea with my fellow polymorphous perverts—Stephanie Clare, Niamh Duggan, Joanna Cupano Bowling, Marcie Bianco, and Irene Revell—on High Street in Oxford. It then grew into a dissertation completed in the History of Science Department at Harvard University under the guidance of Anne Harrington, Afsaneh Najmabadi, Katy Park, and Marwa Elshakry. Alongside these excellent readers and kind mentors, I found colleagues in the program for women, gender, and sexuality studies and was able to make this not-quite history of science project my own. Thanks also to Margot Minardi and Laura Murphy, who were willing to listen to my theory babble. However, the project truly gained flesh during my three wonderful years at New York University's Draper Program. Within this luminous community, I was blessed with excellent students and wonderful colleagues—John Andrews, Rebecca Colesworthy, Robert Dimit Nina Hien, Larissa Kyzer, Georgia Lowe, Theresa Macphail, Steve Moga, Robin Nagle, Ann Pellegrini, and Maia Ramnath—who offered cocktails, invaluable feedback, and friendship. Ultimately, the book was completed thanks to a generous fellowship at the Pembroke Center at Brown University. I thank my colleagues, most especially Meredith Bak, Timothy Bewes, Fannie Bialek, Nadine Boljkovac, Michelle Cho, and Debbie Weinstein for stimulating conversation and help in reorienting my thoughts on perception. Special Thanks to Washington University in St. Louis and the Program for Women, Gender, and Sexuality Studies for their intellectual and financial generosity in this project's final stages.

Throughout these years, I have also been incredibly fortunate to call Stephanie Clare, Jennifer Nash, and Nasser Zakariya dear friends. They tirelessly read multiple drafts, provided encouragement and advice, asked hard questions, and surrounded me with an abundance of care and support. I also owe a large debt of gratitude to Ankur Ghosh, Emily

Bolton, Danny Fox, Larissa Chernock, Ann Weissman, Joseph Cooper, Chitra Ramalingam, and Isaac Nakhimovksy, who are closer to family than friends. I am grateful to them for meeting my angst with adventure, laughter, sharp wit, intellect, and generosity.

I owe the largest debt of gratitude to my family, who have consistently provided me with love, support, and imagination. They have taught me that life shouldn't be taken too seriously and that celebration and gratitude are the nectar of life. Much love to Camille, John, and Thomas Musser.

NYU Press has been excellent to work with. I thank Ciara McLaughlin, Alicia Nadkarni, Tim Roberts, and Eric Zinner for their work in making all of this come to fruition. I especially thank Eric for his insight into the real stakes of this book, which were buried somewhere between words 1 and 80,000. Darieck Scott's and an anonymous reviewer's keen readings helped the manuscript gain its wings. I have also benefited enormously from Ann Pellegrini's and José Muñoz's incisive feedback, gentle shepherding of the project, and generous invitation to be part of the Sexual Cultures series. José even came up with the title this book. It is strange and sad to be writing these acknowledgments in the wake of José's untimely and unimaginable passing. I remain awestruck at their enormous generosity as scholars and friends.

Audiences at Occidental College, Bucknell University, Emory University, Brown University, Oxford University, and Washington University in St. Louis have provided thoughtful and helpful engagement with this project. Thanks to Sikkema Jenkins & Co and Kara Walker for permission to reproduce *The End of Uncle Tom and the Grand Allegorical Tableau of Eva in Heaven*. Thanks also to Luhring Augustine and Glenn Ligon for permission to reproduce *Untitled (I Feel Most Colored When I Am Thrown against a Sharp White Background)*. Portions of chapters 2, 3, 4, and 5 were developed in earlier essays: "Anti-Oedipus, Kinship, and the Subject of Affect," *Social Text* 30, no. 3 (2012): 77–95; "Reading, Writing, Masochism: The Arts of Becoming," *differences: A Journal of Feminist Cultural Studies* 23, no. 1 (2012): 131–50; and "Reading, Writing, and the Whip," *Literature and Medicine* 27, no. 2 (2009): 204–22.

1

Introduction: Theory, Flesh, Practice

MASOCHISM IS A powerful diagnostic tool. Usually understood as the desire to abdicate control in exchange for sensation—pleasure, pain, or a combination thereof—it is a site where bodies, power, and society come together in multiple ways. It can signal powerlessness, domination, or ambivalence depending on one's point of view. As such, masochism allows us to probe different ways of experiencing power. Masochism's rich analytic possibilities stem from its ability to speak across theory and practice, disciplines, and identities. Indeed, masochism's plasticity is my jumping-off point for this book. *Sensational Flesh: Race, Power, and Masochism* brings together a divergent set of debates, historical actors, and theorists under the sign of masochism to reveal the sensations that become attached to difference.

Sensations are fundamentally subjective; they are a condition of existing in a body and are present in more permutations than there are living beings. They are the embodiments of difference. Yet sensations are also the tools that we have for making sense of the world; in this way sensation has an external dimension. Sensation resides at the border of reality and consciousness. It marks the body's existence as a perceiving subject and the world's existence as an object to be perceived, and it serves as the basis for experience. Thus I suggest that *sensation* is an important critical term because it undercuts the identitarian dimensions of experience. If we conceive of experience as the narrative that consciousness imposes on a collection of sensations, sensation provides a way for us to explore corporeality without reifying identity. Here, however, an immediate question arises: If sensation is such an individual concept, how can it be useful as an analytic term? Though sensation can be fully understood individually, we can think of it as occupying certain forms because of its externality. This externality allows us to think about sensation as inhabiting particular forms with a shared (and some might say learned) assumption of the boundaries of each particular category.[1] Though the sensations that I describe in this book are more complex than this, I will use the color blue as an example of what I am talking about. While you and I may perceive the color differently, the fact that we assume that we are experiencing a shared referent allows us to imagine that the color occupies a particular form that is both multiple (we each experience it differently) and singular (we both also experience it as distinct from other colors). This structural aspect of sensation is what gives it its analytic purchase. Sensation is then both individual and impersonal; it occupies a sphere of multiplicity without being tethered to identity.

Given that masochism is about the relationship between sensation and power, it offers a distinct lens for theorizing the ways that difference is embodied. Further, masochism is compelling because it always seems to be in the midst of a critical moment. It was an important term for fin de siècle sexologists, early twentieth-century psychoanalysts, mid-twentieth-century theorists of decolonization, existential philosophers, feminists in the late 1970s and early 1980s, and queer theorists of the 1990s. Masochism means different things to different people at different times and in different disciplines. I take masochism to be a mobile entity; its meaning is always local and contingent, dependent on the speaker and his or her philosophy and worldview. What emerges from thinking about masochism this way is not a portrait of power or sexuality in the modern age but rather a continued fascination with questions of agency, subjectivity, and difference.

Sensational Flesh's reach extends from fin de siècle Austria to midcentury France and concludes in the early twenty-first-century United States. In that space, I will examine various notions of masochism at work. What begins as a literarily influenced sexual practice morphs into a universal aspect of subjectivity, a way to describe a type of relationship between self and other, a subversive mode of desubjectification or resistance to dominant forms of power, and finally a privileged mode of personhood. I have woven together these particular threads of masochism because they illuminate issues of agency, freedom, representation, and experience. Masochism is important not for its essence but because it exists as a set of relations among individuals and between individuals and structures. This mobility makes it a useful analytic tool; an understanding of what someone means by masochism lays bare concepts of race, gender, power, and subjectivity. Importantly, these issues converge on the question of what it feels like to be enmeshed in various regimes of power.

In order to really understand what is at stake in masochism, I suggest we theorize the structures of sensation underlying these performances of submission. In this way, we can attend to the question of flesh and difference. While avoiding edging toward one or several essences of masochism, these structures of sensation move us closer to theorizing embodiment and difference and what it feels like to exist in the space between agency and subjectlessness. In its quest to center the flesh, *Sensational Flesh* produces a counternarrative to that which defines masochism not as a diagnostic space but as an exceptional practice linked to subversive politics. Though I argue that masochism is always politically charged, I caution against always reading it as a subversive practice. By working around the collapse between masochism and subversion, this book explores the territory in between, the space where bodies are embedded in power.

The history of masochism's association with subversion is important, however, because it allows us to see not only why masochism has had such critical purchase but also what gets elided in that collapse—namely questions of difference. While this introduction explores masochism's link with the subversive, the remainder of the book foregrounds other sensational orbits by resurrecting other bodies and histories that are also animated by masochism. Difference and sensation come together to perform a queer of color critique.

An Exceptional Practice: Masochism, Sexuality, and Subversion

> I fancied that I was a prisoner and absolutely in a woman's power, and that this woman used her power to hurt and abuse me in every way possible. In this, whipping and blows played an important part in my fancy, and there were many other acts and situations which all expressed the condition of vassalage and subjection. I saw myself constantly kneeling before my ideal, trod upon, loaded with chains, and imprisoned. Severe punishments of all kinds were inflicted on me, to test my obedience and please my mistress. The more severely I was humiliated and abused, the more I indulged in these thoughts.[2]

These are the confessions of the "first" masochist, an anonymous man who described his sexual practices in a manuscript that he sent to Dr. Richard von Krafft-Ebing, an eminent psychiatrist in Graz, for inclusion in *Psychopathia Sexualis*, Krafft-Ebing's compendium of sexual disorders, in the hopes of enlightening the scientific community about masochism, a term that he invented as an homage to Leopold von Sacher-Masoch's *Venus in Furs*. In 1890, this man was rewarded for his efforts by becoming case 9 in the sixth edition of *Psychopathia Sexualis, Neue Forschungen auf dem Gebiet der Psychopathia Sexualis*. His inclusion reoriented Krafft-Ebing's theory of sexuality by introducing the psychiatric community to masochism and making it one of the fundamental disorders of sexual desire. Masochism, according to Krafft-Ebing, was about submission. He considered it a feminization of man's sexual *rôle*, a perversion that was characterized by passivity and subjection.[3] As a diagnostic category, masochism's "essential element" was "the feeling of subjection to the woman."[4]

I begin with this narrative not only because it marks masochism's first foray into scientific literature but because it also inaugurates its connection to the subversive. Historicizing the trajectory of reading masochism as exceptional—in the sense of "unusual" and in the sense of something that "gestures to narratives of excellence"—exposes the political potency of subversion and the assumptions and silences about bodies, race, and gender that undergird this exceptionalism.[5] This history of exceptionalism, which takes us from Krafft-Ebing through Sigmund Freud, Michel Foucault, Leo Bersani, Lee Edelman, and contemporary queer theory, allows us to begin to understand how masochism functions as an embodied form of social critique and simultaneously how its performative inversions can serve to reinforce the status quo. Further, linking subversion and exceptionalism entails discerning what is deemed subversive for these contexts and how masochism fits into that picture. This means examining different ideologies surrounding sexuality, politics, and pathology.

For Krafft-Ebing, the most compelling aspect of this man's narrative was his explicit desire to invert the conventional social order and submit to a woman. Krafft-Ebing could not understand why men would want to be powerless. The masochist's desire to invert norms and abdicate agency was not only irrational but pathological in the context of nineteenth-century Austria. Masculine submission threatened to upend established social order by placing women in positions of power. Against a backdrop of fears of feminism, lesbianism, and female empowerment, the masochist became a visible symptom of the declining state of manliness and masculinity.[6]

We see evidence of this transgression in case 9's narrative through the liberal use of the passive voice. He is "trod upon, loaded with chains, and imprisoned." Here, the passive voice marks his submission. Literally, he willingly abdicates his agency, but this maneuver is not without complication. The fantasy is enacted so as to focus on his pleasure—both voyeuristic ("I see myself") and sensational—denying agency to his mistress. In describing practices of self-annihilation, he reifies the self, and not just any self, but an agential masculine self. This is submission of a particular type. Here we begin to understand why, despite being articulated as a practice in which one becomes feminized, Krafft-Ebing's formulation of masochism produced a gap between feminization and femininity. Women, though described as passive and lacking in agency, were not usually considered masochists. The naturalization of submission in women made it difficult for psychiatrists to imagine a separate category of female masochists. Symptoms of masochism in men were classified as normal behavior in women; Krafft-Ebing writes that "in woman, an inclination to subordination to man is to a certain extent a normal manifestation."[7] This gendering made female masochism natural and hid female masochists.

Female masochists became legible to Krafft-Ebing only through a masculinization of their desires. One way of accomplishing this was by articulating a cross-gender desire. For example, case 70 in the eighth edition of *Psychopathia Sexualis* expressed her wish to be a male slave rather than a female one because "every woman can be the slave of her husband."[8] She further described herself as "otherwise proud and quite indomitable, whence it arises that I think as a man (who is by nature proud and superior)."[9] Her fantasies of transgressing the boundaries of femininity marked her desire to be whipped as masculine, which rendered her legible as a masochist. This woman's agency, expressed most markedly in her wish for its absence, was a mark of masculinity. It was the female masochist's overt sexuality, however, that was her most masculine attribute. Physicians and social theorists considered displays of autonomous female sexuality threatening for a variety of reasons. They hinted at independence from men and the potential participation in a sexual underworld of lesbianism, masturbation, and miscegenation.[10]

While Krafft-Ebing viewed this willful stance of exceptionalism as a sign of pathology and perversion, it is easy to see how this practice could be rescripted as subversive in that it flew against prevailing societal norms. Indeed, this is the type of reading practice that I argue takes place first with Freud, then with Foucault, and then with Bersani and Edelman. One of the things that I want to emphasize, however, is how focusing on this element of masochism erases the other sensations that are at work. In his original description of masochism, the author of case 9 links his practices and fantasies of subjection with *Venus in Furs'* lush tableaux of domination, providing submission with texture. By doing this, he marks masochism as a fantasy, a practice, an aesthetic category, and a physical sensation. Throughout this book, I seek to reinvigorate these other ways of reading masochism, particularly because reading it as exceptional reifies norms of whiteness and masculinity and suppresses other modes of reading power, agency, and experience.

In Freud's theoretical renegotiation of sexuality, there is no place for Krafft-Ebing's masochist. Freud's theory of sexuality, which is grounded in infantile pleasure, changes the landscape of what can be considered a perversion and why. Using pleasure as a metric and infancy as a mechanism, Freud reclassifies perversions as neuroses and cites infantile experiences, rather than degeneration, as their cause. Though this shift away from degeneration and hereditarian notions of perversion could serve to quell rampant anti-Semitism by portraying Jews (and indeed other ethnicities) as not pathological, the most radical shift in *Three Essays on the Theory of Sexuality* is the move away from the paradigm of perversion toward that of neurosis. For Freud, all perversions can be attributed to arrested infantile development; instead of being the norm, heterosexuality is the culmination of a difficult developmental process. Thinking about perversions as developmental rather than hereditary, coupled with understanding that heterosexuality is an accomplishment rather than a given, radically alters the schema of studies on sexuality. Instead of merely focusing on perversions, they give attention to the mechanism behind "normalcy." What is "dominant" is placed under the microscope, and what could be considered perverse is no longer part of a binary but one end of a spectrum; space "outside" of pathology ceases to exist. This renders attempts at marking the exceptional difficult. Furthermore, after dismissing hereditarian arguments for pathology, Freud argues that this spectrum of sexual "normalcy" is socially relative. What some societies have judged to be abnormal is prized in other societies; more importantly, some societal rules have repressed normal sexual impulses, relegating them to the unconscious and causing neurosis. In a reading that again serves to highlight the specter of complicity, Freud argues that society produces what it pathologizes.

In *Three Essays*, Freud transforms sexuality from a contained system that operates according to the binary of pervert/citizen into the ground for society and civilization. In displacing the pervert, the neurotic becomes simultaneously universal (everyone is vulnerable to repressed desires) and hidden. Despite the visibility of some symptoms, its true root remains in the unconscious. Importantly, this reorganization of pathology as invisible lays the groundwork for mapping both exceptionalism and complicity onto a number of practices; the difference between the two comes down to a matter of framing.

Freud's theoretical and methodological shift also works to reorient masochism. Rather than diagnose someone as a masochist, Freud looks for the presence or absence of masochistic desires. This difference exemplifies his modification of the concept; it is at once spatial (from external to internal), temporal (from present to past), and formal (social to instinctual). While Krafft-Ebing characterized the masochist as a performer attempting to invert social hierarchies in order to gain momentary pleasure from losing power, Freud argues that masochism is a product of polymorphous perversion and mixed-up instincts. In describing its etiology, he writes: "Ever since Jean Jacques Rousseau's *Confessions*, it has been well known to all educationalists that the painful stimulation of the skin of the buttocks is one of the erotogenic roots of the *passive* instinct of cruelty (masochism)."[11] This statement, which focuses on the experience of being beaten, differs markedly from Krafft-Ebing's analysis of Rousseau's condition, which dwells on Rousseau's desire, as a child, to be punished by his domineering schoolmistress.[12] The schoolmistress is absent in his story; the most important element is the stimulation of the buttocks. Krafft-Ebing would term this flagellation, but Freud sees this as emblematic of a deeper merging of pain and pleasure. It is not mere "nerve irritation" but symptomatic of an unconscious association of physical pain with pleasure, a type of internal confusion that leads some adults to seek punishment in order to achieve physical excitation.

Freud's use of the infant's confusion of pleasure and pain as an explanation for sadism and masochism foregrounds the work of the unconscious. Since Freud conceives of pain in opposition to pleasure, masochism is particularly aberrant in his libidinally infused schema: Why would one seek pain? Freud's only response is to imagine that the instincts are confused so that what is painful actually registers as pleasure. Eventually this problematization of pleasure grows into three distinct types of masochism: erotogenic, feminine, and moral. Freud defines erotogenic masochism as receiving pleasure from physical pain

and feminine masochism as a practice that relies on the fantasy of submission in which male actors gain pleasure due to the adoption of the
feminine role and the performance of submission.[13] Moral masochism is
an entirely new entity; it is an unconscious desire for punishment that
manifests itself clinically as almost paralyzing feelings of guilt.

Freud's reworking of masochism transforms it into a way to describe
what is essential about life, namely, negativity in the form of guilt,
shame, and a desire for death. Freud's characterization of life as unstable, chaotic, and yet driven toward stillness, a struggle that is overtly
manifest in masochism, is at odds with Krafft-Ebing's vision of a world
that preserves autonomy and social hierarchies (keeping women and
non-Germanic ethnicities at the bottom). Freud disrupts the concept
of autonomy first by positing the unconscious and then by positing an
unconscious drive toward death and pain. This replacement of order
with chaos allows masochism to be read on myriad levels. It plays both
to narratives of exceptionalism and to those of complicity and normal-
ization. By this I mean that it is at once a marginal perversion and a
necessary universality; it plays on axes of ethnicity and gender, but it is
also beyond these categories; and it challenges autonomy as much as it
negates its very possibility.

Though Foucault's use of S&M to articulate both individual freedom
and communal resistance has been empowering for queer theorists,
his insistence on difference from previous formulations of masochism
occludes the similarity between his theorization of S&M and Freud's.[14]
For both, masochism acts as a space of social critique; in Freud this
manifests as guilt and shame, while Foucault imagines the production of
new pleasures.

In *The Will to Knowledge*, Foucault famously argues that one might
be able to "counter the grips of power with the claims of bodies, pleasures, and knowledges, in their multiplicity and their possibility of
resistance."[15] Bodies and pleasures, Foucault argues, run counter to sex-
desire. By this, he suggests thinking of pleasure as something separate
from a psychoanalytic ethos of lack and the reproductive imperative that
has governed sex. Pleasure, which can be "evaluated in terms of its intensity, its specific quality, its duration, its reverberations in the body and
the soul," offers a frame for thinking about embodiment that exceeds
the disciplinary regimes that define modernity, therefore opening up
different modes of theorizing resistance and power.[16] Further, we can
situate pleasure as one of the possible outcomes of the primary mode of

resistance that Foucault articulates in the second and third volumes of *History of Sexuality*, namely, technologies of the self or asceticism. Foucault argues that asceticism lies at the base of self-formation, ethics, and freedom. For Foucault, freedom is more than resistance; it is creativity and a particular type of relationship to the self and the other that is based on exceeding and subverting the disciplinary boundaries of the body. Freedom, I argue, in this instance is about opening possibilities for thinking about corporeality.

With this in mind, we can examine Foucault's turn toward S&M, which he argues offers freedom because it is a practice in which subjects manipulate bodies and power relations in order to reconfigure their own relationships to pleasure. Foucault's understanding of S&M is historically and geographically specific. In an interview, Bob Gallagher and Alexander Wilson press Foucault to discuss the impact of his work on gay liberation movements in North America. In gay history, 1982 was a year that contained the rosy residue of gay liberation's political fervor, its ethos of sexual abandon, and the taint of anxiety related to Gay Related Immune Deficiency Disease (GRID), which would become known as AIDS after July 1982. The gay liberation movement, which was formed after the Stonewall Riots in 1969, succeeded in demedicalizing homosexuality by removing it from the *Diagnostic and Statistical Manual of Mental Disorders* in 1973; pushed for an agenda of skepticism toward psychiatry, government, and other institutions; and advocated promiscuity and the creation of a homosexual culture. In this moment before the event of AIDS, anxiety was building in American gay communities about the sudden illnesses and deaths of young men; it was not yet linked to sex or bodily fluids, but the perception of a "gay plague," a punishment for homosexuality, was in the air. These undercurrents—the promise of gay liberation, the potential peril of homosexuality, and distrust of institutions like psychiatry, government, and the nation—lend the interview and Foucault's comments on S&M a certain historicity. For example, while Foucault speaks of pleasure, experience, and sex as idyllic and without a mention of safety, the shadow of inadequate governmental response to the crisis looms—"Being homosexuals, we are in a struggle with the government."[17] Importantly, in a statement that will be echoed by later queer theorists, he is also invested in moving homosexuality away from an identity-based category toward a way of being. In response to a question regarding the needs of a gay movement, Foucault says:

What I meant was that I think what the gay movement needs now is much more the art of life than a science or scientific knowledge (or pseudoscientific knowledge) of what sexuality is. Sexuality is a part of our behavior. It's a part of our world freedom. Sexuality is something that we ourselves create—it is our own creation, and much more than the discovery of a secret side of our desires. We have to understand that with our desires, through our desires, go new forms of relationships, new forms of love, new forms of creation. Sex is not a fatality: it's a possibility for creative life. . . . We have to create a gay life. To *become*.[18]

In articulating a desire to move away from the regulation produced by sexual categories, Foucault invokes asceticism and pleasure. He seeks a move toward thinking creatively about what bodies can do and the relationships that they can form when they are unimpeded by normativity. While this interview can be read as a comment on the fear and panic surrounding GRID and the later emergence of AIDS, we can also read it as a death knell for identity politics. One does not have to be immobilized by the idea that there is one way to have sex and to be gay; rather, bodies offer multiple possibilities for creativity.

In light of this, Foucault is asked about the "enormous proliferation in the last fifteen years of male homosexual practices: the sensualization, if you like, of neglected parts of the body and the articulation of new pleasures."[19] He responds by praising S&M as innovative because it allows for an alternate formation of subjectivity by offering new possibilities (separate from modernity's sexual ethos of surveillance, discipline, and control) for being and relating to others. Foucault centers these possibilities on S&M's innovative nongenital practices of pleasure:

[S&M] is the real creation of new possibilities of pleasure, which people had no idea about previously. . . . We know very well what all those people are doing is not aggressive; they are inventing new possibilities of pleasure with strange parts of their body—through the eroticization of the body. I think it's a kind of creation, a creative enterprise which has as one of its main features what I call the desexualization of pleasure. The idea that bodily pleasure should always come from sexual pleasure as the root of *all* our possible pleasure—I think *that's* something quite wrong. These practices are insisting that we can produce pleasure with very odd things, very strange parts of our bodies, in very unusual situations, and so on.[20]

According to Foucault, the practice of S&M redraws the lines between pleasure and eroticism. *Scientia sexualis*, he argues, has privileged genitally based sexuality; S&M's mobilization of a myriad of other body parts for pleasure turns eroticism into a nongenital, creative act. Foucault locates both resistance to a reproductive imperative and freedom in these continuous possibilities of creation and pleasure. In this schema, he posits pleasure and creativity against desire and violence. Desire, he argues, is mired in a psychoanalytic concept of lack and anticipation, while pleasure is marked by a temporality of the present. S&M reorganizes the body to emphasize pleasure rather than identity or discipline; it offers tangible corporeal freedom.

Another important side of S&M emerges in this interview. Beyond thinking about it solely as a practice of the self, Foucault regards it as a type of collectivity, a subculture. As a subculture, S&M is part of dominant society, but it offers a space for difference and possibilities for resistance and freedom by illuminating forms of organization outside of the heterosexual norm. Here, we must remember that Foucault understands S&M as an emergent sexual subculture, which arose as an alternative to 1950s homophile societies as a place for gay men to assert and play with their masculinity.[21] Thinking about S&M as a subculture allows Foucault to imagine alternative kinship structures. Rather than being bound by reproduction, these men are linked through the collective practice of S&M. This subculture offers a space for difference and possibilities for resistance and freedom.

Foucault's delight in the productive potential of S&M is palpable. At various points in the interview he describes S&M as "the use of a strategic relationship as a source of pleasure (physical pleasure)," "the real creation of new possibilities of pleasure," and "the eroticization of power."[22] Underlying this sense of glee is a theory of S&M, a theory of its origins, practice, and ethics. Foucault's S&M is a practice of eroticized manipulations of power involving bodies, pleasure, and pain between men or women. His interest in the eroticization of power signals, not only admiration for a sex practice that functions outside the reproductive imperative, but also a desire to think power in a new modality, to think about not just the power of eroticism but the eroticism of power.

Throughout, Foucault posits S&M as outside: outside of history, outside of current sexual norms and practices, and outside of normative social hierarchies. Given Foucault's insistence on novelty, the pertinent question becomes—what ruptures does he envision as having taken place? Classifying S&M as new marks this practice as different from earlier iterations of masochism; it allows us to read S&M as a practice that is suspended in the present, which offers insight into Foucault's political and ethical sensibilities. By situating S&M as a sexual subculture within same-sex communities, Foucault attempts to align it with a logic that is separate from the reproductive ethos of modernity. In this utopian vision, pleasure is not genitally focused but located in every part of the body. This shift allows for a proliferation of pleasures and opens new possibilities for relations between bodies and people. In short, it creates a new ethics. In producing a narrative of emergence, however, Foucault truncates the history of S&M. He refuses to fold it into the institutional narratives of the history of sexuality and psychiatry.[23] Both of these narratives heavily rely on society's valorization of the concept of modernity, which encompasses the workings of biopower, surveillance, and individuality. Situating S&M against and outside of these regimes suggests hope for, or perhaps signals the birth of, a new episteme, an episteme that works on the level of the community and individual subjects.

Foucault allows us to ask—What does it mean to figure subversion as a bodily act when complicity is the general condition of subjectivity? In terms of Foucault's specific attachment to S&M, we might also ask what possibilities this form of corporeal subversion might offer to those whose bodies might be read differently (because of differences in race, gender, able-bodiedness, etc.) in these dynamics of power exchange. While I think these are valid questions to ask of S&M, to some degree I wonder if they are triggered less by Foucault's commitment to S&M, which he articulates in response to a query specifically about possibilities of freedom for gay men, and more by those who have read these statements as a blanket endorsement for S&M.

Masochism, Queer Theory, and Self-Annihilation

A few years after Foucault's statements on S&M, pleasure, and subversion, AIDS reached the broader American consciousness. Though not formally acknowledged by President Ronald Reagan until 1987, the disease by then had a very public face. Because it first gained notice among gay men, AIDS was linked with homosexuality. This association refocused attention to the homosexual body as potentially pathological and disease ridden while simultaneously scripting homosexual desire, especially among men, as dangerous and symptomatic of a death wish. Rather than being treated as a public health crisis, AIDS was framed as a matter of morality. AIDS, then, reoriented the public's imagination with regard to sexuality, bodies, and pleasures. In 1988, Steven Seidman described some of these shifts:

> AIDS has provided a pretext to reinsert homosexuality within a symbolic drama of pollution and purity. Conservatives have used AIDS to rehabilitate the notion of "the homosexual" as a polluted figure. AIDS is read as revealing the essence of a promiscuous homosexual desire and proof of its dangerous and subversive nature. The reverse side of this demonization of homosexuality is the purity of heterosexuality and the valorization of a monogamous, marital sexual ethic. . . . Liberal segments of the heterosexual media have, in the main, repudiated a politics aimed at the repression of homosexuality. Instead they have enlisted AIDS in their campaign to construct an image of the "respectable homosexual" and to legitimate a sexual ethic of monogamy and romance.[24]

I have quoted extensively from Seidman because his statements underscore the degree to which AIDS permitted the villainization of homosexuality in the name of public health. Seidman argues that this backlash was already under way in response to a national feeling of "social crisis and decline" spurred by "an economic recession, political legitimacy problems stemming from Watergate, military setbacks in Vietnam and Iran, and social disturbances arising from the various civil rights, protest, and liberation movements."[25] Homosexuals, Seidman writes, were seen "as a public menace, as a threat to the family, and as imperiling the national security by promoting self-centered, hedonistic, and pacifist values."[26] If, as Seidman argues, AIDS provided the pretext around which sentiments of hostility coalesced, it also provided the impetus to rearticulate an ideology that placed monogamy and marriage at the center of a national morality. Since monogamy was framed as a matter of public health (despite the scientifically problematic nature of that equation), not adhering to those norms was scripted as a matter of personal failure and societal threat. What should have been read as a failure on the part of governments was treated as a matter of individual responsibility. Though Seidman does not use the term, this shift toward the individual, the private, and the moral clearly adheres to the logic of neoliberalism. Likewise, the response of some gay men to produce an image of a "good" homosexual who is respectable because of his monogamy and therefore not a threat to the nation is one of the origin points of homonationalism.[27]

Against this focus on individual responsibility and private citizens, we have a different context for reading Foucault's discussion of bodies and pleasures. This context gives Foucault's argument that individuals can resist heteronormativity through pleasure a moral overtone of shame and disgust. According to this logic, individual pleasure is dangerous because it causes societal harm and personal destruction, and the AIDS crisis was produced not by the failures of various structures—such as health systems and governments—but by individual selfish pleasures. How, then, can we discuss individual pleasures and subversive technologies of the self when the individual rather than the structure is seen as the problem? This is the context where we truly see the emergence of masochism as exceptional and subversive because analytic attention rests on the individual as agent rather than as a component of a larger structure, as we saw with the disciplined subject or complicit psyche.

Leo Bersani begins to take up the question of the individual in his 1987 article "Is the Rectum a Grave?" The seminal article puts forth the argument that homophobia is connected to a "sacrosanct value of selfhood" that is threatened by "the self-shattering and solipsistic jouissance" of sexuality.[28] Jouissance, here, is more than pleasure; it is, following Lacan, beyond pleasure and pain and beyond identity. Bersani argues that the anality of gay male sex "advertises the risk of the sexual itself as the risk of self-dismissal, of losing sight of the self, and in so doing it proposes and dangerously represents jouissance as a model of ascesis."[29] Here and in *The Freudian Body*, Bersani presents sexual practice and pleasure as a way outside of subjectivity. In the *Freudian Body*, Bersani writes, "Sexuality would be that which is intolerable to the structured self," because, as he goes on to assert, "sexuality—at least in the mode in which it is constituted—could be thought of as a tautology for masochism."[30] It is from the vantage point of celebrating gay male sexuality as a mode of self-annihilation and exceptionalism that Bersani comes to his reading of Foucault on sadomasochism.

In *Homos*, Bersani elaborates on his statement that male homosexual desire is intimately connected to self-annihilation. Bersani draws on Foucault's comments on sadomasochism to further politicize gay male sex by arguing that S&M, "partly as a result of the demonstration [it] is said to provide of the power of the bottoms, or presumed slaves . . . [,] has helped to empower a position traditionally associated with female sexuality."[31] S&M allows Bersani to argue (against Foucault's other statements on friendship and homosexuality) that sex is where the radicality of homo-sexuality lies. For Bersani, "S/M raises, however crudely, important ques-tions about the relation between pleasure and the exercise of power, and invites (in spite of itself) a psychoanalytic study of the defeat, or at least the modulation, of power by the very pleasure inherent in its exercise."[32] Though he is drawing on Foucault, Bersani's investment in sadomasoch-ism hinges, not on its potential to create nongenital pleasure, but on its ability to connect pleasure, power, and self-annihilation. Further moving away from Foucault's understanding of S&M, Bersani writes, "The most radical function of S/M . . . lies rather in the shocking revelation that, for the sake of . . . stimulation, human beings may be willing to give up con-trol over their environment."[33] Bersani's interest in sadomasochism stems from its suggestion that the subject renounces his or her agency. The sub-ject, understood, according to the tenets of liberalism, as rational and possessing agency, wants to relinquish his mastery. Since this is his hold on the world, it is equivalent to self-annihilation. Bersani also invites us to consider sadomasochism through the lens of psychoanalysis, which fuses desire and the death drive into self-annihilation. This is in contrast to Foucault's understanding of S&M as a technology of the self. Bersani's attachment to psychoanalysis, fraught as it may be, also preserves a focus on pleasure as the ultimate aim, which problematizes Foucault's interest in S&M as a community formation even as it may lead to other consider-ations of alternate forms of relationality.

Bersani articulates a vision of sadomasochism as a form of "nonsui-cidal disappearance of the subject," arguing that the desire for masoch-ism originates in the overwhelming sensations that greet newborns and infants.[34] In turn, this understanding of masochism marks sexuality, in psychoanalytic terms, as "an aptitude for the defeat of power by plea-sure, the human subject's potential for a jouissance in which the sub-ject is momentarily undone."[35] Following this logic, Bersani argues that jouissance is "'self-shattering' in that it disrupts the ego's coherence and dissolves its boundaries."[36] Since sexuality is therefore inextricably tied to masochism and self-annihilation, Bersani argues that it can provide a way to conceive of subjectivity without identity.

Bersani is interested in sexuality and sadomasochism insofar as they offer modes of theorizing gay male subjectivity. Bersani's investment in the radicality of gay male sex in tandem with his understanding of sexuality as a masochistic, that is to say, self-shattering, enterprise leads him to argue that homosexual desire is rife with "anti-communitarian" impulses due to its "perverse" structures. In other words, he embraces the negative spin that conservatives placed on homosexuality in the wake of AIDS: that homosexuals were not interested in monogamy, becoming part of the normative community, or upholding the ideals of individuality. Bersani argues that these anticommunitarian impulses are born from the homosexual investment in sameness (homo-ness), which he marks as a mode where there is not an investment in identity or the self. Bersani writes, "New reflections on homo-ness could lead us to a salutary devalorizing of difference—or, more exactly, to a notion of difference not as a trauma to be overcome (a view that, among other things, nourishes antagonistic relations between the sexes), but rather as a nonthreatening supplement to sameness."[37] Bersani's valorization of similarity over difference pushes him toward sadomasochism as a way of creating similarity through the annihilation of the ego.[38]

There are many ways that we can read Bersani and Foucault as articulating parallel claims about pleasure producing a way to exist outside of subjectivity. Foucault describes this as a space exterior to the disciplinary formations of subjectivity, while Bersani fixates on the shattering of the ego. Bersani's use of psychoanalysis is a notable difference from Foucault, though Bersani reads Freud and Foucault as sharing a commitment to thinking pleasure outside of genital sexuality.[39]

While not necessarily calling forth the clinical tradition that Foucault takes issue with, Bersani's invocation of jouissance and self-shattering does announce the fact that he is talking about a different sort of subject and a different sort of masochism, even as the end results—pleasure and protest—are similar. While Foucault is intrigued by the possibilities of pleasure as an externality that the subject produces, Bersani is invested in the subject's depth. That is to say, his masochism is the result of unconscious relations that evoke guilt, shame, and the desire for self-annihilation. Though this destruction of the ego occurs in protest against various regimes of normativity, it is still a subject governed by an interiority and as such enriches our ability to talk about relationality, temporality, and emotion within the framework of masochism, pleasure, and exception.

Within queer theory, others have taken up Bersani's investment in the psychoanalytic subject and articulated the equation of queerness with social disruption and exceptionalism even more forcefully. "Queerness," Lee Edelman argues, "undoes the identities through which we experience ourselves as subjects, insisting on the Real of a jouissance that social reality and the futurism on which it relies have already foreclosed."[40] In *No Future: Queer Theory and the Death Drive* Edelman links the queer disruption of normative narratives to the death drive. For Edelman the death drive, as "the articulable surplus that dismantles the subject from within, . . . names what the queer, in the order of the social, is called forth to figure: the negativity opposed to every form of social viability."[41] Although Edelman does not name it this, we might, following Freud, consider this internal drive toward social death a form of masochism. In contrast to Bersani's description of self-annihilation as internal to the subject and his or her desires, Edelman describes subjects whose futures are foreclosed because of the external dictates of normativity. Instead of working toward a queer project of assimilation to reclaim those futures, he issues a call to arms: "And so what is queerest about us, queerest within us, and queerest despite us is this willingness to insist intransitively—to insist that the future stop here."[42] This explicit link between queerness and its position outside of reproductive time allows us to see that practices of self-annihilation interrupt the subject's linear temporality on both a macro and a micro scale. Queerness, then, in Edelman's reading is inextricable from the death drive, temporal suspension, and masochism.

Homosexuality, queerness, community, self-annihilation, and jouissance are not equivalent terms, yet they are all put in relation to each other against reproduction and modernity. The link between these concepts is masochism, which, I argue, is the term that creates the outside to modernity in this strain of queer theory. Masochism, these theorists argue, dislocates the subject and its claims to agency by replacing it with temporal suspension, sensation, objectification, and passivity. The links between these concepts are facilitated by a shared politics of marginality, which we might understand in keeping with Judith Butler's formation of queerness in "Critically Queer" as "never fully owned but always and only redeployed, twisted, queered from a prior usage and in the direction of urgent and expanding political purposes."[43] As a practice of self-annihilation, S&M lies outside the bounds of liberal subjectivity; it forms the outside to how the subject has traditionally been understood. Jouissance, the queer, homosexual desire, and stasis lie exterior to the folds of liberal subjectivity. In this formation of queerness, sadomasochism is presented as exceptional. Foucault, Bersani, and Edelman all take masochism to mark a privileged space outside the norm; Bersani and Edelman see it as a way to resignify an already marginalized space, while Foucault sees it as the creation of a new possibility for being.

By underlining the link between Krafft-Ebing, Freud, Foucault, Bersani, and Edelman, however, I am doing more than illustrating the way that masochism has been read as enacting a form of social critique; I am pointing to the particular formations of self that undergird these formulations of masochism. Bersani's and Edelman's use of a psychoanalytic account of masochism produces the idea of a universal subject, a subject who is most easily legible in these accounts as a gay white male. This specificity has been much criticized.[44] While Foucault's explicit desire to use S&M to distance himself from prevailing discourses of subjectivity gives us pause, several aspects of his discussion of S&M speak to certain assumptions about identity. Most importantly, Foucault imagines an equivalence of power between partners, such that he describes it as a chess game in which reversals of power are straightforward and part of the practice, rather than located external to the actors. By taking this model of community and self-formation for granted, though it is a part of a particular gay male subculture, Foucault fails to accommodate difference.

Difference occupies a complicated space within queer theory; it is often caught in the collision between theorizing subversion and rescripting agency. The clash between movements to expand rights to marginalized subjects and the desire to work outside of the disciplinary trappings of subjectivity has informed how racial and gendered difference is approached in queer studies. José Esteban Muñoz describes the failure to work with identity as an "escape or denouncement of relationality" that "distanc[es] queerness from what some theorists seem to think of as the contamination of race, gender, or other particularities that taint the purity of sexuality as a singular trope of difference. In other words, antirelational approaches to queer theory are romances of the negative, wishful thinking, and investments in deferring various dreams of difference."[45] Chandan Reddy echoes Muñoz's argument and pushes it further to argue that sexuality as a frame silences race. Sexuality, Reddy writes, "names the normative frames that organize our disciplinary and interdisciplinary inquiries into our past and into contemporary racial capitalism."[46] While sexuality has offered much as a site of analysis in queer studies, especially as a space to examine particular modes of marginalization, it tends to subordinate race and block the other avenues through which race might speak.[47] In discussing Edelman, for example, Reddy wants to historicize his hypothesis in order to open the possibility of subversion and non-normativity to spaces that are not dictated by sexuality. In this way, he seeks to point to networks of affinity between, say, the illegal alien and the queer. He writes that as normativity spreads, "the sinthomosexual [the equation of queerness with the death drive] is not absorbed but displaced onto other cultural subjects and figures. . . . Surely one meaning of the queer ought to be a figure that reveals the corrosive vitality of the death drive that coincides with the establishment of a universal social order."[48] In this reformulation, sexuality is not the only political frame at work; it does not amend race but allows its structure to exist with, sometimes intersecting, sometimes not, that of sexuality.

In short, this history of reading for exceptionalism has disavowed difference in its quest to decenter the subject. This is the omission that Muñoz and Reddy allude to. When sexuality is placed at the core of exceptionalism, other markers of difference are either forgotten or marginalized. What, however, would it mean to see masochism not as a practice of exceptionalism or subversion but as an analytic space where difference is revealed? Here, I would like to take a moment to reemphasize the political potential of masochism's plasticity. Rather than speaking exclusively to subversion, this mobility allows us to see the multiple ways that people experience power and how that shapes the terms of their embodiments. We see glimpses of those spaces throughout my readings of these theorists' concepts of masochism, but I would like to argue for another type of reading practice, empathetic reading, which would center difference, flesh, and multiplicity.

Though thinking about flesh means thinking about embodiment, it articulates a particular relationship to embodiment in that it is mediated through the social. Flesh connects bodies to the external world by emphasizing the various conditions that make bodies visible in particular ways; it is about power and difference. Historically, flesh is the province of marginalized subjects. Even before Simone de Beauvoir wrote that woman is "shut up in her flesh, her home," to equate women and racialized others with flesh was to repeat a Cartesian dualism in which the body was inferior to the mind.[49] Hortense Spillers, for example, describes the transformation of black bodies into flesh as one of the artifacts of the transatlantic slave trade. Spillers writes, "Before the 'body' there is the 'flesh,' that zero degree of social conceptualization that does not escape concealment under the brush of discourse, or the reflexes of iconography. . . . Even though the European hegemonies stole bodies . . . we regard this human and social irreparability as high crimes against the *flesh*, as the person of African females and African males registered the wounding."[50] This dismembering of bodies into flesh is part of the equation of blackness with depersonalization and nonsubjectivity. Spillers argues that this traffic in bodies (and I am using this resonance with Gayle Rubin's essay "The Traffic in Women" deliberately) marks the production of flesh as a tactic of domination. Flesh connotes objectification, woundedness, and a lack of agency. Yet dismissing it is also problematic. As Spillers notes, "The flesh is the concentration of 'ethnicity' that contemporary critical discourses neither acknowledge nor discourse away."[51] As such, flesh occupies a fraught position within studies of difference. It oscillates between being a symptom of abjection and objectification and a territory ripe for reclamation. Despite its resonance with objectification and the negation of subjectivity, flesh has become an important political space. To ignore flesh is to ignore how bodies have been made to speak of difference.

The difficulty in taking on flesh, however, stems from the fear that objectification reifies identity and essentializes subjects in particular ways. We see this ambivalence at work in feminist rhetoric that posits the body as "that which has been belied, distorted, and imagined by a masculine representational logic" while simultaneously seeking to redeem a feminine version of the flesh.[52] This cycle of abjection and resurrection does nothing to move us beyond the impasse of identity categories. The question, then, is how to think about flesh outside of identity while retaining its purchase on theorizing difference. In what follows, I propose moving to sensation as an analytic because it allows us to think about flesh, not as something static and essential, but as something that changes, something that is in motion. In this way differences become a matter of relationships rather than fixed essences unto themselves. The focus on sensation to articulate difference leads us back to masochism and toward empathetic reading.

Through synthesizing various iterations of masochism, empathetic reading allows us to read the affective and sensational currents that run through texts. Drawing on Gilles Deleuze's practice of intensive reading, empathetic reading foregrounds both the corporeality of reading and the "impersonal flows," the affects and sensations that texts produce.

This set of practices brings attention to the ways that sensation shapes representation and allows me to weave together different tapestries of masochism from different voices grouped by sensational affinity, that is to say grouped by the sensations that they arouse in the reader rather than by historical, disciplinary, or identitarian relationships. Following Claire Colebrook, this is a methodology that asks, "What are the forces of potentiality hidden in our experienced encounters?"[53]

Empathetic Reading and Embodied Knowledge

Empathetic reading is a reading practice, a critical hermeneutic, and the methodology that I use throughout the book. As a reading practice, empathetic reading highlights corporeality and the flesh. Some of this work is done by unpacking the historical structures in which each actor is embedded, but more generally it calls attention to the nonidentitarian circuits of embodied knowledge production. In this way I am taking up Elizabeth Freeman's call to "theorize S/M, to historicize its theoreticians, and, most urgently, to *theorize its historicisms*."[54] By taking the writer into account, I seek to make the flesh more visible within the process of knowledge production. In this regard, history of science and feminist theory has been useful. History of science has provided many ways to understand knowledge production as corporeal, oftentimes enlarging our concept of what counts as knowledge and who is a knowledge producer.[55] History of science's particular emphasis on the materiality of practice has allowed me to focus on the sensations that are woven into knowledge transmission, giving weight, for example, to the smell of a whip and the texture of a corset. Feminist and queer scholarship also has a rich tradition of thinking critically about knowledge production and access to knowledge. This work emphasizes the importance of thinking through class, race, gender presentation, and sexuality (among other variables) as coproductive of identities. Feminist and queer theory allows us to think about the fact that different bodies have different types of relationships to power and experience its effects differently. This, then, highlights the importance of understanding experience as complex and multiple. By bringing these related but divergent methodologies together, I hope to emphasize the place of contingency and embodiment at the heart of knowledge production. *Affect, sensation, experience,* and *multiplicity* are the key terms that I seek to emphasize in thinking about reading.

Further, as a reading practice, empathetic reading illuminates how subjectivity and power act in concert with embodied experience. These insights allow us to see *masochism* as a relational, contingent term that describes a plethora of relationships. What comes to the fore through this practice of reading is a series of unexpected sensational affinities. Theorists and practitioners speak to each other in multiple and unexpected ways. Empathetic reading also functions as a critical hermeneutic and methodology in that it highlights how we can discern the structure of sensation in various texts/performances and it works to give those sensations meaning, which in turn allows us to read difference in a sensational mode.

As a marker of difference, sensation reveals something of the underlying structure that binds assemblages together. Gilles Deleuze provides an example of the relationship between assemblages and sensation. In *Francis Bacon: The Logic of Sensation,* he describes Bacon's 1978 painting *Figure at a Washbasin,* which portrays a figure clinging to the sides of a washbasin with his head down. The figure looks as though he is about to jump into the basin, but the rest of canvas—which looks to be the interior of a bathroom—is remarkably static. In his description of the painting, Deleuze writes that "the body-figure exerts an intense motionless effort upon itself in order to escape down the blackness of the drain."[56] Further, he describes this observed desire to escape as waiting for a spasm. This set of descriptions is extremely evocative; Deleuze captures the motion and emotion of the work, yet it is unclear what this tells us about sensation. While he writes that Bacon may have been trying to approximate abjection or horror, Deleuze condenses this into a scream, which "is the operation through which the entire body escapes through the mouth. All the pressures of the body."[57] We might describe pressure as the operative sensation in this piece, then. While pressure might be an unintuitive sensation to ascribe to abjection or horror, the logic of sensation is not that which lies on the surface but that impersonal flow which provides the unity for the whole assemblage. Later in the text, Deleuze analogizes this process of finding the logic of sensation with finding its rhythm. Rhythm is "diastole-systole: the world that seizes me by closing in around me, the self that opens to the world and opens the world itself."[58] This analogy is useful because it illustrates that sensation is something internal to the assemblage that articulates a particular essence, as well as emphasizing that sensation is also something that opens onto others through numerous affective and structural connections. If the rhythm of the piece is pressure, it is something that is articulated through the combination of colors, lines, movement, and so on of the painting, but it is also something that the viewer can identify and connect with his or her concept of pressure. Through this process of connection on the level of sensation, we can start to unpack why abjection and horror—Bacon's stated goals—manifest as pressure. This, in turn, allows us to probe the ways we might connect this sensation of pressure to various experiences of these affects.

This simultaneous internality and externality of sensation is what gives it its analytic charge. Through this dimension we can articulate how sensation is connected to politics, bodies, and feelings. It is these linkages in particular that enliven our understanding of the corporeal and its analytic possibilities. By theorizing sensation we acquire a way to understand structures at a level beyond the discursive. We gain access to how these act upon bodies. Though each body reacts differently, we can read a structure as a form with multiple incarnations and many different affects. All of this is achieved without having to appeal to identity; this is about opening paths to difference.

There is, however, another dimension to using sensation as an analytic tool: namely, the fact that deciphering the structure of sensation requires a particular mode of reading that emphasizes the connections between reader and text/object/assemblage. Deleuze puts forward the methodology of intensive reading as putting the text into conversation with the rest of the reader's world: "This intensive way of reading, in contact with what's outside the book, as a flow meeting other flows, one machine among others, as a series of experiments for each reader in the midst of events that have nothing to do with books, as tearing the book into pieces, getting it to interact with other things . . . is reading with love."[59] This invocation of the readers' world not only introduces contingency and multiplicity but also invites us to examine the fleshiness, or experiential dimension, of the text. Deleuze is not concerned with the meaning of the text or the individual reader. He argues that a book "transmits something that resists coding: flows, revolutionary active lines of flight, lines of absolute decoding rather than any intellectual culture."[60] Deleuze foregrounds contingency and experience as they relate to the body (and state) of the reader. This allows him to be attentive to the flesh while not reifying any connection between experience and identity.

While empathetic reading is centrally concerned with deciphering the structures of sensation that subtend various objects/assemblages/texts, it does so by being attentive to the sensations aroused in the reader. While Deleuze's practice of intensive reading is attentive to readerly sensation, it is not actually invested in the corporeality of the reader. Here is where we part ways; empathetic reading relies on fostering a connection between the corporeality of the reader and the structures of sensation. This emphasis on readerly corporeality allows the objects/assemblages/texts to be grouped by structure of sensation, thereby allowing for promiscuous and queer groupings and underscoring the work of empathy.

Bringing readerly flesh into the production of textual affect brings to mind other work within queer theory on embodied reading. I place Carolyn Dinshaw's queer "touch across time" and Elizabeth Freeman's erotohistoriography alongside empathetic reading. Dinshaw emphasizes the production of history via "a relation across time that has an affective or an erotic component," with political and present consequences for this touching: "What importance do social, cultural, economic, and political constraints and hierarchies have if we speak so blithely of 'reenactment,' 'citation,' 'living with' a figure from the past?"[61] Freeman's vision of erotohistoriography makes more explicit the ways that history can serve the present; she argues that affective temporal relations may produce "reparative criticism" that "insist[s] that various queer social practices, especially those involving enjoyable bodily sensations, produce forms of time consciousness—even historical consciousness—that can intervene into the material damage done in the name of development, civilization, and so on."[62] While both Freeman and Dinshaw underscore the importance of the corporeal links that are forged between the reader, text, and in many cases, the past and present, empathetic reading offers a twist on that methodology by making explicit the consequences of taking *writerly* flesh into account through the juxtaposition of disciplines and histories and empathy.

I argue, therefore, that in addition to forging a relationship with the text, the reader forges a relationship with the writer of the text and his or her subject position. Further, these sensational connections between reader, text, and writer are forged through empathy and identification. In its least vexed form, empathy asks the reader to imagine his or her body in the place of another. Even as I write this I acknowledge that this logic of substitution, the literal replacement of one body for another, can be dangerous, both because it threatens to obliterate the other and because it risks "naturalizing the condition of pained embodiment."[63] Though *empathy* can be a problematic term, I use it to speak about the way that feeling through another can be a space of multiplicity rather than erasure or imperialism.[64] In this I am drawing on Elin Diamond's analysis of identification, or what she terms the slide from "I" to "we."[65] In articulating the political possibilities for identification, Diamond cites Hélène Cixous and Catherine Clément's description of reading as a form of identification: "One never reads except by identification. But what kind? When I say identification, I do not say loss of self. I become, I inhabit. I enter. Inhabiting someone at that moment I can feel myself traversed by that person's initiatives and actions."[66] While Cixous recalls Deleuze's analysis of reading as a process of becoming, she emphasizes the transformation (and augmentation) of self rather than its unmaking. This distinction is critical because it highlights how empathy can work. By preserving the integrity of the self, Cixous draws attention to the way that identification can be a form of inhabitation and multiplicity. Neither self nor other is destroyed, but a lacuna of sensations and feelings binds this hybrid of reader-text-writer. Just as Diamond posits the potential for a politics of identification, "a politics that dismantles the phenom-enological universals of transcendent subjects and objects; that places identity in an unstable and contingent relation to identification; and that works close to the nerves dividing and connecting the psychic and the social," I argue that a critical employment of empathy can produce similar effects.[67] Allowing this multiplicity into the empathetic equation shifts the focus away from understanding the other as unified and trans-parently available to us and invites us to experience affinities on a corpo-real level *with* others through sensation. This dimension of multiplicity is a space where difference can become apparent while still registering the structures of sensation that undergird the text. Empathetic reading, therefore, allows us to grapple with the position of the other while main-taining a sense of the impersonal flows that bind things together.

Masochism's Sensations and Histories

In writing the histories of masochism that form the bulk of *Sensational Flesh*, then, I aim to attend to questions of flesh and sensation. Practi-cally, this has meant paying attention to particular bounded histories in order to see how they might speak to larger questions about the multiple types of relationships that we have with power. Broadly speaking, these histories focus on power's work in the process of othering, the types of intimacy that power cultivates, the depersonalization enacted by power, and the self's tendency both toward and against cohesion. Though I have separated each structure of sensation into a different chapter, I do not meant to suggest that they do not operate in tandem or even at odds with each other. These histories are meant to enliven our thinking about masochism by presenting contradictions, various imaginaries, multiple forms of power, and diverse responses to that power. Further, I see these disparate embodiments as part of larger conversations within queer theory on antinormativity, precarity, queer of color critique, and new materialisms, though the chapters do not explicitly engage with queer theory.

The second chapter, "Specters of Domination: Patriarchy, Colonialism, and Masochism," picks up where my history of exceptionalism leaves off and analyzes masochism, not as a mode of subversion, but as a symptom of the normative. It does this, first, by exploring the relationship between masochism and white male privilege as it was articulated in feminist debates about patriarchy and lesbian sadomasochism in the United States in the early 1980s; and, second, by analyzing Frantz Fanon's meditation on colonialism as a pathology that produces white masochism.

Debates about female sexuality in the 1980s revolved around the place of patriarchy in structuring female desire. Some radical feminists argued that sexuality was being used to continue to oppress women. Overt displays of sexuality such as pornography and sadomasochism were deemed especially pernicious because of their ties to masculinity and patriarchy. If heterosexual sex was bad, pornography and sadomasochism exacerbated the power imbalance between the sexes and reinforced the notion of passive femininity. In this way, I see these arguments as heirs to a fin de siècle sexological linkage between female sexuality, deviance, and masculinity. Though these debates most directly respond to radical feminist proclamations of sexual liberation, which were initiated in part by a rejection of Freud and other nineteenth-century sexologists, their ideology echoes this historical linkage between masculinity and sexual desire.[68] Additionally, this close association between women and passivity played into cultural ideas of women as willing victims in rape, abuse, and domestic violence. The assumption that women unconsciously wanted to be abused was a contentious point of the American feminist movement.[69]

These arguments against S&M's subversive quality gain depth when juxtaposed with Fanon's analysis of masochism and colonialism. In *Black Skin, White Masks*, Fanon conceptualizes masochism as inherently white, understanding it to be part of the affective residue of racism.

Speaking from the position of the colonized, Fanon provides an analysis of the psychic tolls of being subject to domination. Thus I add a racialized dimension to this collusion between masculinity and masochism. By unpacking the ways that masochism can function to stabilize regimes of domination, this chapter resonates with recent critics of queer theory's focus on the antinormative. In her discussion of fake orgasm, Annemarie Jagose notes that critical consensus has moved toward the idea "that transformative political potential attaches by default to queer sexual practice, that is the non-normativity of queer erotic practice that makes it recognizable as political."[70] In the face of this push toward the antinormative, Jagose argues that a turn toward normativity and other configurations of sexuality might actually offer more potential for queer analysis: "Pushing against the commonsense plausibility that credits certain transgressive acts and identities with resistant potential, I am suggesting instead that the more valuable insight afforded by Foucault's call to bodies and pleasures is the recognition that one's relation to the disciplinary system of sexuality is necessarily articulated with regard to historically specific and bounded sites of contestation."[71] By looking at those who refuse to prize S&M and masochism as subversive, this chapter augments our understanding of the disciplining of sexuality. These local histories of masochism illuminate the contours (white, male) of a particular mode of freedom while expanding on what it feels like to be othered. Both Fanon and radical feminists articulate feeling dominated as part of the process of othering, a process in which voyeurism, antisociality, and detachment come together as the structure of sensations that inform these types of relationships to power. In this way, while I am speaking about two very particular case studies, they serve to show what is at stake when power is formulated as a binary: that is to say, when it is seen as something that one possesses and the other lacks.

The next chapter responds to the crushing weight of normativity by analyzing literary representations that thematize submission. "Objectification, Complicity, and Coldness: *The Story of O*'s Narratives of Femininity and Precarity," *Sensational Flesh*'s third chapter, examines literary representations of submission and femininity to articulate what complicity feels like. Using *The Story of O* as a starting point, this chapter looks at the ways that submission has been understood as a performance of femininity in the context of postwar France. I argue that *The Story of O* produces a link between femininity, objectification, and recognition through masochism by foregrounding aesthetics and other models of agency under conditions of constraint. In this way, I read *The Story of O* as one of the spaces of cruel optimism that Lauren Berlant discusses in her analysis of life under neoliberalism. Berlant writes, "In cruel optimism the subject or community turns its treasured attachments into safety-deposit objects that make it possible to bear sovereignty through its distribution, the energy of feeling relational, general, reciprocal, and accumulative. . . . In a relation of cruel optimism our activity is revealed as a vehicle for attaining a kind of passivity, as evidence of the desire to find forms in relation to which we can sustain a coasting sentience, in response to being *too* alive."[72] In her formulation of cruel optimism, Berlant connects fantasies of change, manifested as a desire for passivity and an investment in materiality, to the reality of structural powerlessness.

Though Berlant is invested in life under the slow death of neoliberalism, the performances of femininity under the heavy hand of patriarchy of the immediate postwar period and earlier offer a similar model of confined subjectivity. Ambivalence toward gender, then, is at the heart of the *Story of O.* This ambivalence, embodied by the sensation of coldness, allows us to see the ways that femininity is embedded within prevailing discourses of power. Though this has some resonance with the fear that S&M relies upon an implicitly masculine subject, I read *The Story of O* as a narrative about complicity and the conditions that attend precarity. First, I read the novel in conjunction with Simone de Beauvoir's *The Second Sex*, in which she argues that masochism is a mode of complicity with feminine objectification that impedes freedom. Next, I read Gilles Deleuze's "Coldness and Cruelty" and Sacher-Masoch's *Venus in Furs* as producing parallel narratives of female complicity with patriarchy even as they strive to describe female agency. Finally, I read *The Story of O* through Jessica Benjamin and Jean Paul Sartre to understand complicity as the compromised outcome of seeking recognition. While this narrative focuses on femininity to underscore how coldness and an attention to aesthetics mark these situations of complicity, the larger question guiding this chapter is that of complicity and precarity. I want to examine what types of power structures complicity can produce and how these reveal strategies to deal with one's overwhelming precarity. In contrast to the second chapter's emphasis on thinking about power as a matter of "us" and "them," this chapter locates relations to power on an intimate, subject-constituting level, echoing Berlant's attention to structures of fantasy and subjectivity.

The conditions that foreclose agency are the subject of the fourth chapter, "Time, Race, and Biology: Fanon, Freud, and the Labors of

Race." By looking at the affective labor of subject formation, this chapter directly engages with recent work in queer of color critique. In *Aberrations in Black*, Roderick Ferguson describes the aims of a queer of color critique as "an epistemological intervention . . . [that] denotes an interest in materiality, but refuses ideologies of transparency and reflection, ideologies that have helped to constitute Marxism, revolutionary nationalism, and liberal pluralism."[73] Queer of color analyses make visible the "manifold intersections that contradict the idea of the liberal nation-state and capital as sites of resolution, perfection, progress, and confirmation."[74] This chapter continues that project by looking at these foreclosures of agency at the level of individuals.

The chapter takes up the question of race, recognition, and the laboring body by focusing on becoming-black as a sensation of becoming-biological and of depersonalization. Through a close reading of Fanon's historically situated description of racialization during colonialism, I look at the ways that the racialized male body has been described as an ahistoric plane of suffering and explore what work the spectacle of the black body in pain does to produce narratives of black atemporality and becoming-biological in conjunction with white guilt and liberal subjectivity. This chapter examines the racial dynamics at work in the concepts of empathy and sympathy to compare the shame of racialization with the affects produced by the masochism of the liberal subject as articulated by Sigmund Freud. In linking becoming-black with what I term "stickiness," or the weightiness of being overdetermined, with ahistoricity, and with labor, I analyze the work of Glenn Ligon as illustrating how race has been understood as affective labor and as offering a model for moving beyond that space.

"Lacerated Breasts: Medicine, Autonomy, Pain," the book's fifth chapter, looks at the explicitly sadomasochistic practice of Bob Flanagan, "supermasochist" and performance artist; Audre Lorde's reflections on cancer; and Deleuze's theorizations of illness and masochism. Through an analysis of Flanagan, Lorde, and Deleuze, this chapter examines desubjectification by focusing on illness, pain, and their attendant affects. The first half of the chapter grapples with different models of producing subjective coherence in the face of illness by paralleling Flanagan's participation in S&M and Lorde's practices of memoir. The second half of the chapter investigates the potential empowerment of desubjectification as it is worked through by Deleuze and Lorde.

By foregrounding the agency of pain, we see the work of new materialisms in action. If animacy, according to Mel Chen, "helps us theorize current anxieties around the production of humanness in contemporary times," this chapter looks toward two disparate modes of decentering the subject to understand what the political costs of such a move might be.[75] In the face of his own illness, Deleuze imagines masochism as a step away from the discipline of modernity and subjectivity; it allows for the opening of new possibilities for thought and life. The most developed form of this argument is his work with Félix Guattari on the Body without Organs (BwO), which they describe as an anti-Oedipal formation of becoming. We might see this idealization of desubjectification as akin to the models of masochism as a form of exceptional subversion, but I would like to stress that sexuality, subjectivity, and agency work very differently in the BwO. I turn to Lorde's reading of the erotic as another mode of desubjectification. She writes toward a communal self, scripting agency and sexuality as affects of this plurality.

Ultimately, what is at stake in each of these debates within queer theory and each of these local histories is the relationship between subjectivity, sexuality, and agency. The final chapter of *Sensational Flesh*, "Conclusion: Making Flesh Matter," looks at the work of Kara Walker to probe the relationship between black women and the flesh. Through an exploration of how one might "play" with history, this chapter probes the limits of individual performance and agency and asks what it might mean to truly conceive of black female subjectivity. By looking at black female masochism, this chapter argues that our understandings of masochism have been shaped by particular framings of sexuality, subjectivity, and agency and asks how we might think otherwise.

Sensational Flesh tells several stories about masochism and S&M in order to explore experience and sensation as connected to theory and practice. By placing flesh and difference at the center of knowledge production and circulation, it opens alternate modes of understanding circuits of power. This work centers sensation to look at how people experience power and subordination in a variety of disciplinary situations. At its core, *Sensational Flesh* is about how difference is made material through the particular understandings of sexuality, subjectivity, and agency; and ultimately the book works to produce a new mode of thinking sexuality.

2

Specters of Domination: Patriarchy, Colonialism, and Masochism

IN HER 1979 essay "The Meaning of Our Love for Women Is What We Have Constantly to Expand," Adrienne Rich seems to have directly taken up Michel Foucault's provocation that S&M is an emergent sub-culture within the gay world. But in contrast to Foucault's discussions of creativity, eroticism, and freedom, Rich fixates on violence, power dif-ferentials, and self-destruction: "On the other hand, there is homosex-ual patriarchal culture, a culture created by homosexual men, reflecting such male stereotypes as dominance and submission as modes of rela-tionships, and the separation of sex from emotional involvement—a cul-ture tainted by profound hatred for women. The male 'gay' culture has offered lesbians the imitation role-stereotypes of 'butch' and 'femme,' 'active' and 'passive,' cruising, sado-masochism, and the violent, self-destructive world of gay bars."[1] Here, S&M is assumed to contaminate the world of lesbianism. Rich rationalizes this distance by arguing that S&M is part and parcel of patriarchy. This chapter interrogates the ide-ologies and sensational structures that allow Rich to align S&M, patri-archy, and the butch as axes of domination that work *against* lesbianism and feminism. On the one hand, Rich's comment speaks more generally to the distrust many radical feminists felt toward butches (and mascu-linity) in the 1970s and 1980s. On the other hand, the connection that Rich draws between butches and S&M speaks to the delineation of a particular sensational orbit for patriarchy.

In unpacking the sensations that attach themselves to the distance that Rich and other radical feminists want to produce between feminism and patriarchy, this chapter interrogates the specter of domination from two disparate positions—that of the butch within radical feminism and the black man within colonialism. In both of these formulations, mas-ochism is figured as a manifestation of patriarchal and colonial power. The feminist panic regarding S&M in the 1980s was explicitly about defining feminist possibilities of female sexual expression; its detractors saw lesbian S&M as a practice that invited masculinity into the bedroom.

This conflation of S&M with masculinity and domination unintention-ally reunited femininity and passivity such that S&M was read as a (con-demned) performance of patriarchy—regardless of the acts performed. These sentiments coalesced into anxiety about the butch, who was also figured as masculine and dominating. In the second half of the chapter, I turn to Frantz Fanon to show how the black man is turned into a specter of domination under colonialism. In Fanon's writing, being subjected to the sensational regime of colonialism results in feeling objectified and overexposed. By focusing on the role of masochism in Fanon's descrip-tion of the harms of colonialism and the place of S&M as a particularly pernicious axis of patriarchy for radical feminists, this chapter locates the cluster of sensations that undergird these systems of domination as having to do with distance.

S&M, Patriarchy, and the Drive toward Separation

Looking backwards, the focus on lesbian S&M within radical feminism might seem peculiar, but lesbian S&M seemed to offer a lens to study patriarchy by bringing issues of gender, agency, eroticism, and violence to the fore. In her remarks on the infamous 1982 Barnard conference on sexuality, a British feminist, Elizabeth Wilson, wrote that she found "it curious that one particular, and arguably rather marginal sexual prac-tice should have come to occupy such a key space in the discussion of sexuality."[2] Wilson went on to hypothesize that S&M "sometimes seems to have to do with sexual outlawry and the dark side of self and forbid-den desires. Perhaps feminism really has done something to lesbianism in confusing it with non-eroticized love between women, so that some lesbians have been attracted to other, more deeply 'forbidden' ways of insisting that lesbianism *is* about sex."[3] Wilson's comments highlight several axes of contention within American feminism in the early 1980s. In a moment when some feminists argued that focusing on sexuality was a symptom of the insidious nature of patriarchy and that pornography and promiscuity degraded women by reducing them to sexual objects, feminists who were invested in seeking liberation through sexuality were accused of being blind to its pernicious aspects. The arguments against lesbian S&M were the product of a set of overlapping assump-tions: that the task of feminism was to end violence against women, that S&M was about violence and patriarchy, and that sex between women had more to do with mutual respect than with eroticism. The underlying unity of these arguments against S&M was that feminism had to keep femininity (and women) safe from the incursion of patriarchy. Further, by framing patriarchy as separate from femininity and feminism, these arguments expressed their experiences of patriarchy as structured by sensations associated with distance, namely voyeurism and antisociality. This, in turn, figured lesbian S&M as a practice of domination character-ized by invasion.

Jane Gerhard describes the ideological convergence behind anti-S&M sentiment as a merging of antipornography feminism, cultural femi-nism, and lesbian separatism.[4] Though each strain of feminism had its own concerns, they overlapped in their belief in an essential feminin-ity that was separate from patriarchy. For lesbian separatists, this mani-fested itself as the idea that lesbianism was fundamentally different from and more egalitarian than heterosexuality, or, as Gerhard writes, that lesbianism seemed to offer "an emotional and political alterna-tive to heterosexuality."[5] The project of cultural feminism "celebrate[d] women's bodies as unique and their sexuality as independent of 'male models' of genital sex."[6] Antipornography feminists, on the other hand, were invested in illuminating the societal and personal harm that het-erosexuality (in its numerous patriarchal guises) produced. Antipornog-raphy feminists, Gerhard writes, "tended to conflate social power (or, in the case of women, social subordination), heterosexuality, and the unconscious in a way that paralleled theories of women's difference. The anti-pornography movement interpreted heterosexual intercourse as an expression of men's power over women and the penis as a weapon in the larger effort to keep women submissive to men and male power."[7] Taken together, these ideologies position femininity in opposition to patriar-chy. This logic mobilized feminism as a discourse that protected femi-ninity from the violence that patriarchy produced on both the structural and the individual level.

Radical feminism's move away from a politics of sexual liberation toward a woman-centered, nonheterosexual ideology is exemplified by Adrienne Rich's 1980 essay "Compulsory Heterosexuality and Lesbian Existence." Rich frames her essay as an intervention against patriarchy's insistence on heterosexuality and a plea for feminism to make space for lesbianism. She argues for a woman-centered feminism to incorporate a plethora of different types of relationships between women in order to rally against patriarchy's denigration of these homosocial bonds:

"Women's choice of women as passionate comrades, life partners, co-workers, lovers, tribe, has been crushed, invalidated, forced into hiding and disguise."[8] Throughout the essay, Rich argues that patriarchy, which manifests as domination and violence, has suppressed femininity's nurturing qualities, which are exemplified in the bond between mother and child. A particularly pernicious site of this oppression is pornography, which Rich describes as "a major public issue of our time" because it relays the message that "women are natural sexual prey to men and love it; that sexuality and violence are congruent; and that for women sex is essentially masochistic, humiliation pleasurable, physical abuse erotic. But along with this message comes another, not always recognized: that enforced submission and the use of cruelty, if played out in heterosexual pairing, is sexually 'normal,' while sensuality between women, including erotic mutuality and respect, is 'queer,' 'sick,' and either pornographic in itself or not very exciting compared with the sexuality of whips and bondage."[9] In the objections that Rich presents to pornography, we can see an essentialized image of women as nurturing and egalitarian, a characterization of heterosexuality as violent and oppressive, and a desire to remove lesbianism from the sphere of the pathological and the pornographic. Rich writes toward a space and a feminism where woman-identified women are able and encouraged to express their love. In this context we can clearly see the separate spheres assigned to femininity/feminism and patriarchy. Sensual, egalitarian femininity was contrasted with patriarchy's investment in heterosexuality, masochism, violence, and pornography.

As we see with Rich's alignment of S&M with violence, humiliation, physical abuse, and heterosexuality, feminists argued that S&M was a pernicious extension of patriarchy because it coerced women into participating in this masculine sphere of unequal power distribution through a cooptation of eroticism. In her introduction to *Against Sadomasochism*, a 1982 radical feminist analysis of S&M, Robin Ruth Linden writes:

> Throughout *Against Sadomasochism* it is argued that lesbian sado-masochism is firmly rooted in patriarchal sexual ideology, with its emphasis on the fragmentation of desire from the rest of our lives and the single-minded pursuit of gratification, sexual and otherwise. There can be no doubt that none of us is exempt from the sphere of influence of patriarchal conceptions of sexuality and intimacy. For this reason, I believe that the recent interest by some women in

sadomasochism is testimony to the profoundly alienated and objectified conceptions of erotic desire that our culture has produced and
from which lesbians and feminists are by no means exempt.[10]

Linden frames interest in S&M as a form of alienated compliance with
patriarchy that manifests itself as an individual drive toward pleasure at
the expense of feminist political progress. In this reading, S&M focuses
on the individual instead of the collective and threatens to separate
women from their sources of feminine power, thereby isolating them
from the collective projects of feminism and female empowerment.
S&M, then, is experienced as a practice that produces distance between
women and feminism *and* a practice that threatens to contaminate feminism by breaching the distance between it and patriarchy.

Voyeurism, Alienation, and Other Practices of Distancing

These logics of distance are manifest at the level of sensation. Perhaps
unsurprisingly, given the kinship between arguments against S&M and
those against pornography, one of the prevailing descriptions of patriarchy is that it is (among other things) a form of scopic violence, but
there is more to the sensation of looking than the ocular. Like arguments against S&M, feminist arguments against pornography stress
the costs of patriarchal domination for society at large and women in
particular. Radical feminists argued that the pornography industry
exploited women and that pornography itself eroticized domination
and perpetuated violence against women vis-à-vis the internalization
of patriarchy. In short, pornography, like S&M, was thought to be a
practice that, at its best, misrepresented women and female pleasure
and, at its worst, objectified and dehumanized them. In pornography,
much of this objectification happened on the level of the visual; pornography was domination via the power of looking. As an example of
this connection let us turn briefly to Andrea Dworkin's and Catharine MacKinnon's work against pornography. In their proposed antipornography ordinance, Dworkin and MacKinnon are explicit about
this equation of looking with domination, going so far as to define
pornography as "the graphic sexually explicit subordination of women
through pictures and/or words."[11] Though the US Supreme Court ultimately vetoed this ordinance, its formulation is instructive because

it encapsulates the equation of visual objectification with patriarchal violence.

While arguments against S&M were not as oriented toward representation and visuality as arguments against pornography, I argue that unpacking the sensations that characterized domination results in a similar connection between looking and S&M. Some women explicitly voiced the link between practices of S&M and feeling visually dominated. Marissa Jonel, who contributes an essay to *Against Sadomasochism*, writes about the surveillance that her former lover performed as a continuation of her submission after the end of their S&M relationship. Though Jonel is careful to draw a distinction between her abusive relationship and S&M, she is resolutely against S&M, arguing that "sm almost ruined my life."[12] Most tellingly, Jonel describes her abuse as linked, not with pain, but with surveillance. She writes, "I was a virtual prisoner in my home" and describes this incarceration as a combination of isolation and constant monitoring: "Although we didn't live together any more, my role continued as a masochist. I saw no other women and was kept under careful watch by telephone and visits from my lover."[13] Here, Jonel equates S&M with abuse and being watched with being dominated.

In many ways, Jonel voices the explicit connection between domination and voyeurism that has already been described at length by philosophers like Michel Foucault, Louis Althusser, and Jean Paul Sartre. In *The Birth of the Clinic* Foucault discusses the objectifying and dehumanizing medical gaze, which separates doctor from patient, and in *Discipline and Punish* he describes the panopticon as a model for the internalization of the gaze.[14] Through Foucault we gain insight into the ways that subjects are formed through power; more precisely, we have been given tools to understand how power and vision collude to work on bodies. While these examples from Foucault illustrate the workings of power on a macro level, it is clear that power and the gaze also operate on the scale of the individual. We see this tangibly in Althusser's famous description of being hailed by the police in "Ideology and the Ideological State Apparatus," but we can also turn to phenomenology, which has its own way of illuminating the work of visuality in constructing the subject. While Sartre argues in *Being and Nothingness* that looking objectifies the other, he also argues that the process of looking is what helps to constitute one's subjectivity. Sartre is ultimately most interested in exploring what it means to oscillate between seeing and being

seen, being-for-others and being-for-itself, but his theorization of looking as central to producing subjectivity is important because it links the
gaze with autonomy and individuality. The gaze establishes the difference between the self and other by figuring their relationship in terms
of distance. Taken together, Foucault and Sartre show us that vision is a
complex sense that cannot be restricted to the ocular; looking is an act
that produces objects, consolidates subjectivity, and enacts domination.
Thinking about the way power and vision commingle through distance
is central, I argue, to understanding the sensation of domination.[15]

In this regard, discussions of S&M also move beyond the strictly
visual toward articulating an affective link between power and distance.
In order to show the collision between distance and domination, I turn
to an essay by Elizabeth Harris that is also in *Against Sadomasochism*.
Harris's essay links sadomasochism with estrangement and alienation.
After an S&M scene ends in her tears, she writes, "I had not felt such
anguish in a long time and wanted to cry or scream it out. . . . When I
finally stopped crying I felt estranged from my partner and our relationship and sadomasochism."[16] This estrangement, which she experiences
as anguish, resonates with the distance radical feminists imagine is created within women when they participate in S&M. If S&M is a practice of patriarchy, it is a betrayal of, or distancing from, one's essential
femininity. Here, I am reading alienation and estrangement as psychic
modes that coalesce around the sensation of distance. Though alienation
and estrangement are feelings that arise from a disruption in consciousness, articulating the ways that they conjure up the physical sensation
of distance speaks to the interconnectedness of affect and structures of
sensation.

Loosely following Foucault, Sartre, and Althusser, I argue that we
consider this discussion of distance, both psychic and literal, as another
permutation of voyeurism. What does it mean to theorize voyeurism
as a form of distance? Film theory, which has been invested in unpacking spectatorship, among other things, is useful in this regard. In "The
Imaginary Signifier," Christian Metz brings together psychoanalysis and
semiology to bear on film. He argues that film produces an all-perceiving
subject; the spectator sees everything except for the "one thing only that
is never reflected in it: the spectator's own body. In a certain emplace-
ment, the mirror suddenly becomes clear glass."[17] Metz's description of
the position of the spectator is explicit about the power that the spectator feels through looking. He labels the spectator "all-perceiving" and

"all-powerful" because his or her absence from the screen allows for this fantasy of domination over that which he or she sees.[18] In short, the cinematic spectator is a voyeur—something that Metz characterizes not by domination but by distance. He writes that "the voyeur is very careful to maintain a gulf, an empty space, between the object and the eye, the object and his own body: his look fastens the object at the right distance, as with those cinema spectators who take care to avoid being too close or too far from the screen."[19] In fact, Metz argues that cinema itself is predicated on the power imbalance of this simultaneous absence and presence; he terms this a technique of the imaginary, which "provides unaccustomed perceptual wealth, but unusually profoundly stamped with unreality."[20]

Metz's analysis of voyeurism as a sensation having to do with distance and power offers a way to characterize these critiques of S&M as having to do with a logic of distance and voyeurism. Voyeurism emphasizes the power imbalance between parties; the voyeur invades the scene and responds to it without requiring the consent of the watched. This formulation resonates with a radical feminist analysis of S&M as a practice without the possibility of consent that adheres to the logic of patriarchy. S&M is pernicious because it produces alienation and antisociality. When applied to a theorization of patriarchy and domination, this conglomeration of sensations—voyeurism, alienation, and antisociality—illuminates the fact that patriarchy can be read as a form of domination that relies on controlling the distance between parties.

We can see some of the effects of that distance and antisociality at work in Laura Mulvey's analysis of phallocentrism at work in narrative cinema. Not only are women not given a space as spectators, but their presence as objects to be looked at is seen as a distraction from the plot—even in the imaginary realm, women function only as decoration. In her 1973 essay "Visual Pleasure and Narrative Cinema," Mulvey argues that woman's presence on screen correlates to her place in patriarchal society. She writes, "Woman then stands in patriarchal culture as signifier for the male other, bound by a symbolic order in which man can live out his phantasies and obsessions through linguistic command by imposing them on the silent image of woman still tied to her place as bearer of meaning, not maker of meaning."[21] In Mulvey's reading, the scopophilic impulse objectifies woman because she *represents* rather than produces meaning. Not only is the gaze in this situation predicated on distance, but it creates and perpetuates that distance. It produces women as objects who are not to be engaged, thus reinforcing their status as nonagential beings. And in this way it also reproduces a social separation according to gender. Taken together, this articulates the logic of patriarchy that radical feminism rallied against. Through this example we see clearly that the sensation of domination is dependent on an economy of distance, which foregrounds the practices associated with maintaining distance (in this case looking) and the feelings associated with that, described here as alienation and isolation. The structural coherence that emerges from this examination of patriarchy rewrites practices of lesbian S&M as having to do with antisociality and inequality rather than sexuality or violence. In terms of theorizing radical feminist responses to S&M, we become able to recognize their critiques of S&M as occurring on a deeper level than a kinship to patriarchy: we can see how their understanding of the assemblage of S&M was related to distance, scopophilia, and antisociality, all of which were in opposition to the sensations that they wanted to correlate with feminism, namely eroticism and mutuality.

The Politics of Penetration: Analyzing Debates about the Butch and the Dildo

If feminism's task was to enable female sexuality to flourish apart from patriarchy and its ethos of domination, lesbian S&M was a symptom of patriarchal contamination and linked with masculinity. In opposition to radical feminism's focus on woman-centeredness, lesbian S&M was likened to abuse, and its practitioners were described as adhering to traditional gender norms where masculinity and butchness were linked with domination and femininity was linked with passivity.[22] Because lesbian S&M was seen as emulating patriarchal, masculine forms of domination through the eroticization of power, some radical feminists perceived it as reinscribing the notion of women as passive victims. Choosing submission or choosing to dominate was a sign of false consciousness, a sign that one was under the thrall of patriarchy. Sadomasochistic acts were lumped with rape and domestic abuse as a form of violence against women.[23] Domination was masculinized while submission was coded as feminine. In a retrospective analysis of these debates, Judith Butler highlights the problematic nature of this gendering: "[These positions] offer an analysis of sexual relations as structured by relations of coerced subordination, and argue that acts of sexual domination constitute the social meaning of being 'a man,' as the condition of coerced subordination constitutes the social meaning of being a 'woman.' Such a rigid determinism assimilates any account of sexuality to rigid and determining positions of domination and subordination, and assimilates those positions to the social gender of man and woman."[24] In figuring S&M as a patriarchal practice, radical feminists reentrenched gender norms surrounding masculinity and femininity. Femininity was associated with community, love, and mutuality, while masculinity was equated with domination, violence, and selfishness. While the practice of S&M was linked to masculine practices of patriarchy, the individual embodiment of these fears about masculinity and patriarchal contamination was the butch and the micropolitics of penetration. Radical feminists mapped anxieties about domination, masculinity, and a politics of distance onto her body. Though the butch was only tenuously linked with S&M, figurations of her provide a further window into the politics surrounding radical feminist critiques of patriarchy and the sensations that were connected to patriarchal domination.

The hostility toward butches that Rich voices at the beginning of this chapter echoes the overriding sentiments of radical feminism of the 1970s and 1980s. Woman-centered lesbianism and feminism demonized the iconic lesbian butch/femme couples of the 1950s and 1960s as imitative of heterosexuality.[25] Though both the butch and the femme were criticized for internalizing patriarchy, the butch, the more visible of the pair, carried the additional burden of masculinity, which was even further proof of patriarchal compliance. In part, this disdain for masculinity can be attributed to historical causes. Sexological literature of the early twentieth century labeled lesbians inverts, which is to say their desire for women was characterized as masculine and they were described as possessing masculine physical traits and a masculine sexual appetite.[26] This masculinization of women's desire for women in terms of both character and quality (aggressive instead of the prevailing paradigm of feminine passivity) pathologized both female desire and lesbianism. As radical feminists worked to reorient female sexuality and lesbianism on their own terms, they emphasized the femininity of female desire and read any conjunction of women and masculinity as a symptom of patriarchal oppression.

While patriarchy and domination are characterized by a nonengaged distance, the butch provides a different analytic metric for understanding

the traversing of difference, namely, she speaks to the political implications of penetration, which radical feminism coded as a sexual practice
of domination.[27] In her most feared specter, as masculine and dominating, the butch wields the phallus or dildo. While submission had its own
problematic dynamics, the notion of a woman who wanted to dominate,
or worse, penetrate other women was particularly pernicious. Heather
Findlay describes this convergence in her analysis of the dildo wars:
"Some lesbians have debunked the dildo and its notorious cousin the
strap-on, calling them 'male-identified.' . . . Distaste for dildos, especially
'lifelike' ones, is based on the conviction that a dildo represents a penis
and is therefore incompatible with 'woman-identified' sexuality. . . . The
critique of the dildo . . . has developed in tandem with radical feminist
attacks on butch-femme and sadomasochism . . . [, which] hold that
both practices reproduce a 'heteropatriarchy' based on masculine and
feminine sex roles." [28] In Findlay's description of the tensions at work in
these debates, we explicitly see the collapse between S&M, the butch,
patriarchy, and the dildo. In addition to symbolizing the desire to penetrate, the dildo's status as nonanatomical phallus represented a willful
and gleeful adoption of dictates of masculinity.

By suggesting penetration (even in fantastical form), a woman with a
dildo threatened radical feminist modes of sexual intercourse. The dildo
marked a departure from a feminist ideology that imagined female sexuality as outside of patriarchy and lesbian sex as explicitly nonpenetrative.
Colleen Lamos neatly summarizes the heteronormative assumptions of
this position as exemplified in the writings of Marilyn Frye: "As recently
as 1990 Marilyn Frye announced, remarkably, that '"sex" is an inappropriate term for what lesbians do': Lesbians don't 'have sex,' because that is
a 'phallic concept' implying coitus."[29] Some of these analyses of lesbianism went so far as to displace individual female pleasure and desire with
the generalizable desire for community among women—Lamos notes
that according to Nett Hart "Lesbian desire is not directed at individuals
but 'is for the community formed by the self/mutual love of women.'"[30]
Bringing these threads together, we can see that the dildo represents the
possibility of individual sexual pleasure in penetration, which operates
in tension with the feminist ethos of collectivity; Lamos argues that the
dildo "rejects traditional feminist claims to a moral superiority based
upon supposed female innocence, powerlessness, and purity from which
has issued a politics of resentment and vengeance."[31] Penetration, like
S&M, was marked both as antisocial and as an invasion of female space.

In order to fully illustrate how distance operates as a sensational undercurrent for these feminist debates on S&M, butches, and penetration, I offer a brief glimpse at Lynda Hart's and Judith Butler's resignification of the dildo in the 1990s. Since they are writing from a frame that is not invested in keeping masculinity and femininity separate or reinforcing the link between femininity and feminism, they read the dildo as a form of subversive citationality that calls attention to the phallus's lack rather than reading it as a symptom of patriarchal imitation.

For radical feminists, the falseness of the phallus was due to its conflict with an essential notion of femaleness. It was problematic because it bridged the gap between masculinity and femininity. In her analysis of the feminist problem with the lesbian phallus, Butler writes that "the phallus signifies the persistence of the 'straight mind,' a masculine or heterosexist identification and, hence the defilement of betrayal of lesbian specificity; secondly, the phallus enters lesbian sexual discourse in the mode of a transgressive 'confession'; . . . it's not the real thing (the lesbian thing) or it's not the real thing (the straight thing)."[32] In other words, the phallus is read as a violation of lesbian modes of sexual intercourse because it is perceived as a desire for the masculine (against the idea that lesbianism should be about the protection of a female space) and because it is perceived as an admission that heterosexual vaginal intercourse is preferred to other modes of intercourse. In her rereading of the phallus, Butler turns to psychoanalysis to argue that the phallus need not be linked to masculinity and can actually be read as an open signifier rather than specifically tied to masculinity or male genitalia. Butler then reclaims the phallus for lesbian sexuality, extending its parameters beyond the dildo and articulating, in psychoanalytic terms, the work that the lesbian phallus does: "Consider that 'having' the phallus can be symbolized by an arm, a tongue, a hand (or two), a knee, a thigh, a pelvic bone, an array of purposefully instrumentalized body-like things. And that this 'having' exists in relation to a 'being the phallus' which is both part of its own signifying effect (the phallic lesbian is potentially castrating) and that which it encounters in the woman who is desired (as the one who, offering or withdrawing the specular guarantee, wields the power to castrate)."[33] A woman wielding the phallus is subversive; she threatens the notions of a subservient woman, and she threatens traditional masculinity by illuminating its redundancy (she, too, can castrate). As we can see, Butler's rescripting of the dildo moves away from a logic of difference that situates masculinity and femininity as separate spheres. It is precisely the bridging of distance between masculine and feminine that allows for this subversion.

Hart argues that the link between the dildo and lesbian S&M allows us to read lesbian S&M as social critique through its reliance on mimicry, specifically phallic mimicry. By illuminating the elements of performance at work in sexuality, lesbian S&M challenges notions of the real: "If we think of the erotic interplay of lesbian s/m as resignifications that are no doubt enabled by certain heterosexual or homosexual models but at the same time dissonant displacements of them, we might move toward a better understanding of their erotic dynamics and better grasp the political and ethical controversies they have raised."[34] In crude psychoanalytic terms, Hart argues that masochism can be read as a delicate dance with power (the phallus): male masochism is a relinquishing of the phallus, and female masochism is an impossibility because the woman has nothing to give up.[35] Even as the purposeful denial of equating power with the phallus can be read as an act of self-annihilation, in many ways it serves to reinforce the connection between masculinity, power, and domination. But, as Hart points out, "To a certain extent, the controversy about whether s/m is 'real' or performed is naïve, since we are already in representation even when we are enacting our seemingly more private fantasies."[36] While the link that Hart makes between the subversive nature of the lesbian phallus and the social critique articulated by lesbian S&M appears to parallel connections that radical feminists made between the patriarchy, the politics of penetration, and S&M, Hart is not invested in reifying separation. Her analysis, like Butler's, emphasizes the impossible line between fantasy and reality as it is embodied in the phallus and S&M. The question of maintaining separate masculine and feminine spheres and the underlying importance of sensing distance either as isolation or as contamination are not at issue.

Radical feminists' collapsing of gender roles, sexual practices, and power dynamics produced a structure where domination, masculinity, and patriarchy were aligned with distance, voyeurism, and antisociality. While S&M and penetration offer glimpses of what happens on an individual level when patriarchy sullies the sphere of feminism and femininity, S&M also provides a template for understanding domination on a macro level using the same logic of sensation. In making their arguments about these connections, radical feminists linked both contemporary and historical patterns of global domination such as slavery, colonialism, and the Holocaust to S&M because these, too, were manifestations of a patriarchal relationship to power and distance. This scalar analogy had wide-reaching effects for radical feminism—it increased the stakes for taking S&M seriously as a danger to society and opened the conversation to race in an explicit fashion.

By connecting colonialism and fascism to S&M, radical feminists made a case that S&M was especially dangerous because, in contrast to submission on the part of the colonized or otherwise dominated, it required choice. Robin Ruth Linden writes: "For women and other oppressed peoples, the historical and pragmatic significance of oppression is that it is always a received rather than chosen condition. Indeed, it is difficult to imagine even having the *option* to embrace the conditions of oppression."[37] Sarah Lucia Hoagland elaborates on the dangers of linking liberation with willful submission:

> Aside from entrapment in patriarchal logic, the idea that trusting means submitting suggests we have not yet taken ourselves seriously enough. I do not find Blacks as a political group claiming that engaging in masochism (or sadism) is consistent with Black liberation. Nor do I find Jews as a group claiming the political right or necessity of engaging in masochism (or sadism) in the name of Jewish liberation. I do not mean by this that no blacks or Jews engage in sado-masochism. My point is that I see no one attempting to argue from within those political communities that submitting to (or dominating) another in the community is consistent with liberation.[38]

By asking how liberation could look like submission, Hoagland highlights the difficulty that feminists encountered theorizing consent within patriarchy. Robin Morgan historicizes S&M by analogizing its harm to women with slavery and the Holocaust: "Here we can encounter the virulently anti-feminist thought of such Freudians as Marie Robinson, whose book *The Power of Sexual Surrender* is to women what a tome called *Why you Know you Love it on the Plantation* would be to Blacks or one titled *How to be Happy in Line to the Showers* would be to Jews."[39] Her argument that S&M represented a form of subjugation similar to slavery or genocide implied that individual acts of S&M constituted a continuation of these painful legacies.

In these narratives, we can see that enlarging the scope of anti-S&M feminism from protecting femininity from contamination to protecting Others (the enslaved, the colonized, etc.) from the pernicious machinations of masculine power worked to feminize these groups and racialize the practice of S&M (both submission and domination) as white. In a moment of harmony between black feminism and antipornography feminism, sadomasochistic acts were read as racist and imperialist.[40] In her short story "A Letter of the Times or Should This Sado-Masochism Be Saved?" Alice Walker gives voice to a professor who experiences a sense of betrayal at viewing a documentary on S&M that features a black woman who calls herself a slave. In describing the documentary, Walker writes, "The only interracial couple in it, lesbians, presented themselves as mistress and slave. The white woman, who did all the talking, was mistress (wearing a ring in the shape of a key that she said fit the lock on the chain around the black woman's neck), and the black woman, who stood smiling and silent, was—the white woman said—her slave."[41] This contemporary and willful reclamation of an identity (or nonidentity) that embodied generations of harm offends the professor in Walker's story (and presumably Walker herself). Walker describes the hurt and pain that this representation of history inflicts, not only on her character, but on those whom she is trying to teach: "All I had been teaching was subverted by that one image, and I was incensed to think of the hard struggle of my students to rid themselves of stereotype, to combat prejudice, to put themselves into enslaved women's skins, and then to see their struggle mocked, and the actual enslaved *condition* of literally millions of our mothers trivialized—because two ignorant women insisted on their right to act out publicly a 'fantasy' that still strikes terror in black women's hearts."[42] Walker's disgust with S&M has to do both with the perceived continuum between the institution of slavery and sadomasochism and with the residual trauma of slavery. She cannot separate the idea of the slave from its history of racism, especially when embodied by a black woman who submits to a white woman. Indeed, the black woman, further the black lesbian, was frequently figured as the position of absolute powerlessness within the framework of 1980s feminism.[43] This reading of black femininity as a site of perpetual duress and domination precluded the possibility of reading submission as anything but violent and painful. As Walker makes clear, S&M toggles between domination between individuals and domination on a macro scale.

Sullied States: Colonialism, Racism, and Masochism

The racialization of domination is one area where feminist arguments against S&M and patriarchy unexpectedly converge with Frantz Fanon's exploration of the psychoanalytic dimensions of colonialism. While feminist arguments against S&M indict the racism of the practice, Fanon provides another perspective on the matter. In his explicit analysis of masochism as a product of colonialism, we are able to read around the radical feminist ethos of protectionism in order to explore the sensations that coalesce around distance in Fanon's description of the experience of the colonized. Though this is a subtle inversion of the radical feminist framework, which situates S&M as the overarching structure of domination, it allows Fanon to argue that colonialism and racism (rather than masochism) are pathological. Through Fanon, we see colonialism as a performance of white submission, where the victim (the black man) is also produced as the feared specter of domination. The politics and sensations of distance are still very much at work in this narrative, but here these tactics are being mobilized *against* the perspective that we are privy to, that of the black man.

When the world is subject to Fanon's gaze in *Black Skin, White Masks*, we are given the tools to experience what being a black man under colonialism feels like. Fanon describes many feelings and sensations of desubjectification, but most important to my narrative here is the painful separation that he describes between the colonizer and the colonized. Quite simply, "The black man is not a man."[44] Central to this production of distance is "unconscious masochism."[45]

In a particularly evocative passage, Fanon describes the link between masochism and colonialism through an analysis of Uncle Remus stories. These stories focus on the heroic antics of Br'er Rabbit, who outwits his animal predators, Br'er Fox and Br'er Bear. White Americans, he argues, identified with Br'er Rabbit but then realized that they were problematically valorizing blackness and its aggression, since Br'er Rabbit was widely considered a stand-in for a slave. This allowed them to imagine that the Negro's aggression was turned toward them, which gave them a reason to feel guilty for their domination. Central to this masochistic imaginary was the specter of the aggressive black man: "The Negro makes stories in which it becomes possible for him to work off his aggression; the white man's unconscious justifies this aggression and gives it worth by turning it on himself, thus reproducing the classic schema of masochism."[46] Like the domineering woman in *Psychopathia Sexualis*, this trope served two purposes. It allowed blacks to have access to agency, even if it was located in the imaginary; and, Fanon argues, it made whites feel both justified in their racism and punished for it. In articulating a connection between the treatment of blacks in America and Sigmund Freud's notion of moral masochism, Fanon argues that white practices of domination are laced with the guilty pleasures of masochism.

The masochism that Fanon describes is a complex psychic formulation. In accounting for it, he argues that it is born from white America's initial "sadistic" aggression toward the black man, which is swiftly "followed by a guilt complex because of the sanction against such behavior by the democratic culture of the country in question," given that overt discrimination is recognized to be incoherent with the ideals of democracy.[47] Additionally, Fanon argues that this aggression is "tolerated by the Negro," which is to say that he lacks the ability to combat it, and that in the white man it results in masochism (and produces guilt and shame at his behavior).[48] Though Fanon uses the term *masochism*, it differs from the moral masochism that Freud describes, which involves the reactivation of the Oedipus complex and guilt by potentially provoking parental (but now subsumed by the superego) ire. The initial violation committed by the white (American) man was that of wanting to unnecessarily punish the black man. This desire, which Fanon terms sadistic, thereby coding it as erotic, violates the white familial credo of democracy and equality. The result is guilt, which he terms masochism because of the pleasure this narrative of personal suffering evokes for the white man.

Fanon's equation of the superego with a national character, democracy, is strikingly different from Freud's description of the superego as a punishing parent. It raises the question—How, indeed, can democracy punish? The answer to this lies with understanding Fanon's radical break from a family-centered psychology toward one centered on nationality and race. Democracy punishes the white man, Fanon seems to argue, by revealing him to be perverse and making him feel guilty. The white man's desire to hurt the black man shows that he has failed to absorb the lessons of the family/nation while simultaneously revealing these goals to be impossible. There is a break in the system; but unlike Freud's concept of moral masochism, this does not result in punishment from the superego. As a concept, democracy cannot act in this way; it becomes nothing more than an ideal that is not reached, and *that* becomes the new familial reality. Unlike Freud's moral masochist, who becomes paralyzed by his inability to resolve his or her new Oedipal crisis and continually seeks punishment, Fanon's white masochist is not particularly impeded by this guilt. Though he seeks to self-punish, this punishment does not occur at any actual social cost to the white man; the actual burden is felt by the black man through the production of various sensations of distance.[49]

A Negro Is Raping Me: Fear, Masochism, and the Black Man

One of the tangible ways that the white man's guilt manifests itself as a problem for the black man is through the creation and perpetuation of the myth of the dominating, threatening black man. Fanon analyzes this specter in his "explanation of the fantasy: *A Negro is raping me* [un nègre me viole]."[50] Fanon offers this as a twist on Freud's "A Child Is Being Beaten." In Freud's narrative, a child fantasizes about another child being beaten because he or she wants paternal affection. Freud suggests that this fantasy about another child is actually a fantasy about the child's masochistic desire to be beaten by his or her father as punishment for his or her Oedipal desires. Fanon replaces the child with an adult woman and argues that her fantasy of punishment is to be raped by a black man: "I wish the Negro would rip me open as I would have ripped a woman open" (Je souhaite que le nègre m'éventre comme moi je l'aurais fait d'une femme).[51]

Immediately it is clear that this fantasy is embedded within a discourse of naturalized female masochism. The woman does not just want to be raped but wishes violence upon her body. This voiced desire for evisceration defines the white woman in terms of her predisposition for pain. She is presented as voraciously sexual with an appetite for destruction. In addition to this characterization of her desires, Fanon's analysis of this fantasy further naturalizes white femininity's relationship to pain by making a link to the work of Hélène Deutsch and Marie Bonaparte, "both of whom took up and in a way carried to their ultimate conclusions Freud's ideas on female sexuality," which is to say, they argued for an innately female biological desire for pain.[52] Fanon argues that this fantasy was "the fulfillment of a private dream, of an inner wish," and that consequently "it is the woman who rapes herself."[53] With these words, Fanon indicates that the fantasy is not about a fear of the black man but about the white woman's subconscious desire to hurt herself. Fanon argues that she does this by imagining herself as a Negro and endowing that imagined man with violent, carnal desires, which she then imagines being turned on herself or any other woman. Noticeably absent from Fanon's analysis is any suggestion of homosexual desire, despite the familiar transpositions of lesbianism onto blackness and masculinity. Fanon, here and elsewhere, places the possibility of lesbianism, as Ann Pellegrini writes, "beyond all imagining."[54]

As presented, "A Negro Is Raping Me" complicates our understanding of female masochism as described in "A Child Is Being Beaten." The beloved father is no longer the locus of agency and desire; narratively, he has been replaced by the Negro. What does the white woman's submission mean in this context? It is difficult to see this substitution of Negro for father as neutral. Though it is tempting to read it as a way to recuperate black agency, the narrative elides this possibility by reducing Fanon's narrator to an always-willing, always-desiring, always-sexual body. In this situation, the Negro is equated with his penis, which looms larger than life in the racist imaginary. Fanon argues that this conflation of the black man with his penis is one of the main qualities of Negrophobia, which manifests as sexual panic that takes the form of fear and desire. The myth of the large black penis only serves to emasculate the black man.[55]

The Negro's impotence is further signaled by his inability to actually substitute for the punishing father of Freud's narrative. Though the menacing black penis offers the possibility of physical pain, the Negro does not serve as a superego for the woman. The woman's punishment for her desire to be raped occurs, not at the hands of the Negro, but within the realm of the white psyche. The fantasy is formed in anticipation of harsh societal judgment against her desires, which represent the persistent paranoid fear of white femininity being violated by black men. The woman voices what Fanon imagines to be the deepest fear/desire of white patriarchy. The woman will not actually be punished for this fantasy, but its effects are especially real to the black man, resulting in the social castration of black men. As Diana Fuss writes, "Fanon's deconstruction of this fantasy takes place in an historical context when fabricated charges of rape were used as powerful colonial instruments of fear and intimidation."[56]

It is important to remember, however, that the words Fanon attributes to a white woman in his articulation of her interracial white fantasy are not actually hers but what Fanon imagines her thoughts to be. The female figure in "A Negro Is Raping Me" is not actually given agency. As such, she parrots both patriarchal and colonial logic. While this fantasy is emblematic of colonial racism, the woman's words, indeed her presence, actually serve to triangulate Fanon's relationship with white masculinity. Fanon's analysis of this fantasy, then, is less about white women and black men than it is about the relationship between white men and black men and the psychic costs of being an empty symbol of domination.

If we reread "A Negro Is Raping Me" alongside "A Child Is Being Beaten" with this alternate logic in mind, the black man becomes the child with the unconscious wish to be beaten, and the white man, whom Fanon equates with the European nation, fills the paternal role. By placing the black man in the place of the child who wants to be punished, Fanon effectively rewrites psychoanalysis for the colonial subject.

This begins with his critique of the Oedipus complex, which he argues does not apply to the Antillean. He writes, "It would be relatively easy for me to show that in the French Antilles 97 per cent of the families cannot produce one Oedipal neurosis."[57] Fanon's reluctance to universalize the Oedipus complex can be traced to the demographics of family in Martinique in the early twentieth century. Martinique's historical reliance on a slave economy created a norm in which black workers were beholden to seasonal work, which separated both men from women and parents from their children.[58] Though Fanon was raised in a middle-class home with both of his parents, the nuclear family was not common in Martinique. Stuart Hall describes the specific historic conditions of French colonialism as conducive to fleeting and often coercive relationships between white men and black women, which produced offspring who were often raised in the absence of paternal figures and families that were frequently separated for economic benefit.[59] In her assessment of the legacy of slavery on the contemporary African American family, Hortense Spillers connects the literal absence of the father with the pathologization of the black family, arguing that this is related to a pervasive and pernicious perception that the black family is aberrant, a violation of the psychoanalytic family unit. Spillers writes, "The 'Negro Family' has no Father to speak of—his Name, his Law, his Symbolic function mark the impressive missing agencies in the essential life of the black community."[60] Importantly, however, Fanon does not use this to dismantle psychoanalysis altogether but rather to give an example of the difference between blacks and whites.

As a result of these structural constraints, Fanon provides an alternate, colonial reading of the Oedipus complex. In his explicit revision, he describes the rape of the mother and the killing of the father as actions of the white man. In this rescripting, he quotes the Senegalese poet David Diop: "The white man killed my father / Because my father was proud / The white man raped my mother / Because my mother was beautiful."[61] The poem has several resonances with the Oedipal myth: the father is killed and sexual access to the mother is transferred. The protagonist, however, is not the son, though he is implicitly the narrator, but the white man, and the mother is not married to him but raped. This retelling of the Oedipal myth illustrates the fragility of the Negro family.

This jettisoning of family leads Fanon to argue that the Antillean "has therefore to choose between his family and European society."[62] Indeed, we can see a white national superego and the specter of black masochism at work in Fanon's self-punishing declaration that "it is normal for the Antillean to be anti-Negro. Through the collective unconscious the Antillean has taken over all the archetypes belonging to the European. . . . I am a white man. For unconsciously I distrust what is black in me, that is, the whole of my being."[63] While I will discuss Fanon's description of guilt and shame at his blackness in another chapter, I position the black man in place of Freud's child to show how the impact of this substitution on the psychic structures of race and colonialism. Fanon wants us to believe that the Negro, without agency and without a nuclear family, is not affected by the Oedipal myth. Neither the father's death nor the transfer of maternal sexual access leads to the phallus because of blackness.[64] Yet we can complicate this family drama by incorporating our reading of "A Negro Is Raping Me" into the black man's version of "A Child Is Being Beaten." This suggests that if the black man is the child, his unconscious Oedipal struggle is with the white man as father. The anxieties of colonialism become folded into a psychoanalytic tableau of colonialism, masochism, and relationships between men.

Fanon also complicates radical feminist readings of penetration by illustrating the ways that the Negro is not actually there, which is to say that the penetrative act that he describes in "A Negro Is Raping Me" can be read as either a masochistic desire for punishment on the part of the white woman or a masochistic desire for recognition from the Negro vis-à-vis the white democratic superego. Though he penetrates, it is clear that Fanon's Negro does not possess the phallus. This collapse between the ideal of domination and the reality of nonagency points to the way that domination is tethered to objectification.

Though he started off as a feared enemy, at this end of this narrative the black man occupies a nebulous place. He is left without agency.

His masochism is unrecognizable because, like the girl's masochism in "A Child Is Being Beaten," it becomes folded into his subjectivity and naturalized; unlike the white man's masochism, it is not a performative subversion of authority. Instead, it is marked by impotence—impotence in the face of his mother's rape and impotence in his own rape of the white woman; this impotence marks the black man's nonrecognition by society. The black man is more than just emasculated; his masculinity is illegible, and, as I wrote earlier, "The black man is not a man."[65] Man is a phallic subject, while the Negro is "a zone of nonbeing, an extraordinarily sterile and arid region, an utterly naked declivity."[66]

Vision, Othering, and Race

Fanon's discussions of race and colonialism also bear witness to the importance of vision to understanding the power of colonialism. Most saliently, Fanon argues that blackness is a product of the (white, colonial) gaze. In Fanon's discussion of objectification, however, we see the perils of being perceived as a threat. In an oft-cited passage of *Black Skin, White Masks*, Fanon describes an encounter with a boy on a train. Upon seeing the black narrator, the boy says, "Look, a Negro!"[67] While this interpellation launches Fanon's discussion of the phenomenology of blackness and the formation of racial consciousness, which will be discussed in a later chapter, it is pivotal to locating domination within the sphere of visibility. Though the boy's order that the rest of the train car look at the narrator is first articulated in French as "Tiens, un nègre!"— which more literally translates as "there [you have], a Negro"—before switching to the more optically oriented "Maman, regarde le nègre . . ." (Mother, see the Negro), it is clear that looking is an act of domination.[68] This scene and, indeed, much of *Black Skin, White Masks* attests to the violence that looking produces. The boy's statement is a declaration of visible difference that additionally alerts us to his position within the power structures that create that difference. Having seized the power of looking (and classifying), the boy attempts to direct the rest of the car to partake in this scopic pleasure. Moreover, Fanon makes it abundantly clear that this colonializing look does not stop at the skin but orients bodies and structures the psyche.

Not only is looking a sign of domination, it is very much a privilege. Fanon's discussion of "A Negro Is Raping Me" underscores this aspect.

In his elaboration of this fantasy, Fanon focuses on black men's objectification by the white female gaze: "The women among the whites, by a genuine process of induction, invariably view the Negro as the keeper of the implacable gate that opens into the realm of orgies, of bacchanals, of delirious sexual sensations."[69] This equation of the black male body with sexual prowess is part of the landscape of blackness and masculinity; it becomes knowledge that is attached to the white colonizing gaze. Chillingly, the social impotence that I argue Fanon's analysis *actually* describes is also predicated on the visual. We see this most clearly in the case of Emmitt Till. Till, a fourteen-year-old African American boy from Chicago visiting relatives in Mississippi, was murdered and had his eyes gouged out on August 28, 1955, three years after *Black Skin, White Masks* was published in France. Till was accused of having had inappropriate contact with a white woman—she claimed that he had touched her, others argued that he had whistled at her, and still others said that he had looked at her. William Chafe, a civil rights historian, writes that he was "lynched because he allegedly had leered at a white woman."[70] The positing of looking as a motivation for retribution lays bare the connection between looking and domination.[71]

Radical feminism articulates a logic of patriarchy that relies on distance, antisociality, and voyeurism, and Fanon's critique of colonialism illuminates colonialism's dependence on systems of hierarchy so as to highlight the distance between the colonized and the colonizer. Fanon's pain is a result of coming to understand not only that that distance exists but also precisely how large it is and how difficult it is to navigate. As Pellegrini writes, "The comma separating *Black Skin* from *White Masks* marks the socio-psychical looking glass through which racialized subjects see reflected in the white gaze their own alterity, radical otherness, inferiority."[72]

Nicholas Mirzoeff describes the work of visuality in these situations as "a series of operations that . . . classifies by naming, categorizing, and defining—a process Foucault defined as 'the nomination of the visible.'"[73] Mirzoeff connects this process of othering and distance with the political projects of colonialism and slavery. Indeed, we can see how an order dependent on voyeurism produces difference and distance between the colonizer and the colonized and, in this case, between the white and the black man.

In Fanon's description of colonialism, we can see how distance and voyeurism collude to regulate the colonial subject and how crippling objectification prevents meaningful connection, thereby enacting a form of antisociality. Colonialism, then, also opposes community and recognition. Fanon's interest in the visual aspects of domination adheres to his articulation of patriarchy as a mode of objectification. To be rendered an object is to be visible, but it is also to be cut off from agency, communication, and volition. While we can see the ways that antisociality and distance operate within this formulation, it is the power of looking that exerts the most pull. Given his interest in describing the ways colonialism has harmed blacks and his understanding of black men as victims of colonial structures so as to enact changes, the sensation of looking, which emphasizes the power imbalance between the viewer and the scene, is an apt aspect of domination for him to focus on.

Exposure and Objectification

Through Fanon we see the ways that sensations of distance produce a logic in which colonialism makes the black man into a feared specter of domination through the workings of masochism. In writing from the perspective of the colonized, Fanon figures colonialism as a regime that articulates a separation between the colonizers and the colonized, who experience this separation as a form of social isolation. We also gain insight into how being caught in this web of sensations renders visibility pernicious. It produces not just objectification but exposure and vulnerability. Though radical feminists do not use this language, the vulnerability of femininity is precisely what is revealed in their framing of patriarchy. In their fierce guarding of femininity, they fail to notice that they have made the butch a scapegoat for patriarchy in ways somewhat analogous to how colonialism mobilized fear around the black man. In concluding this chapter, I would like to bring these discourses of hypervisibility and vulnerability to bear on the black butch. Given that the butch appears to bring together the problematics of exposure that Fanon reveals to be part of racism and the fears that radical feminism articulates around masculinity, discomfort around the black butch is emblematic of these regimes built on this particular structure of sensation, yet we also glimpse something that appears to be outside of this framework.

In turning toward the black butch, we should first acknowledge that the trope of the domineering butch possesses racial overtones. Beyond the predominately white composition of many radical feminist groups, it is important to remember that female innocence was generally figured as belonging to white women. Owing to legacies of slavery and racism, black women were already read as separate from an economy of innocence and femininity.[74] In addition to naming the black woman the perpetual victim, these discourses worked to masculinize her, thereby aligning her with the butch. As Siobhan Somerville has pointed out in her examination of early twentieth-century sexology, in relationships between women blackness became code for masculinity: "Black was to white as masculine was to feminine."[75] Black women were seen as corrupting forces; their overt sexuality was read as masculine and was generally described as oozing into perversion. In this way, I want to argue that the black butch could also be seen as a coded way to refer to all black lesbians regardless of gender presentation. Further, in the world of S&M, we find this mix of blackness, masculinity, and perversion in the pervasive stereotype of the black butch top. Much as Fanon argues that white masochism produces the specter of the threatening black man, Lynda Hart argues that this stereotype is a racialized atonement for historical grievances. By producing an aesthetic of white female submission to black butchness, it inverts social hierarchy: "White lesbians often assume that all women of color, particularly black women, are butch (and top butches at that), a complicated recognition that, I think, contains elements of social and historical guilt, which becomes eroticized (hence it is the white lesbian's historical legacy/ revisionism and her strategy for overcoming it that makes submitting to a woman of color pleasurable)."[76] Adding this racial element to the specter of the butch complicates the equation of patriarchy with S&M and domination in many ways. Most concretely, it brings to the fore a series of contradictions that undo the relationship between the butch, S&M, and domination. It is clear that this "desired" black butch is linked to domination because she is coerced into occupying this space. She, like the black man, is made into a dominating figure regardless of where her own desires lie.

Audre Lorde's biomythography *Zami: A New Spelling of My Name* offers an examination of this forced role playing and the costs of associating blackness with masculinity and domination. *Zami* offers an unexpected bridge between anti-S&M feminist politics and Fanon. Writing in the early 1980s from within the radical feminist community, Lorde sets her narrative in the 1950s, largely in New York City. Her portrait of a black lesbian, a woman who is mired in multiple frames of domination, speaks to Fanon's portrait of the colonial black man who is trying to make sense of his place in postwar France. Lorde's text illuminates the complexities of the black lesbian subject's relationship to patriarchy and masculinity and allows us to look more closely at the economies of domination, submission, sadism, and masochism.

Zami presents us with the narrative of Audre, who illustrates the links between blackness and masculinity as she navigates the difficulties of being young, black, and gay. In trying to understand the space between these communities, Lorde writes: "It was hard enough to be Black, to be Black and female, to be Black, female, and gay. To be Black, female, gay, and out of the closet in a white environment, even to the extent of dancing at the Bagatelle, was considered by many Black lesbians to be simply suicidal. And if you were fool enough to do it, you'd better come on so tough that nobody messed with you. I often felt put down by their sophistication, their clothes, their manners, their cars, and their femmes."[77] In Lorde's telling, the combinatory effect of inhabiting the points of intersection of these three realms of persecution—blackness, gayness, and femaleness—is to create a tough external, masculine shell. Lorde frames this space as necessary for the survival of the self, the alternative being suicide. Audre, Lorde's narrator, experiences this space of masculinity as thrust upon her by the external dictates of female beauty. She writes that occupying this space is somewhat liberating because "I felt I didn't have to try so hard. To be accepted. To look femme. To be straight. To look straight. To be proper."[78] Yet she also demonstrates discomfort with overt butchness: "I wasn't cute or passive enough to be a 'femme,' and I wasn't mean or tough enough to be a 'butch.'"[79] As a role that society seemed to demand of these women and that they took on because of the hardships that they faced, the black butch frightens Audre: "The Black women I usually saw around the Bag were into heavy roles, and it frightened me. This was partly the fear of my own Blackness mirrored, and partly the realities of the masquerade. Their need for power and control seemed a much-too-open piece of myself, dressed in enemy clothing. They were tough in a way I felt I could never be."[80] Audre's fear of the butches in the bar stems both from the way they wield power and from her identification with them, which is rooted in her understanding that her blackness aligns her with masculinity.

If masculinity is a posture that black lesbians must adopt, it is a fraught form of embodiment. As Judith Halberstam notes, Audre's frustration with butchness extends to the realm of the sexual; Audre "finds herself playing the role of baby butch to both black and white lovers and often in the position of love maker rather than the object of another woman's sexual attentions."[81] In the narrative, she experiences this non-reciprocity as a rejection of both her body and her love. She describes sexual encounters with Bea as leaving her "distraught and ravenous, I would come up for air, raving like a maniac, a sex fiend, a debaucher of virgins."[82] Audre's nonidentification with the masculine role is made worse by her lover's inability to appreciate her efforts. This masculinity, inhabited, but not completely owned, is a delicate thing. On the one hand, it produces a space for Audre in the lesbian community, but on the other, it leaves her vulnerable.

Audre occupies a space that is between domination and submission. She must negotiate the terrain of her own desires while grappling with the contradictions within her subject position. This is similar to how Fanon's Negro must navigate the complicated aftermath of colonialism; in the white world his masculinity is both challenged and envied. The performative subversion of masochism, then, becomes a mark of dominance. Masculinity and masochism are tied together in a complex drama marked by possessing, disavowing, and lacking the phallus. Patriarchy and colonialism both mask their power by producing the butch and the black man as threatening figures even as both are actually linked to these structures of domination in altogether different ways, ways that are marked by exposure and vulnerability.

This connection between looking, exposure, and objectification that the black man and the butch point to is the underside to the discussions about domination and voyeurism. Though I have hinted at how masochism might be involved in theorizing submission and negotiating agency within spaces of constraint, in the chapter that follows, the questions of vulnerability, objectification, and complicity become central.

3

Objectification, Complicity, and Coldness: *The Story of O*'s Narratives of Femininity and Precarity

FOR A BOOK that has engendered so much commentary, *The Story of O* begins unassumingly, with a walk in the park: "Her lover one day takes O for a walk in a section of the city where they never go—the Montsouris Park."[1] From there the narrative progresses rapidly. René, her lover, deposits O at Roissy, a castle, where she is stripped, penetrated orally, anally, and vaginally and taught how to submit. After her initiation, the narrative ricochets between S&M tableaux and descriptions of O at work. O is given to another lover, goes away for further training, and is pierced and branded as a sign of her bondage to Sir Stephen. In one of two endings offered, O has become a living statue in an owl costume; in another, she asks to die because her lover has lost interest in her.

The novel caused an immediate stir when it was published in France in 1954.[2] Written by Pauline Réage (later unmasked as Dominique Aury), *The Story of O* won the Prix de Deux Magots for emerging voices in literature but was also subject to censorship from the French government. One of the main axes of contention was the identity of the author. Pauline Réage was previously unknown: Was she really a woman? Could women write such erotica? In his introduction to the text, the publisher Jean Paulhan pleads ignorance but argues that the text suggests that the author, whoever Réage might actually be, is really a woman.[3] As evidence, he points to her attention to detail—"the green satin dresses, wasp-waist corsets, and skirts rolled up a number of turns (like hair rolled up in a curler)"—and to the narrator's persistent selflessness: "When René abandons O to still further torments, she still manages to have enough presence of mind to notice that her lover's slippers are frayed, and notes that she will have to buy him another pair. . . . It is something a man would have never thought of, or at least would never have dared express."⁴ The connection that Paulhan draws between aesthetics, selflessness, and femininity forms the core of this chapter.

The question of Réage's gender matters because it speaks to larger issues of agency and submission. Most immediately, this gender confusion is a continuation of assumptions that masochism carries a masculine valence and represents patriarchal power structures. Indeed, there is much in *The Story of O* to support that reading. Some of Paulhan's statements on the matter, for example, further this association between masochism and masculinity. Even as he expresses certainty about Réage's femininity, he writes that the central character, O, "expresses a virile ideal. Virile or at least masculine."⁵ By this Paulhan implies that O functions as a sort of masculine wish fulfillment: "Rare is the man who has not dreamed of possessing Justine."⁶ Though pleased with the text, he cannot quite comprehend its narrative of submission as a feminine desire: "So far as I know, no woman has ever dreamed of *being* Justine."⁷ In order to reconcile both the desire for submission and the courage that he imagines it would take to write about that desire with femininity, Paulhan resorts to placing Réage in a masculine genealogy: "Woman you may be, but descended from a knight or crusader."⁸ Paulhan's statement resonates with the radical feminist claim that sadomasochistic practices are the result of an internalization of patriarchal notions of masculine domination and female submission. Paulhan claims O as male fantasy, and, indeed, when Aury revealed herself to be Réage, she said that she wrote *The Story of O* as a love letter to Paulhan in order to impress and titillate him with her ability to emulate the Marquis de Sade. In this vein, one could also argue that O's submission is emblematic of Michel Foucault's description of the subject's relation to power. Foucault's conception of power as diffuse and pervasive, his theoretical emphasis on the impossibility of resistance outside of power, and the productive power of repression can easily be mapped onto O's submission.⁹ Indeed, as readers, we see O as a subject formed through these matrices. What could be read as an abstraction is made concrete through the physical changes O undergoes at the direction of René and Sir Stephen. As men (with power) who look, they produce this new version of O.¹⁰ I suggest, however, that we read *The Story of O* otherwise. Even as it illuminates the constraints of life for women within patriarchy, it also reveals spaces of agency. O is desirous of and complicit in her own objectification. Rather than diagnose this as a mode of false consciousness, this chapter provides a sustained examination of the production of self as it is manifest in an attention to aesthetics and an affective coldness.

The Story of O offers a window into this discussion because O's submission is presented not as something innate or inevitable but rather as something that she chooses. Within the world of the book, her masochism is symptomatic of her fraught relationship to power. When O is framed as complicit in her own objectification, complicity emerges as a mode of self-fashioning in which agency and aesthetics collide. In order to make this argument, this chapter presents several different readings of *The Story of O*. First, I turn to Simone de Beauvoir's *The Second Sex* to parse out the gendered implications of theorizing complicity as a form of agency. Next, I position *The Story of O* against Gilles Deleuze's reading of *Venus in Furs*. If O represents not just a mode of submission but a mode of femininity, the feminine domination in *Venus in Furs* presents its own process of objectification. Finally, I turn toward Jessica Benjamin's argument that *The Story of O* is a narrative about recognition and love in order to argue, through a reading of Jean Paul Sartre, that they form the other side of objectification and coldness. In this chapter, coldness, objectification, recognition, and aesthetics emerge as crucial components to understanding complicity as a modern response to power.

Muddling the Story of O(bjectification)

O offers us a glimpse of what it is like to be embedded in French patriarchal society in the 1940s. When we look more closely at the dynamics underpinning this submission to read O as an agent who is complicit in her objectification, however, we begin to see her attachment to aesthetics not merely as a symptom of her objectification but as something that plays an important role in her process of self-making.

As Paulhan notes in his introduction, aesthetics figure prominently in *The Story of O*. Attention to O's wardrobe is an essential part of the narrative. This begins at Roissy, where she is given "a long dress with a full skirt, worn over a sturdy whalebone bodice gathered tightly at the waist, and over a stiffly starched linen petticoat."[11] In addition to its aesthetic charms, the outfit is designed to facilitate access to O's body: "Everything that lay beneath [was] readily available."[12] When she returns to Paris she wears more conventional clothing, but she is permitted to wear only what meets, first, René's, then, Sir Stephen's approval. While

O willingly submits to her lovers' fashion dictates, she is also a woman who is invested in appearance—not only her own but that of others. By trade, O is a fashion photographer. Susan Griffin argues that this fact locates O as "an extraordinary woman, a woman who transcends the traditional social roles for women."[13] Indeed, this is an arresting profession to bestow upon a female character in France in the 1950s. Her status as a professional separates her from the aspirations of French postwar femininity, which expected women to be childbearing and domestic. Her career enables O's independence—she lives alone and seems to be financially solvent—and it allows her to play with the gaze.

As a fashion photographer, O fixes the image of femininity for women. However, as Roland Barthes notes of *Elle* in the 1950s, fashion magazines portray femininity for men; he describes the magazine as a "feminine world . . . a world without men but entirely constituted by the gaze of man."[14] Barthes argues that this creation of an all-female space allows for illusions of female agency but that in reality men possess control because they have priority: "Love, work, write, be business-women or women of letters, but always remember that man exists, and that you are not made like him; your order is free on condition that it depends on his; your freedom is a luxury, it is possible only if you first acknowledge the obligations of your nature."[15] In Barthes's assessment, O's professional autonomy is illusory. While she has the camera, she is actually embodying the male gaze. But there are breaks in that logic. First, we can see that possessing this gaze ties O to a position of agency, which she uses to objectify other women. Griffin speaks of this disparagingly ("As the fashion photographer, she takes the same sexual attitude toward women, and in particular the women who fall under the lens of her camera, that men have taken toward her"), but I argue that this is one way that we can read O as negotiating her own agency through the use of aesthetics.[16]

O's relationship with Jacqueline, the model that she and René seduce, is emblematic of O's embrace and modification of the male gaze. Jacqueline enters the novel as an object in front of O's camera. O is immediately drawn to her because of the beauty of the photographs that she produces, but her pursuit does not begin until she encounters Jacqueline while she is with René. O's objectification of Jacqueline initiates the relationship: "O was looking at Jacqueline and could feel René's eyes following her gaze. Jacqueline was wearing a ski outfit, the kind that only movie stars who never go skiing wear. . . . O said to herself that no one could resist the desire to drink of that green and moving water beneath the silvery lashes, to rip off her sweater to lay his hands on the fairly small breasts."[17] In O's rhapsody to Jacqueline's appeal, she slides neatly into a masculine observational position, describing, not her desire to touch Jacqueline, but her understanding of Jacqueline as desirable to men. When O says that no one could resist Jacqueline, she is thinking not of herself but of men, specifically René. The duality of O's subject position—embodying both masculinity (as René) and femininity (as herself)—complicates Griffin's assessment of O as transparently reiterating the male gaze.

O's embrace of her feminine subject position is evident in her sexual relationships, in which she is careful to describe her pursuit of women (and men) as separate from any discourse of masculinity. Réage writes:

> O had a fairly clear idea of what she was looking for in the young women she pursued. It wasn't that she wanted to give the impression she was vying with men, nor that she was trying to compensate by her manifest masculinity for a female inferiority which she in no wise felt. . . . She enjoyed the pursuit . . . for the complete sense of freedom she experienced in the act of hunting. She, and she alone, set the rules and directed the proceedings (something she never did with men, or only in a most oblique manner).[18]

Rather than seeing her same-sex relationships as a form of masculine mimicry, O experiences her pursuit of women as an agential form of self-expression. This difference is made explicit when she contrasts her relationships with women with those she has with men. With women, she directs; with men, she submits. The juxtaposition between the self she inhabits in the world of women and the self that she inhabits among men is central to O's understanding of herself. Crucially, this divided self gives her the opportunity to see how men perceive and respond to her. She uses insight from her relationships with female lovers to unpack the power dynamics between men and women: "The power she acknowledged that her girl friends held over her was at the same time a guarantee of her own power over men. And what she asked of women (and never returned, or ever so little), she was happy and found it quite natural that men should be eager and impatient to ask of her."[19] Though she sees herself as embodying a traditionally submissive role with the men in her life, the sense of powerlessness that she experiences when she "directs" the relationship allows O to experience her submission as its own form of agency. While O might inhabit the male gaze, it is clear that she does not do so at the expense of her own sense of agency. O's own objectification is especially arresting, then, because it is something that she desires as a sign of power over men and because it is a practice in which she is complicit.

By foregrounding O's complicity, I am challenging Griffin's description of *The Story of O* as a story of self-annihilation, where O "must learn that she does not exist. She becomes only an image to herself."[20] O's agency truly comes to the fore in her aesthetic transformation. O's journey toward objectification begins with the cosmetic. On the car ride to Roissy, René tells her that she is wearing too much clothing and that she must roll her stockings down and remove her underwear. Learning to submit, it seems, begins with learning what to wear. In further emphasis of the importance of aesthetics, O is stripped of her clothing, made up, and given a dress that provides easy access to her breasts and genitals. When the process is finished, O is allowed to examine herself to see what submission looks like: "When she was properly made up and prepared— her eyelids penciled lightly; her lips bright red; the tip and halo of her breasts highlighted with pink; the edges of her nether lips roughed; her armpits and pubis generously perfumed, and perfume also applied to the furrow between her thighs, the furrow beneath her breasts, and to the hollow of her hands—she was led into a room where a three-sided mirror, and another mirror behind, enabled her to examine herself closely."[21] Not only is O made up so that the femininity of her body is highlighted, but she is made to look as though she is in a perpetual state of arousal (via rouge), and potential points of entry—mouth, vagina, anus—are emphasized. O's makeover produces her as a body to be consumed visually (and olfactorily). It is striking, however, that the space that we see this consumption most markedly is in the mirror. O submits to her own gaze.

O's self-conscious participation in this economy of aesthetics is what Foucault would describe as a technology of the self. Technologies of the self are practices "which permit individuals to effect by their own means or with the help of others a certain number of operations on their own bodies and souls, thoughts, conduct, and way of being, so as to transform themselves in order to attain a certain state of happiness, purity, wisdom, perfection, or immortality."[22] Makeup, perfume, and clothing allow O to become closer to her ideal submissive posture. While her goal is self-annihilation, it is her agency that enables this process. Indeed, agency is central to technologies of the self, but we should remember that constraint is also at work. Technologies of the self are but one strand in determining action. While O is shown to embrace and enact her transformation into submission, her relationship to the male gaze also calls attention to how technologies of the self interact with other technologies, most specifically technologies of power.[23] *The Story of O* illustrates the ways technologies of the self, though a recourse for individual agency, do not take place separately from other realms of power. Indeed, Sandra Bartky has already argued that Foucauldian notions of power must be reevaluated to account for femininity by taking into account the male gaze, its power over women, and its embeddedness within capitalism.[24] By being complicit in her own objectification, O exhibits agency within constraint.

Femininity, Masochism, Narcissism

> The most devastating mirror which O (and the female reader) is given in this vision is the image of other women.
> —Susan Griffin, "Sadomasochism and the Erosion of Self"

The Story of O is more than just the story of one woman; one can read it, as Griffin does, as a statement about femininity. For this reason, putting it in conversation with Simone de Beauvoir's *The Second Sex*, which was published five years earlier in 1949, is illuminating because we can examine O's complicity and submission as a phenomenon that Beauvoir associates with femininity.

Like *The Story of O*, *The Second Sex* was a best seller and was quickly translated into English.[25] In *The Second Sex*, Simone de Beauvoir offers a comprehensive reading of philosophy, history, psychoanalysis, literature, and her own phenomenological examination of what it is to be a woman. Ultimately, she argues that women are masochists. Beauvoir uses the term as a way to emphasize the complicity involved in women's status as society's perpetual Other. Transcendence is gendered, Beauvoir argues, and female masochism reflects the paucity of choices that are available to women.[26] Masochism is born from female objectification under the male gaze and women's compliance with the dictates of patriarchy. Because it has to do with image, Beauvoir also argues that masochism is intimately connected to narcissism. Beauvoir writes, "Masochism is an attempt not to fascinate the other by my objectivity, but to be myself fascinated by my objectivity in the eyes of the other."[27] Masochism is an obsession with the state of being an object.

Already, we can see parallels with *The Story of O*. As we see in her interactions with her lovers, O understands that the feminine position vis-à-vis the male gaze is submission, and she fulfills her desire to be objectified by participating in sadomasochistic relationships. There are, however, some marked contrasts with *The Story of O*. First, Réage's novel is framed as a brief interlude in O's life; it begins with her decision to submit to René and ends dramatically with two forms of ultimate surrender—becoming an object (a statue) or dying. In *The Second Sex*, Beauvoir portrays masochism as the cumulative effect of a lifetime of complicity—masochism is something that one must choose again and again and again. This altered temporality produces a vast difference in the affective charge between the two—O unselfconsciously desires her objectification, while Beauvoir's masochists are filled with guilt and shame at their choices. We might argue, then, that while *The Story of O* suggests that O has agency within a sphere of constraint, *The Second Sex* is a portrait of femininity where agency exists in a field that is continually being winnowed and the constraints of patriarchy are almost all-consuming—even aesthetics does not provide a recourse for Beauvoir's masochists.

Beauvoir produces this bleak image by constructing a chronological narrative of the various circumstances unique to each stage of life that situate women as objects. Though each phase is marked by a different relationship to objectification, Beauvoir argues that the process starts in childhood. Young girls are trained to think of themselves as beautiful objects, which leads to narcissism (and subsequently opens the door for masochism). While the girl learns to take pleasure in being an object for others, as she gets older she begins to realize that she is doing so at the cost of her individuality. She believes that she has value only as an object and blames herself for her objectification. This self-blame leads to guilt, shame, and ultimately masochism because the young woman "considers herself to blame for submitting her ego to others, and she punishes herself for it by voluntarily redoubling her humiliation and slavishness."[28]

In Beauvoir's narrative, complicity is functioning very differently from the way that it did in *The Story of O*. Whereas O's complicity manifests itself in her aesthetic choices, Beauvoir frames complicity as the disavowal of choice. Masochism is the result of a set of disavowals that have to be made repeatedly. There are always, Beauvoir argues, alternative behaviors to masochism, namely sexual pleasure, reciprocal romantic relationships with the same or the opposite sex, and careers: anything that allows a woman to be a subject so that she is not dependent on a parent, lover, or child to act as a mirror of herself. In not recognizing those options, masochists turn away from possibilities of subjectivity and freedom.

Here we see that voluntarism and circumstance form an uneasy alliance for Beauvoir. Women, she argues, are drawn to idealize objectification because of their unequal structural status. As much as Beauvoir sees women as responsible for their situations, she also blames patriarchal society for creating the circumstances that make alternatives to objectification unviable.[29] She argues that Man, the general category of men, "wants woman to be object: she *makes* herself an object; at that very moment when she does that, she is exercising a free activity. Therein is her original treason; the most docile, the most passive, is still a conscious being."[30] Beauvoir's acknowledgment that patriarchy has the power to frame women's desires is powerful. This is where we see Beauvoir most aligned with *The Story of O*. Beauvoir, however, is angry at women for choosing to participate in their own objectification—terming it their "original treason." Complicating matters is the fact that true objectification is an impossibility and women still retain some agency; Beauvoir writes, "Mais tout existant, si éperdument qu'il se renie, demeure sujet" (But all existents remain subjects, no matter how passionately this is disavowed). Masochism, then, is marked by a fundamental ambiguity. Women are limited by their status as dependents of men, but they are still subjects with free will. More specifically, it is free will with societally specific restrictions. Beauvoir exhibits horror at the constraints of modern womanhood *and* disdain for what she sees as women's weakness, their complicity.

This ambiguity is the affective marker of complicity, and it manifests itself in several ways throughout *The Second Sex*. Beauvoir argues that these women, by failing to acknowledge their own agency, have cut off possibilities of transcendence and are effectively trapped in the matter of their own bodies. Additionally, this foreclosure of agency limits the possibilities of authentic interaction with others. Both of these aspects of complicity are experienced as dimensions of coldness.

Beauvoir describes these female masochists as parasites who dwell on their own victimization and argues that they had been made to feel as though they are victimized by society because they know that they are living under conditions of oppression: "Woman herself recognizes that the world is masculine on the whole; those who fashioned it, ruled it, and still dominate it today are men."[31] This stance prevents them from taking action and makes masochism seem like the path of least resistance. Beauvoir writes, "She does not consider herself responsible for it; it is understood that she is inferior and dependent. . . . Shut up in her flesh, her home, she sees herself as passive before these gods with human faces who set goals and establish values."[32] This sense that masochism is the "easy path" reinforces the relationship between guilt and a woman's failure to take responsibility for herself and the actions that she is capable of producing.

In linking willful submission to objectification, masochism disrupts the possibilities of love and the erotic.[33] It is a symptom of an inauthentic relationship with the other. As Beauvoir writes, "Masochism by no means represents the normal and happy flowering of feminine eroticism."[34] While an authentic relationship with the other is founded on mutuality and eroticism, masochism disrupts the ethos of mutuality with a focus on one partner. In this way Beauvoir links masochism and sadism, speaking out against a model of eroticism offered by the Marquis de Sade. In a move that Audre Lorde would later echo in her critique of S&M, Beauvoir argues that sadism is an antisocial model of sexuality. In 1952, Beauvoir was asked to write an introduction to Sade's *Justine*, which was being reissued as part of the growing intellectual interest in Sade.[35] Sade and his work called to mind an idealized eighteenth century—a time before industrialization, capitalism, and the bourgeoisie were in full bloom; he represented liberation on both sexual and social fronts.[36] The resultant essay, "Must We Burn Sade?," exonerates Sade for his violence and argues that his valorization of cruelty when framing encounters with the Other is authentic in the way that it relates freedom and the flesh. In this assessment Lorde and Beauvoir disagree, but Beauvoir argues that sadism thrives on these pleasures of cruelty, which Debra Bergoffen describes as "depend[ing] on a simultaneous valorization and degradation of the particular individual in its fleshed humanity."[37] Beauvoir's main issue with Sade is his model of the erotic—it is based on the individual and does not account for relationality. We see this critique of antisociality at work her essay: "The victim is never more than a symbol; the subject possesses himself only as an imago, and their relationship is merely the parody of the drama which would really set them at grips with their incommunicable intimacy."[38] Not only is the lack of relationality isolating, but it prevents both parties from reaching transcendence.[39] Sexuality, for Beauvoir, is where embodiment and ethics come together. It is not a space for a singular individual, which is the problem with both sadism and masochism, but a space for people to embrace mutual freedom through pleasure. Beauvoir argues that the subject can be free only when the Other is also free.[40] Masochism, or inauthentic living, can be avoided if equality is attained in love and society: "It is possible to avoid the temptations of sadism and masochism when two partners recognize each other as equals."[41]

In its most pernicious guise, this self-punishment and inability to form an authentic relationship to others takes the form of frigidity— "Wounded in her vanity, she feels resentment against him and against herself, and she denies herself pleasure."[42] Beauvoir reads frigidity as the self-inflicted punishment a woman produces because she is being-an-object for a lover. Here, I would like to take Beauvoir's discussion of frigidity literally and read it as a sensation that we can attribute to ambiguity. Since she is writing from a perspective of both distance from and closeness to the problems of femininity, her discussion of coldness teeters between the representational and the experiential. I argue that coldness is a manifestation of ambivalence and that we can see this juxtaposition between an external shell and an inner vulnerability in Beauvoir. She frames frigidity, one of masochism's symptoms, as an act of female agency against the patriarchal order: "In bed the woman punishes the male for all the wrongs she feels she has endured, by offering him an insulting coldness."[43] Beauvoir's use of frigidity is complicated. Since frigidity is a symptom of objectification, it is emblematic of an inappropriate relationship with the Other. It is the mark of a failed erotics and poses a particular problem for women because it prevents transcendence. Even if, following Alison Moore, we read the emergence of frigidity as a sort of somatic protest, a "contest[ation of] prevailing notions of normative feminine desire, or defen[se of] the rights of women to maximum pleasure," its intrinsic corporeality is inescapable.[44] Frigidity marks the point at which the body occludes affect. This coldness, this corporeality at the expense of affective transmission, characterizes objectification.

Coldness puts a new spin on Beauvoir's statement that the masochist is "shut up in her flesh, her home."[45] Given Beauvoir's well-known descriptions of the female body as antagonistic, especially during pregnancy, the prospect of being trapped within female flesh evokes a certain amount of terror.[46] Beauvoir describes woman as "the victim of the species" because she must bear the pain of menstruation, coitus, and childbirth in an effort to sustain the species. The contrast between men and women is manifest, for Beauvoir, at the cellular level: "The sperm, through which the life of the male is transcended in another, at the same instant becomes a stranger to him and separates from his body so that the male recovers his individuality intact at the moment when he transcends it. . . . On the contrary . . . , first violated, the female is then alienated—she becomes, in part, another than herself. She carries the fetus inside her abdomen until it reaches a stage of development that varies according to species."[47] In particular, Beauvoir sees maternity as intrinsically alienating for woman because it limits her ability to attain subjectivity. When woman is not actively maternal, she can reach the same pinnacle as man, but "this individuality is not laid claim to; the female renounces it for the benefit of the species, which demands this abdication."[48] Woman sacrifices herself for the good of the species. Woman emerges as a creature imprisoned by her body, which prevents her from reaching transcendence.[49]

These statements allow us to explore what it means to think about coldness as a property of being in one's body while simultaneously being alienated from it. In Beauvoir's model of masochism, the feminine is not quite passive but rather an aesthetic: a mode of being where being-looked-at is the only objective and the dichotomy between subject and object is threatened. Here, I would like to pick up on the thread that Beauvoir begins when she links narcissism with masochism. While aesthetics provided an outlet for O's agency, in Beauvoir's scenario aesthetics are a symptom of being trapped within objectification. One wants and uses objects in order to be more easily legible as an object. Though she does not dwell on it, the accumulation of things and an attention to appearance are marks of complicity.

Of Ideal Mistresses and Mothers: Illusions of Female Power

Aesthetics and coldness are not just markers of submission; they also find their way into discussions of masochism when women are in power. Rather than arguing that these concepts are intrinsically linked with femininity, I suggest that Gilles Deleuze's analysis of masochism allows us to see feminine power as another form of complicity that also trades on coldness and aesthetics.

Deleuze's 1967 essay "Coldness and Cruelty" is emblematic of his innovative reading style in that his reading of Sacher-Masoch, what he termed his "Présentation de Sacher-Masoch," is faithful but perverse— it demonstrates a logic that Sacher-Masoch is perhaps not quite conscious of creating. Beyond this, it also gives us a sense of an early model of Deleuze's thinking about masochism as a way to access freedom. In particular, Deleuze focuses on Leopold von Sacher-Masoch's Venus in Furs. Deleuze argues that Venus in Furs functions as a guide for understanding how to become a masochist. First, Severin (the masochist) enters into a contract with Wanda (the dominant); the masochist uses the contract to suspend reality and exist in his own fantasies where he is submissive. Training the dominant is crucial to the masochistic enterprise, according to Deleuze: "We are dealing . . . with a victim in search of a torturer and who needs to educate, persuade, and conclude an alliance with the torturer in order to realize the strangest of schemes."[50] In Sacher-Masoch's universe, Severin's goal is to become a slave, which is to say that he removes himself from any possibility of agency or desire. Deleuze reads this as an attempt to reach transcendence (and rid himself of paternal law, which Deleuze equates with the pernicious workings of modernity) through a dialectical relationship with the torturer (Deleuze describes this as the rise of the oral mother, the maternal holder of the phallus). After this process, Severin is "reborn" as a new man without the need of a woman; Deleuze calls this phase the "new sexless man."[51] Deleuze describes this narrative as composed of three disparate elements: "the story in which [Sacher-Masoch] relates the triumph of the oral mother, the abolition of the father's likeness and the consequent birth of the new man."[52]

Here I am using Deleuze's analysis of Venus in Furs and Venus in Furs itself as paratexts to The Story of O. If The Second Sex showed that The Story of O can function as an allegory for femininity under the conditions of patriarchy, Venus in Furs and "Coldness and Cruelty" show us a world where women are ostensibly agential and in control, yet where their agency is illusory. The masochist grants these women agency and they are complicit in the effort to hide their structural powerlessness.

The lynchpin of Deleuze's understanding of masochism is the "triumph of the mother," which is how he describes the power of the woman in charge in Venus in Furs. Though the conceptual agent behind the masochistic schemes is the masochist, the person who actually carries out the actions is the heroine or Ideal Mistress. Deleuze is particularly enamored of her because he argues that she upends paternal law and disrupts conventional understandings of psychoanalysis that place the father at the center of order. Deleuze writes that the Ideal Mistresses in Sacher-Masoch's fiction "have in common a well-developed and muscular figure, a proud nature, an imperious will and a cruel disposition even in their moment of tenderness and naïveté."[53] The main characteristic of the dominant, however, is coldness: "The trinity of the masochistic dream is summed up in the words: cold—maternal—severe, icy—sentimental—cruel."[54] This coldness is not apathy but, according to Deleuze, the disavowal of sensuality. Sensuality still exists, but it is protected through the mechanism of disavowal: "The coldness is both protective milieu, cocoon and vehicle: it protects supersensual sentimentality as inner life, and expresses it as external order, as wrath and severity."[55] This protection allows for the Ideal to be realized because it creates a space for an alternative way of being. In Deleuze's reading, the Ideal Mistress's coldness manifests itself as a surface effect. It is the result of an affective detachment; the aesthetic dimension camouflages the inner vulnerability. Here, we return to Beauvoir's territory. As with Beauvoir's masochists, coldness acts as a sensation to distance the Ideal Mistress from her authentic emotions. Unlike Beauvoir's masochists, who experience this as pain, Deleuze's Ideal Mistress uses this detachment to fixate further on the realm of the aesthetic.

In order to flesh out this connection between the aesthetic and coldness, let us turn directly to *Venus in Furs*, Deleuze's source material. Sacher-Masoch's invocation of a "cold, cruel" woman dressed in furs and high heels, a woman who frequently brandished a whip and demanded worship at her feet, became Deleuze's version of the Ideal Mistress, the counterpart to his masochist. As in *The Story of O*, the pages of this text are rife with descriptions of clothing: "Another fabulous outfit! Russian boots of mauve velvet lined with ermine, a dress of the same stuff gathered by narrow bands of fur, a short jacket matching the rest, tight fitting and also lined with ermine. She wears a tall ermine toque in the style of Catherine the Great, with a plume fastened by a diamond clip, and her red hair lies loose over her back. Thus she climbs onto the driver's seat and I take my place behind her. How she whips the horses! The team flies at breakneck speed."[56] Wanda's fur, Slavic background, and evocation of aristocracy are all components of her appeal. Her costume is a visual signal of her power. The combination of fur, high heels, and makeup not only signals feminine tropes of autonomy but also brings issues of class and ethnicity to the surface. The link to "eastern Europe" extends beyond the legend of Catherine the Great and the wearing of furs; it also stands in for a nostalgia regarding modernity.[57] "Eastern Europe" is figured in the late nineteenth century by empires in the West as a landscape that existed before modernity, where aristocracy reigned at the expense of technological progress.[58] The Slavic woman's tie to the premodern and the exotic characterizes her as barbaric without actually being threatening; her status as an ethnic minority prevents that.[59] In *Venus in Furs*, Wanda's ethnicity combined with her status as an aristocrat lends her an aura of decadence and impenetrability. Here, aristocratic women are stereotyped as possessing a voracious appetite and a disregard for the cost of their desires. Further, this conspicuous consumption is figured as socially irresponsible and morally corrupt. Wanda is coded as vain and cruel even before she is linked to masochism.

The female vampire is another feminine trope that is relevant to this nineteenth-century portrayal of sexual domination. Writers such as Bram Stoker and Charlotte Brontë combined the legend of the sixteenth-century Hungarian Elizabeth Bathory, who killed servant girls to bathe in their blood in an attempt to rejuvenate her skin, with fantasies of unbridled female seduction. This resulted in the idea of the female vampire as a wanton seductress who used her sexuality to attain admirers and then abuse them.[60] In this way, the female vampire is the most direct antecedent of the Ideal Mistress in masochism. Her callous approach to her paramours is symbolized by her vanity. Her attention to appearance, which emphasizes her red lips, pale skin, and immaculately styled hair, is all-encompassing; she is frequently depicted holding a mirror, and her suitors are left to gaze at her in admiration, presumably losing all sense of their own subjectivity and allowing themselves to be abused by her.

While both of these stereotypes are central to the aesthetic dimensions of coldness, the best measure of Wanda's objectification and coldness is the fact that we are continually presented with her as an object. She is first introduced to the reader as the subject of a painting: "It was a large oil painting done in the powerful colors of the Flemish school, and its subject was quite unusual. A beautiful woman, naked beneath her dark furs, was resting on an ottoman, supported on her left arm. . . . Her right hand played with a whip while her bare foot rested nonchalantly on a man who lay on the ground before her like a slave, like a dog."[61] Though she is portrayed as having power, the fact that this is introduced in painted form marks this power is illusory. That is to say, she appears powerful but does not actually possess any power. This absence of power is further confirmed by Sacher-Masoch's insistence on linking her to nineteenth-century iconography of female domination. Bram Djikstra describes these symbols of female domination as containing a combination of coldness and sexuality and as including women who were only partially available for male conquest—chimeric women, statues, and Greek goddesses.[62] Sacher-Masoch plays on these tropes throughout *Venus in Furs*. Wanda appears as a statue of Venus in Severin's dream, and later in the text her high heels recall the statue's pedestal. She is often described as feline, and her penchant for furs aids in this chimeric illusion. Through Sacher-Masoch's descriptions, it would appear that Wanda's power resides in her ability to aesthetically call upon other images of domination. As an object, she stands in for domination.

In fact, Wanda provided such a potent image of domination that *Venus in Furs* was cited by real men who wrote to Richard von Krafft-Ebing to describe their masochistic tendencies. For example, case 9 in *Neue Forschungen* described the influence of Sacher-Masoch in the construction of a masochistic fantasy by stating: "Here there may have been a conscious imitation of the 'Venus in Furs.' It seems to me that the writings of Sacher-Masoch have done much to develop this perversion in those predisposed."[63] This preoccupation with *Venus in Furs* extended to its visual elements and is a consistent thread through the narratives provided by other case studies that Krafft-Ebing presents. One man wrote that "he noticed that he was attracted and satisfied only by women wearing high heels and short jackets ('Hungarian fashion'). . . . He was charmed by ladies' calves only when elegant shoes were on the feet."[64] Even Krafft-Ebing's inaugural masochist, whom I discussed in chapter 1, focused on the aesthetic. First, he wrote that in childhood he "reveled in the sight of pictures of commanding women, particularly if, like queens, they wore furs."[65] Later, after some experimentation with prostitutes, he confessed that neither intercourse nor nudity held any appeal for him: "The real object of my interest was the attired woman. In this velvet and furs play the most important part."[66] Image, for this man, was everything. The aesthetic dimensions of masochism even led Krafft-Ebing to subsume fetishism, which he described as latent masochism, under the rubric of masochism. The aesthetic formed an important component of these masochists' fantasy lives and rendered masochism visible to the outside world through the commodification of these symbols.

Despite knowing the details of her wardrobe, however, the reader of *Venus in Furs* knows very little about Wanda's actual desires. In this way, we can begin to see another way that she embodies the maternal in a Beauvoirian sense. Wanda's beauty and coldness are her appeal. While she banters with Severin about slavery and draws up a contract for his submission, we do not have knowledge of her interior life.[67] In fact, her detachment from her own interiority manifests itself as an enthusiasm for learning (acquiring skills that Severin values), which is treated as her greatest virtue. Of this dynamic Djikstra writes, "The masochism, then, of the late nineteenth-century male, and his manipulation of the image of woman as an all-destroying, rampaging animal was an expression of his attempt to come to terms with the implications of his own marginalization. . . . It was not at all a backhanded compliment to woman's power over him; it was rather the creation of a surrogate master who could be sacrificed—indeed, destroyed if necessary."[68] Even in the dominant position, objectification is still at work.

In many respects the Ideal Mistress is a figment of the masochist's imagination, culled from various cultural sources. Her paraphernalia and demeanor—furs, coldness, whips, and high heels—imply domination, but her agency and her desire for control are actually the masochist's. The Ideal Mistress's control is superficial. The masochist is in command, but he wants to disavow his agency. Nowhere is this lack of female agency made more transparent than in Wanda Sacher-Masoch's *Confession de ma vie*, the memoirs of Leopold von Sacher-Masoch's former wife. Though she was not the inspiration for *Venus in Furs*, her autobiography describes her relationship with Leopold in similar terms.[69] Wanda was a poor divorcée when the couple married in Graz in 1873. After the wedding, Wanda wrote out a contract that had been dictated by Leopold that made him "[Wanda's] slave until [his] last breath" and required Leopold to "completely give up [his] Self" because "[he] ha[s] nothing besides [her]; [she] is everything for [him]."[70] According to Wanda, the union produced three children and much misery. Leopold was constantly looking for lovers, and Wanda was forced to wear fur and beat him daily. He also pressured her to take a lover who would act as her master. The pair separated in 1883 but never divorced. Wanda was extremely embittered by the experience and urged for feminist interventions in the institution of marriage. She wrote, "Why does the *feminist movement* not intervene here? Why does it not advance to the root of the evil, so as to sweep away all of this old rotten institution of marriage—so contrary to our modern thoughts and feelings?"[71] The figure of the Ideal Mistress brings the problem of female agency to the fore; while attempting to showcase its glory, it reveals itself to be nothing more than illusion, a type of feminism without women.[72] This paradox is also apparent in *Venus in Furs*. Ultimately, Wanda abandons the practices of domination in favor of being submissive, saying, "Women need to have a master to worship."[73]

While it is clear that Deleuze's interests lie with the masochist, the Ideal Mistress provides a counterpoint to our discussion of complicity and femininity. Though the masochist is the one who submits, we know from Deleuze that he actually possesses control. In this way, his submission is akin to the masochistic performances of domination that I discussed in the previous chapter. The Ideal Mistress's submission, then, and her coldness are complex. Though she dominates, it is superficial; she is still submitting to various forms of structural authority. Her coldness marks her ambivalent position as possessing agency but lacking power. It is also significant that Deleuze is explicit about the connection between her femininity and her coldness because it illustrates something about a more general reading of femininity and cruelty. Deleuze's descriptions of the Ideal Mistress echo Djikstra's assessment of femininity in fin de siècle art. Femininity, he argues, was portrayed as cruel and domineering, but this was without substance: women were actually disempowered.[74] Coldness, then, is a peculiar sensation because it is the sensation of ambivalence; it illuminates the disempowerment of affective detachment while preserving a veneer of agency.

Though Deleuze and Beauvoir articulate coldness in different ways, there are significant overlaps. Deleuze argues that the affective detachment and aesthetic attention that characterize coldness are useful for thinking about alternatives to a patriarchal order. In his analysis of *Venus in Furs*, he reads the male masochist's desire for a strong woman as a way to "exclude," "nullify," and "humiliate" the father.[75] In Deleuze's understanding, the Ideal Mistress/Mother organizes the masochist's world: "The masochist experiences the symbolic order as an intermaternal order in which the mother represents the law under certain prescribed conditions; she generates the symbolism through which the masochist expresses himself."[76] This exclusion of the father and promotion of the mother is made possible by the contract, which I will discuss in a later chapter, but whose role is to allow the masochist to "liberate himself in preparation for a rebirth in which the father will have no part."[77]

According to Deleuze, "Masochism proceeds by . . . a positive, idealizing disavowal of the father (who is expelled from the symbolic order)."[78] In a later interview he described these contradictions as laying the groundwork for *Anti-Oedipus*, the antipsychiatry text coauthored with Félix Guattari: "I thought I'd discovered things about the specious unity of sadism and masochism, or about events, that contradicted psychoanalysis but could be reconciled with it."[79] While Deleuze valorizes the Ideal Mistress's coldness and maternity as a way to provide liberation from the paternal order for the masochist, Beauvoir allows us to understand the costs of this. She argues that maternity and coldness are detrimental for women because they are states where women are trapped in alienated bodies without hope of transcendence. Taken together, however, Deleuze and Beauvoir do more than expand our theorization of coldness: they open ways for us to think about aesthetics and gender. Given the continuities between Deleuze's Ideal Mistress and Beauvoir's masochists, we might ask what this says about feminine agency and the possibilities of female domination.

While these aesthetic symbols of domination serve to titillate and excite men, they prevent women from attaining transcendence as Beauvoir would recognize it because women are still reduced to objects and not agents. They cannot be free because they want to be objects—interestingly, this desire is manifested through consumption. In Sacher-Masoch's narrative, female agency can be disavowed because the mistress takes initiative only at the masochist's bidding. For Beauvoir, the perversity of masochism lies not in the masculine objectification of women but in women's desire for this state. Even as a woman's choices are determined by her situation, her complicity is central to the masochistic bargain.[80]

Returning to *The Story of O* makes the similarity between the Ideal Mistress and the female masochist even more evident.[81] What brings O into kinship with Wanda is the attention paid to her appearance. In being a slave, she is not just a sexual object but an object-to-be-looked-at. In this objectification and attention to the aesthetic, Wanda and O are emblematic of what Beauvoir argues is the persistent objectification of women. Through her tutelage of Natalie, O even embodies a perverse model of the maternal as she trains the younger girl, Jacqueline's sister, how to be subservient even as she shields her actual desires from her protégée. What is most illustrative of O's fraught dance between agency and submission occurs at the end of the novel when O is turned into an object, becoming either a corpse or an owl statue. O achieves transformation by donning a mask. Réage writes, "The most striking, and the one she thought transformed her most and was also most natural, was one of the owl masks . . . no doubt because it was composed of tan and tawny feathers whose colors blended beautifully with her tan; the cope of feathers almost completely concealed her shoulders, descending half way down her back and, in front, to the nascent curve of her breasts."[82] O blends into her surroundings so much so that "not once did anyone ever speak to her directly. Was she then of stone or wax, or rather some creature from another world?"[83] Through the use of feathers, which recall Wanda's furs, O becomes an object. Yet her willingness to engage with these systems, which we might describe as an amalgam of capitalism, modernity, and patriarchy, in an agential manner—she makes manifest the inevitable—is a symptom of her coldness. She is both trapped in her body and detached from the affective realm of others.

Tainted Love: The Problem of Recognition

Though femininity is where Beauvoir's and Deleuze's reading of coldness and aesthetics meet, the key term that I have been emphasizing is *complicity*. Femininity functions as the backdrop for these discussions of complicity because we have been discussing the possibility of agency under the conditions of patriarchy. In this section, I would like to reframe the discussion by reading *The Story of O*'s emphasis on complicity as a narrative about recognition and love. If complicity is the mode that O uses to achieve her goals, what she hopes to achieve is the possibility of recognition. Likewise, we can read love as her affective (and aesthetic) response to the coldness that complicity produces. In attempting to parse O's motivations rather than the effects of her complicity, it is important to remember that Réage writes *The Story of O* as a love story. Love is a thread that runs beneath my discussions of complicity so far: O submits so that she can receive love, Beauvoir frames a woman's lifetime of objectification as a problem of love, and Deleuze's masochist delights in the possibility of stern maternal love. These discussions of love center on the possibility of recognition, but more precisely they traffic in understanding precarity. In other words, love and recognition are the fantasies that motivate complicity.

In her reading of *The Story of O*, Jessica Benjamin highlights the importance of recognition for O. As a woman, it is not something that she can produce on her own, but Benjamin argues that her submission to Sir Stephen provides O with recognition as a subject. Benjamin is invested in the narrative of O's love. Her reading of objectification, however, hinges on the notion that those without power seek recognition. O wants to be an object so that she is recognized as having been a subject. Benjamin writes, "Once we understand submission to be the *desire* of the dominated as well as their helpless fate, we may hope to answer the central question, how is domination anchored in the hearts of those who submit to it?"[84] The more O submits, the more recognition she gains. In describing the novel, Benjamin writes, "What we shall see, especially in voluntary submission to erotic domination, is a paradox in which the individual tries to achieve freedom through slavery, release through submission to control."[85] Indeed, Benjamin's efforts to tie submission to recognition hinge on the importance of mutual recognition for independence and the tension, which Jean Paul Sartre also elaborates in *Being and Nothingness*, between "asserting the self and recognizing the other."[86] Just as Sartre frames masochism as an overinvestment in recognition, or, as he terms it, being-an-object for the other, Benjamin writes that the inability to deal with this tension transforms itself into self-annihilation: "The conflict between the desire for autonomy and the desire for recognition can only be resolved by total renunciation of self. It illustrates powerfully the principle that the root of domination lies in the breakdown of tension between self and other."[87] *The Story of O*, then, is a fantasy about submitting to an Other "who is powerful enough to bestow his recognition as she gains it, though vicariously."[88] This obsession with recognition leads to a fascination with objectivity and offers another perspective on masochism and complicity as a performance of the self. Submission, from Benjamin's perspective, is O's only recourse for agency under a system in which she has no actual power. Through submission, which she links to love, she gains recognition, which provides her with access to power.

In order to understand recognition's role in submission and why complicity might be appealing, I turn to Sartre. Like Beauvoir, Sartre condemns masochists not only because they attempt to trade their subjectivity for objectivity but because they enjoy it, despite (and perhaps even because of) the absolute failure of this enterprise: "The more he tries to taste his objectivity, the more he will be submerged by the consciousness of his subjectivity—hence his anguish."[89] But Sartre is more deeply concerned with the effect that this objectification has on the possibility of relating to others. In seeking self-annihilation, the masochist views himself as an object and therefore treats others as objects to be used in furthering their own goal of objectivity: "The masochist ultimately treats the Other as an object and transcends him toward his own objectivity."[90] Here, Sartre cites Sacher-Masoch's novels, and we can recall the preceding analysis of the illusory nature of feminine power in *Venus in Furs*. For Sartre, masochism is most pernicious because it disrupts authentic relationships by making it impossible for the subject to grant recognition to the other. While Beauvoir takes issue with these inauthentic relations because they create a problem for transcendence, Sartre frames them as an ethical dilemma about the ability to love authentically. According to Sartre, love requires the ability to bestow recognition on the beloved and vice versa. Thus it requires one to recognize the beloved as an agential subject who is exercising his or her freedom to return both love and recognition.[91] In love, then, one becomes fascinated with the Other, the way that one is an object for the Other, and the Other's freedom.[92]

This is the central node of difference between Sartre's version of masochism and Beauvoir's. While Beauvoir frames masochism in terms of the male gaze, Sartre explains masochism as a pathological extreme of love and desire for recognition. In masochism, the subject imagines him- or herself as relying entirely on the Other for existence, thereby attempting to more fully become an object for the other and to annihilate his or her own subjectivity and transcendence: "Instead of projecting the absorbing of the Other while preserving in him his otherness, I shall project causing myself to be absorbed by the Other and losing myself in his subjectivity in order to get rid of my own."[93] Further, Sartre argues that the masochist "refuses to be anything more than object" and revels in the shame of this state: "I rest upon the Other, and as I experience this being-as-object in shame, I will and I love my shame as the profound sign of my objectivity."[94] Shame in this context goes beyond acknowledging that one is always simultaneously a subject and an object. Loving this shame means tipping the balance away from the self and subjectivity toward the Other and objectivity. Another way of analyzing this would be to return to Benjamin's reading and to argue that the masochist becomes obsessed with being recognized.

Indeed, we see this dynamic at work in *The Story of O*. O takes pride in her bondage and feels that her submission is emblematic of the depth of the love she shares with her master. Réage writes, "No pleasure, no joy, no figment of her imagination could ever compete with the happiness she felt at the way he used her with such utter freedom, at the notion that he could do anything with her, that there was no limit, no restriction in the manner with which, on her body, he might search for pleasure."[95] O enjoys Sir Stephen's objectification of her and his use of her body for his pleasure. Her detachment from affect, her coldness, allows her to understand this desire as emanating from him and not from a desire to please her. O reads this unmediated, almost nonintersubjective desire as love: "Her absolute certainty that when he touched her, whether it was to fondle or flog her, when he ordered her to do something it was solely because he wanted to, her certainty that all he cared about was his own desire, so overwhelmed and gratified O that each time she saw new proof of it, and often even when it merely occurred to her in thought, a cape of fire, a burning breastplate extending from the shoulders to the knees, descended upon her. As she was there, pinned against the wall, her eyes closed, her lips murmuring 'I love you.'"[96] In this narrative, love is operating within a dynamic of self-annihilation and objectification.

The problem with this masochism/love is the abdication of freedom (manifest as the ability to grant recognition) and the production of guilt and shame. The renunciation of freedom is not in the service of increasing the importance of the Other, but it glorifies objectivity and lack of freedom. In a moving passage, Sartre compares masochism to vertigo; both are pathologies in which the senses imagine (and respond to) an impossible (and therefore impotent) action: "Masochism is characterized as a species of vertigo, vertigo not before a precipice of rock and earth but before the abyss of the Other's subjectivity."[97] In the case of vertigo, the body fears falling even in situations where a fall is impossible, rendering it more likely to actually fall and making motion difficult. In masochism, the subject attempts to "correct" for subjectivity by performing objectivity into "the abyss of the Other's subjectivity," an act that in reality is an impossibility. For Sartre, the actions of masochism call attention to the impossibility of denying subjectivity because "in order to cause myself to be fascinated by my self-as-object, I should necessarily have to be able to realize the intuitive apprehension of this object such as it is for the Other, a thing which is on principle impossible."[98] The masochist is performing for the Other, but "the more he tries to taste his objectivity, the more he will be submerged by the consciousness of his subjectivity."[99] Sartre is arguing that the masochist's attempts to produce him- or herself as an object require a substantial amount of agency on the part of the subject, therefore reifying his subjectivity and producing the Other as object by ignoring the desires of the Other. The masochist usually treats the Other as an object in his quest for his own objectivity, thus granting the Other precisely what he has worked for. But this paradox, which leads Sartre to label masochism a "failure," is ultimately what draws masochists to it as a vice. In this self-defeating quest for objectivity, the masochist finds pleasure: "It is sufficient here to point out that masochism is a perpetual effort to annihilate the subject's subjectivity by causing it to be assimilated by the Other; this effort is accompanied by the exhausting and delicious consciousness of failure so that finally it is the failure itself which the subject ultimately seeks as his principal goal."[100] Masochism for Sartre is a "perverse" expression of the subject's subjectivity. I say "perverse" because masochism reduces the Other to object in the quest to make the subject an object, thereby producing an effect inverse to the stated desire. Here, we see echoes with my previous examination of masochism as a form of domination because Sartre's masochist ultimately annihilates his/her beloved.

Masochism, in this context, is indicative of an overly aggressive desire to be the object of the gaze, which Beauvoir describes as a feminine position. Though Sartre focuses on masochism's masking of subjectivity, his argument that it relies on recognition is useful for understanding masochism as a strategy to gain agency in a situation of compromise. Here, we might push our analysis of masochism as a form of feminine complicity to ask what it means for Sartre to discuss it in these terms without the invocation of women. In part, this condemnation of submission can be read as symptomatic of a pervasive anxiety about masculinity that Carolyn Dean attributes to postwar France. Sartre's desire to distance the subject, who can be read here as implicitly male, from submission is "derived from a history of male lack rather than male potency, and the historicity of [this] work is inextricable from this perception of male lack."[101] Against this crisis in masculinity, submission is feminine, but women are forgotten.

By examining masochism as a pathological extreme of love we cannot help but reencounter gender and the problems particular to women in postwar France. Beauvoir writes extensively on the difficulty of love in *The Second Sex*. Quoting Byron, she writes, "Man's love is of man's life a thing apart; 'tis woman's whole existence."[102] Women are faced with a paucity of options, so love becomes a justification for their objectification: "She chooses to desire her enslavement so ardently that it will seem to her the expression of her liberty. . . . Love becomes for her a religion."[103] Beauvoir is careful not to confuse love and masochism—masochism is volitional and centered on objectification, while love is "a dream of ecstatic union"—but the relationship between the two is fraught.[104] In theory love can offer transcendence, but in reality it isolates and "offers a sterile hell as ultimate salvation": "On the day when it will be possible for woman to love not in her weakness but in her strength, not to escape herself but to find herself, not to abase herself but to assert herself—on that day love will become for her, as for man, a source of life and not of mortal danger."[105] While she sees that potential in the erotic, Beauvoir writes against the possibility of love for women because they cannot enter into the situation as equals.

Here, it might be useful to think about what love means in this particular context. If Sartre positions masochism as an inauthentic version of love, love, a situation into which both parties enter into with free will, is founded on a utopian notion of agency. Like Beauvoir's concept of the erotic, it is achievable only when everyone is equal. It is, then, an impossible situation when one's agency has been composed, as it were, in submission. If, however, the dictates of modernity, especially those of postwar France, imply that everyone has submitted and, further, that all are complicit in their own submission, we can use *The Story of O* to guide our understanding of love as a form of recuperating compromised agency through recognition.

Recognition, Subjectivity, and Precarity

In this chapter, I have used *The Story of O* as a lens to think about the sensational currents that attend to complicity. Reading *The Story of O* against *The Second Sex*, *Venus in Furs*, and "Coldness and Cruelty" reveals that O's complicity is a product of her relative powerlessness in a patriarchally ordered world. Coldness and an interest in aesthetics are spaces for us to locate pockets of agency within this world. In tandem with this, reading *The Story of O* through Benjamin and Sartre illuminates recognition's role as a motivating force for this submission and love as the affective undercurrent to this regime of coldness and complicity. Here, I would like to take a brief detour through the racial dynamics of these texts so that we can see more carefully the way this structure of coldness and drive for recognition animate the prevailing logic of complicity. By highlighting other modes of precarity and other relationships to the aesthetic, I illustrate the limits of this logic of submission and complicity.

Though arguments about the possibility of reading *Venus in Furs* as an allegory of ethnic struggle are potent, they are less easily applicable to *The Story of O*.[106] O is not ethnically marked, though the fact that Sir Stephen is British can be read as a play on colloquial descriptions of S&M as the "English Vice."[107] The racial subtext of the narrative, however, centers not on Sir Stephen but on Norah, "the mulatto maid." She serves Sir Stephen and deals extensively with O. She has the key to O's rooms and is charged with preparing O for Sir Stephen. In addition to dressing and undressing O, Norah also whips her. In this way we can read Norah as both Sir Stephen's servant and his proxy. This ambiguous status is very much felt by O, who feels "a kind of pride" at being seen by Norah and expresses a deep fear of Norah's opacity. Réage writes,

> O never got used to these preparations, and taking off all her clothes in front of this patient old woman who seldom looked at her, and never said anything to her, was as much of an ordeal as being naked in front of the valets at Roissy. In felt slippers, the elderly woman drifted here and there in silence like a nun. As she followed her, O could not take her eyes off the two points of her madras kerchief and, every time she opened a door, her thin brown hand, seemingly as hard as the wood, on the porcelain doorknob. At the same time, together with the awe she felt in Norah's presence, there was another, entirely opposite, but not, O thought, contradictory feeling: she derived a certain pride from the fact that this servant of Sir Stephen (what, exactly, was her relation to Sir Stephen? His view of her? Why had he entrusted her with this role of dresser, which she seemed so poorly suited for?) was witness that she too—like others, perhaps, whom she likewise guided about the apartment and attended to, who knows?—was worthy of being used by Sir Stephen.[108]

There is a lot of information in this passage, but one of the most important things we learn is that O views Norah as an interruption to her intimacy with Sir Stephen. This is not the interruption of another lover, however; O dismisses that possibility by likening her to a nun and continually referring to her status as elderly. In O's inability to understand Norah or the sphere of intimacy that she occupies ("What, exactly, was her relation to Sir Stephen? His view of her? Why had he entrusted

her with this role of dresser, which she seemed so poorly suited for?"),
we clearly see that Norah's presence speaks to a different structure of
sensation, one predicated not on recognition but on labor. O does not
understand it because *complicity* is not its dominant term. The difference
between O and Norah is marked by race and age and signaled by Norah's
unobtrusive presence (in contrast to O's interest in aesthetics) and her
opacity (the text is narrated from O's perspective). While Norah is part
of the tableau of domination, she is present not because she desires but
because she serves.

We see a similar economy of labor and affect in *Venus in Furs*. Wanda
employs three black women to deal with Severin while she watches.
This scene in Florence is emblematic of how these women are treated
throughout the novella.

> She rang. The black girls appeared.
> "Tie his arms behind his back."
> I remained on my knees and let them tie me up. . . . The blacka-
> moors tied me to a stake and amused themselves by pricking me
> with golden hairpins . . . while Venus in Furs stood by, watching the
> scene.[109]

These women are as beholden to Wanda as Severin is, but their labor
also goes unnoticed. While they obey her orders, their link to Wanda is
not rendered explicitly erotic, unlike Severin's stake in obedience. We
are to assume that they are servants, not slaves. More, they are invisible.
It takes a while before Severin even notices the features of one of the
women, whom he has described as a demon and a blackamoor: "For the
first time, I noticed her noble, almost European features, her statuesque
bust that seemed chiseled in black marble."[110] We might be tempted
to call this moment a step toward recognition, but since that Severin
persists in objectifying her by likening her to a statue, that conclusion
would be mistaken.

These women are participants in the drama, but their labor is read as
an extension of their masters' desires. The seamlessness of this allows us
to consider these women technicians of domination. I use this phrase
to highlight the labor involved, its invisibility, and the opacity of their
affect. In describing the invisibility of technicians, Steven Shapin writes,
"Technicians' work was transparent when the apparatus was working as
it should and the results were as they ought to be."[111] Facilitating these

women's invisibility are their class, gender, and race. It is not difficult to read their invisibility as emblematic of their lack of institutional and societal power as black women in Europe. We can also read their invisibility as emblematic of the silences that surround black female sexuality. As Hortense Spillers writes, "Black women are the beached whales of the sexual universe, unvoiced, misseen, not doing, awaiting *their* verb."[112] Affectively, this invisibility is produced as the withholding of emotion or affective opacity. This emotional reserve connects Wanda to Norah and produces an arresting resonance with the trope of the stone butch. Judith Halberstam discusses the stone butch as a figure who has been read as pathological. She writes, "Masculine untouchability in women has become immutably linked to dysfunction, melancholy, and misfortune."[113] Further, Halberstam argues that the stone butch's emotional unavailability, read as a "combination of emotional abuse and selfishness," is particularly problematic for black women because "it could also signify the sacrificing of the black butch's desire to be white woman's pleasure."[114] Though Halberstam is explicitly describing lesbian sexuality, this subordination of desire and figuration of black women as emotionally pathological also fits into our understanding of Norah and of Wanda's black servant girls. This reserve is different, however, from the coldness that I have been discussing throughout the chapter. While Wanda and O are also emotionally withdrawn, their coldness is a manifestation of their aesthetic choices and submission to the male gaze. Norah and the black servant girls are read as reserved without the associated aesthetic dimension. Though they are also trapped in their bodies, as black women, their emotional remove is projected onto them rather than produced by them.

This emotional pathos extends to Norah's inexplicable (to O) relationship with Sir Stephen. Without any understanding of this relationship, we know only that O has, in the words of Sir Stephen, "genuine reasons for being afraid of Norah."[115] The clue to unpacking this terror comes from the collapse that Réage and Paulhan enact regarding black bodies and their imagined site of origin. Just as Wanda's Slavic origins figure into our understanding of her cruelty, Norah's blackness is tied to the Caribbean, specifically Barbados. This is not just because Barbados was a British colony at the time that Réage wrote but because the link is articulated in Paulhan's introduction to *The Story of O*.

Paulhan's introduction, an essay entitled "Happiness in Slavery," begins with a narrative of a revolt in Barbados. Contrary to what we might expect, it was not a slave revolt but a request for their former master "to take them back into bondage."[116] The workers presented a notebook of grievances, but their former master refused to make them slaves, and for this they killed him. Paulhan speaks wistfully of the lost notebook and says, "In short, this notebook would seem even more heretical today than it did some hundred and thirty years ago: today it would be considered a dangerous book."[117] Paulhan is speaking of the perception that the abdication of freedom is irrational in the contemporary climate. Indeed, the previous chapter's analysis of masochism as a masculine form of submission argued that this notion of irrationality had to do with the assumption of a masculine, individual, white subject. More heretical, I argue, is Paulhan's ultimate explanation for the slave revolt: "But I suspect that he was not telling the truth, which is that Glenelg's slaves were in love with their master, that they would not bear to be without him."[118]

I argue that we can read Paulhan's invocation of love as a reference to either the love that O performs in her submission to Sir Stephen or the love, measured by attendance and obedience and marked by a financial exchange, that Norah has for him. By naming Norah's labors love, this "love story" provides a sharp contrast to O's understanding of love. We gain a new perspective on what is at stake in O's self-conscious objectification, and we also gain a way, as Evelynn Hammonds suggests, to examine how "the structure of what is visible, namely white female sexualities, shape those not-absent-though-not-present black female sexualities."[119]

The "perverse" love that Sartre and Benjamin ascribe to masochism is a love composed of objectification, self-making, and aesthetics. Norah's invisible labor, which Paulhan describes as love, but which we should understand through the matrix of racialized inequalities, allows us to particularize narratives of complicity. In these scenarios, love, which becomes equated with recognition, relies on the superficial, and masochism becomes a way to understand one's embeddedness in a world of surfaces.

Coldness and complicity, in being linked with masochism and love, become survival strategies for women in patriarchal society. But they can also be seen as much more than that. In particular, I want to place this discussion of submission in its historical context. Against the echoes of French complicity during World War II and the turbulent aftermath of rebuilding and restructuring, submission became an important philosophical issue. The mid-twentieth century was a precarious moment for France. It had weathered two wars on its own soil at substantial cost:

lives were lost, land was damaged, the economy was rocky, and the country was politically unstable.[120] In addition to this, some of France's colonies and *départements d'outre-mer*, including Algeria, Indochina, and Madagascar, launched their own campaigns of independence.[121] The period of rapid postwar industrialization and the wars of decolonization had profound effects on ideas of normative French identity, which was becoming solidified as white, Catholic, and bourgeois.[122] In addition to considering the linking of complicity, free will, and submission to structural—state and societal—norms, conceptualizing submission involves thinking about gender. Is submission, in this context, a feminine act, and, if so, what does feminine submission feel like? The anxiety about submission can be read as symptomatic of a pervasive anxiety about masculinity that Carolyn Dean attributes to postwar France. The desire to feminize submission is "derived from a history of male lack rather than male potency, and the historicity of [this] work is inextricable from this perception of male lack."[123] Finally, read against multiple decolonization efforts, these examples of race and submission become more complicated. In the assumption that love lies behind submission we see the emergence of a rationalization for colonialism. The wish for an authentic love that offers recognition and is premised on free will actually describes a relationship of economic and political submission and dependence. In this context, the ambivalent submissive posture that marks these subjects of modernity is revealed to rely on the domination of others.[124] Here, it is worth noting that Frantz Fanon's *Black Skin, White Masks* was published in 1952, two years before *The Story of O*. The next chapter will take up Fanon's discussion of objectification and examine the relationship between the laboring black body, whiteness, and masochism.

4

Time, Race, and Biology: Fanon, Freud, and the Labors of Race

IN *BLACK SKIN, White Masks* Frantz Fanon brings up the popular linkage between blackness and biology several times. At one point, parroting Octave Mannoni, who lived in Madagascar for decades and wrote on blackness, he writes, "To suffer from a phobia of the Negroes is to be afraid of the biological. For the Negro is only biology. The Negroes are animals. They go about naked. And God alone knows."[1] Later, channeling other popular opinions, he writes, "The Negro symbolizes the biological. First of all, he enters puberty at the age of nine and is father at the age of ten; he is hot-blooded, and his blood is strong; he is tough. As a white man remarked to me not long ago, with a certain bitterness: 'You all have strong constitutions.'"[2]

In these passages, inhabiting the biological is negative; it means occupying a sphere that is separate from civilization. It suggests a body governed by its own instincts rather than societal rules. It is a body marked by sexual potency, a body where virility and fecundity, rather than intelligence and agency, are related to health. This link to the biological also produces its own logic of temporality. Equating the Negro to the biological invokes nineteenth-century beliefs about race in evolutionary biology which held that Africans were less evolved and therefore closer to animals. This insistence on the Negro's primitive origin marks him, and gender is very important here, as distinct from modernity. In particular, he is imagined to be atemporal. This untimeliness links black bodies to a rawer, more violent, and more sexual form of embodiment.

Importantly, this atemporality and becoming-biological are also markers of a particular relationship to labor and capitalism. Here, I want to embed Fanon's discussion of becoming-biological as a form of racialization in midcentury France in a historical trajectory that includes the transatlantic slave trade and the contemporary fetishization of black bodies as symptoms of socioeconomic devastation. The laboring black body haunts *Black Skin, White Masks* and informs Fanon's understanding of how blackness has been read as biological. Labor in this context relies on the interconnectedness of several narratives: the historical commodification of black bodies in the slave trade, the specter of sexual exploitation through the idea of a primitive black sexuality, and the affective work of producing white subjectivity as a contrast to scenes of black suffering. These are contexts in which the black body is produced as depersonalized biology rather than subject. By arguing that the Negro stands in for the base level of humanity through a process of becoming-biological, I link the depersonalization of labor with affective processes of racialization and the sensation of stickiness.

The othering of the black body and the spectacle of the black body as biological matter is the central theme of this chapter. I argue that the specter of the biological black body, a body so marked by its embeddedness in suffering and pain, constitutes an affective framework for understanding race. This particular mode of black objectification (or enfleshment) allows for an understanding of whiteness as an affective state that requires an other to project him- or herself against and that this coproduction of white subjectivity and black objectification, which I read through this discourse of the biological, is reliant on a structure of sympathy and empathy. The resultant depersonalization, I argue, is experienced as atemporality and stickiness.

Shame and the Suffering of Blackness

> The black is a black man; that is, as the result of a series of aberrations of affect, he is rooted at the core of a universe from which he must be extricated.
>
> —Frantz Fanon, *Black Skin, White Masks*

Central to Fanon's critique of colonialism is his phenomenological description of becoming-black. Here, he makes two related claims: one, that the black man, the Negro, is not a subject, in that he does not possess agency; and two, that the process of becoming-black is marked by pain and suffering.

Blackness, in Fanon's universe, begins with interpellation: "Look, a Negro!"[3] This hailing disrupts the narrator's sense of himself as a sovereign subject, a subject who could possess mastery over the world.

Instead, he discovers that he is an object, which is to say that he has no agency and is controlled by other people's images of him. This moment of objectification catches the narrator by surprise and undoes his sense of self. Fanon describes the loss of agency and subjective coherence in physical terms: "I burst apart" (J'explosai), "the corporeal schema crumbled."[4] After the fragmentation produced by this violent objectification, Fanon's narrator is reorganized—"My body was given back to me sprawled out, distorted, recolored, clad in mourning in that white winter day."[5] This reorganization, I argue, is the narrator's recognition of his blackness. In becoming-black, he has become racialized, physiologically reduced to a large, willing penis (as we saw in a previous chapter), and, significantly, he grieves the loss of the subjectivity that he now realizes he never possessed.

Further, the fact that this realization takes place in the metropole, France, complicates the terms of objectification. The Antillean man was confronted with the fact of his blackness, which was a trait that he had been taught to equate with savagery and evil, and he also understood himself to be distant from Europe, which stood for whiteness and the nation. The resulting schism between individual, nation, and family was traumatic. Fanon writes, "The Negro's inferiority or superiority complex or his feeling of equality is *conscious*. These feelings forever chill him [À tout instant, ils les transitent]. They make his drama. In him, there is none of the affective amnesia characteristic of the typical neurotic."[6] The combination of a delayed shattering of the self, a new understanding of the self as black, and the overwhelming flood of conscious feelings is deeply problematic and creates a nonsubject who is, Fanon writes, "rooted" by these affects to the core of a difficult universe, a universe of suffering. Despite the fact that becoming-black is a process of anatomization and becoming-biological, the suffering Fanon describes is psychological; it is the pain of inhabiting a hated body, a hated body that does work for others.

Like Freud's melancholic, in whom "one part of the ego sets itself over against the other, judges it critically, and, as it were, takes it as its object," Fanon's narrator internalizes the lost object—the subject he imagined himself to be—and becomes a being who occupies multiple positions.[7] Fanon writes, "I existed triply: I occupied space. I moved toward the other . . . and the evanescent other, hostile but not opaque, transparent, not there, disappeared. Nausea . . ."[8] While Freud's melancholic unconsciously identifies with the abandoned object, Fanon's narrator experiences his fragmentation and multiplicity consciously. His relationship with these parts of himself is difficult. He describes the simultaneous responsibility for "my body, my race, for my ancestors," but does not dwell on the affective relationship he has to them.[9] Here Diana Fuss's understanding of trauma offers another way to examine the affective consequences of this denial of identification. Using Freud, Fuss defines trauma as "another name for identification, the name we might give the irrecoverable loss of a sense of human relatedness."[10] The alienation from subjectivity that Fanon's narrator feels upon his interpellation as a Negro is a mark of his identification with whiteness. His realization of this gap occurs on a multitude of levels.

Body is the narrator's current configuration in the world, race is the way he is viewed by others, and ancestors are his attachment to the past. Fanon's narrator experiences his present as an uncomfortable corporeality that makes itself known as nausea. Nausea, which Sartre describes as "the 'taste' of the facticity and contingency of existence," is a reminder that consciousness is corporeal and that access to the external world is mediated.[11] In addition to how he experiences his subjectivity, Fanon's narrator has to contend with the way he is seen by others and his relationship to this label. Fanon's narrator experiences his relationship to race, the structure that defines him as black and inferior, as one full of "shame. Shame and self-contempt" (La honte. La honte et le mépris de moi-même).[12]

Through Eve Sedgwick we can understand shame as embedded in a structure of consciousness, sociality, and identity. Even as shame suggests a distance from one's identity, it also works to solidify that identity. Sedgwick writes, "Shame floods into being as a moment, a disruptive moment, in a circuit of identity-constituting identificatory communication. . . . But in interrupting identification, shame, too, makes identity. In fact, shame and identity remain in very dynamic relation to one another, at once deconstituting and foundational, because shame is both peculiarly contagious and peculiarly individuating."[13] In Sedgwick's understanding of shame, it is not the subject who is imperiled but his or her relationship to identity. Shame alienates the subject from him- or herself while reifying the contentious identity. This is the tension that we see at work in Fanon. The narrator's shame stems from being interpellated as something undesirable; his sense of self has been abased. There is no way for him to reconcile the difference between the way others perceive him and the way he perceives himself. This rupture leads to self-contempt and nausea, which are indicators of the narrator's alienation from society and the self. Taken together, these emotions—shame, self-contempt, and nausea—are markers of a consciousness that overwhelms the self. Rather than open the narrator to a multitude of possibilities, they anchor him further to his body.

Fanon's narrator experiences his being as a collection of unhappy affects. It is a conglomeration of feelings that we might attach to the concept of suffering. Though Fanon wants to put these emotions aside, he recognizes that he is historically tied to them: "But I rejected all immunization of the emotions. I wanted to be a man, nothing but a man. Some identified me with ancestors of mine who had been enslaved or lynched: I decided to accept this. It was on the universal level of intellect that I understood this inner kinship."[14] In part these affects are rejected because they are useless for conceiving of agency or sovereignty, but it is also because Fanon recognizes that this constellation of affects gets at the heart of what it is to be a black man. Fanon is explicit about the relationship between suffering and blackness, writing that "the Negro suffers in his body quite differently from the white man."[15]

For Fanon the key variable in the racialization of suffering is the black man's place, or lack thereof, in history, which has denied him mastery and kept him as a laboring body under these conditions. Fanon writes, "Though Sartre's speculations on the existence of The Other may be correct (to the extent, we must remember, to which Being describes an alienated consciousness), their application to a black consciousness proves fallacious. That is because the white man is not only The Other but also the master, where real or imaginary." Fanon is explicit about how Sartre's philosophy (and by extension Hegel's) cannot be thought of as universal because it cannot apply to the black man, who does not have the agency to be radically free.[16] This means that the master-slave dialectic cannot be applied to black men. He argues that despite the ideals of democracy, the white man cannot admit that the black man is his equal.[17] For Fanon this persistent search for impossible satisfaction marks both subjectivity and society. It suggests that the only possible way out of this unresolvable dualism, is for the slave to act—bringing about the end of history, which Fanon interprets as breaking the deterministic pattern set forth by the condition of the master/slave.[18] Action, however, is something that belongs to white men because in the eyes of white society the black man inhabits a space of atemporality, objectification, and suffering. The abolition of slavery is not enough to bring recognition; being a black man means being objectified and awash in a sea of affect.

Recognition, Gender, and the Laboring Body

This racialization of suffering returns us to the biological. It is not just that the black man is reduced to his body; it is that he has been reduced to a dismembered body. Further, in finding kinship with the lynched and enslaved, Fanon hints at the association between black masculinity and the penis. This is an important association, not only because it underscores that the black man does not possess the phallus, as I argued in a previous chapter, but because it produces immense repercussions for Fanon's discussion of gender.

Throughout the text, Fanon evinces a certain discomfort with attributing sexuality to black men. In part, I argue this is because he views sexuality as the province of whiteness. Both the white woman and the white man desire the black man: "The Negrophobic woman is in fact nothing but a putative sexual partner—just as the Negrophobic man is a repressed homosexual."[19] Nowhere, however, does he describe sexual desire on the part of the Negro. When he speaks of desire for the white woman, it is about recognition rather than sexuality: "I wish to be acknowledged not as *black* but as *white*. . . . Who but a white woman can do this for me? By loving me she proves that I am worthy of white love."[20] Since the Negro does not have recognizable sexuality, he, specifically his penis, is a sex object. Moreover, this reduction to objectivity is not only an erasure of subjectivity and its potential for desire and sexuality but a replacement of those concepts with labor. As I argued previously, the black man's penis produces pleasure for others through the black man's work. The lack of access to sexuality is another symbol of the black man's objectification, anatomization, and commodification. Fanon channels this erasure of subjectivity and sexuality into rage against women. This has the effect of marginalizing women in his text. He treats white and black women as commodities; they are exchanged between white and black men, but their own agency and desires are trivialized.[21]

In a harsh reading of Mayotte Capécia's *Je suis martiniquaise*, Fanon illustrates what Rey Chow describes as an inability to reconcile female sexuality with community.[22] Capécia's novel tells the story of a woman, Mayotte, who decides that she will marry a white man because of the hardships women of color face. She never marries but is impregnated by her white lover, who then abandons her. Literary critics such as Cheryl Duffus, Jennifer Sparrow, and Susan Andrade argue that Capécia's narrative is a historically accurate portrayal of the plight of the black Martinican woman, who had few avenues for upward mobility within the structures of colonialism.[23] Fanon, however, describes her novel as "a vast delusion."[24] He argues that Mayotte treats the white man with pathological deference—"She asks nothing, demands nothing, except a bit of whiteness in her life"—because she is obsessed with whiteness.[25] He condemns this desire as "infantile" because it explicitly relates whiteness with financial and social success.[26] Fanon's quarrel with the black woman is that she rejects blackness—she turns away from the overtures of the Negro or mulatto man, and she disavows her own blackness. Fanon universalizes black women's desire for whiteness and white men: "I know a great number of girls from Martinique, students in France, who admitted to me with complete candor—completely white candor— that they would find it impossible to marry black men (get out of that and then deliberately go back to it? Thank you, no). Besides, they added, it is not that we deny that blacks have any good qualities, but you know it is so much better to be white."[27] Fanon's dismissal of the black woman is framed against her imagined prior rejection of the black man. Because he assumes that she prefers whiteness, he leaves her outside of his discussion of recognition and community. Chow argues that "Fanon's admittance of the sexual agency of the woman of color signifies her inevitable expulsion from her community" because her tendencies (real or imagined) toward miscegenation threaten Fanon's utopian vision.[28] Fanon's vision of community is a world of men, a world of radical solidarity. Importantly, it is also a world without homo- or heterosexuality.

Fanon's desire for recognition, then, is framed as solidarity. In the introduction to *Black Skin, White Masks*, Fanon writes that this book is a way "toward a new humanism . . . / Understanding among men . . . / Our colored brothers . . . / Mankind, I believe in you."[29] Fanon's turn toward brotherhood is one that goes beyond race toward the end of oppression, toward love: "I, the man of color, want only this: That the tool never possess the man. That the enslavement of man by man cease forever. That is, of one by another. That it be possible for me to discover and to love man, wherever he may be."[30] Though David Macey and Stuart Hall speak to the historical and geographic specificity of *Black Skin, White Masks*, it is important to recognize Fanon's own attempts to forge bonds with other colonized black people. After he joined the Algerian resistance movement, he took on Algerian citizenship and considered himself part of the Algerian nation. Though this move has been either maligned by scholars as a refusal of national identity (Gates) or hailed as a step toward postcoloniality (Bhabha), I read it as a part of Fanon's discomfort with sexuality and black femininity.[31]

By focusing on recognition and what he calls Hegel's "being for others," Fanon changes our understanding of the Hegelian dialectic.[32] The abolition of slavery is not enough to bring recognition; being a black man means being objectified. Recognition and subjectivity are possible through two different avenues in Fanon's world—love and conflict. Love, however, is impossible. In his relationships with white women, the Negro, according to Fanon, is seeking recognition, as I have already mentioned. To repeat, he writes, "I wish to be acknowledged not as *black* but as *white*. Now—and this is a form of recognition that Hegel had not envisaged—who but a white woman can do this for me? By loving me she proves that I am worthy of white love. I am loved like a white man. I am a white man."[33] The rape fantasy that I analyzed in the second chapter does not qualify as a type of recognition because it validates only the Negro as phallus; it fails to acknowledge his subjectivity. These interracial relationships based on mutual recognition are rare, according to Fanon, but meaningful because they signal a willingness to look beyond the Negro as a phobogenic object and see a man. Given his refusal to acknowledge interracial love between a white man and a black woman, Fanon's admiration for this particular mode of coming to consciousness is interesting and conflicted. Fanon disavows false versions of these couplings, saying, "This sexual myth—the quest for white flesh—perpetuated by alienated psyches, must no longer be allowed to impede active understanding," but he allows for the possibility of love in a restructured world.[34] This narrative provides a counterpoint to his discussion of the Negro rape fantasy by refusing to reflect on female desire in these relationships, which he terms authentic love. In these special cases, he envisions a white woman who is not motivated by lust or desire but who simply recognizes the man beneath the blackness. The difficult part of this coupling is not the white woman's inability to bestow recognition but the black man's ability to accept it. Once he accepts her recognition, he can accept himself as a man.

The other path to recognition is conflict. In Hegel's vision, the slave demands recognition and fights for his freedom, thereby becoming a subject. Fanon's interpretation of the historical reality behind slavery locates the freeing of slaves with the white man, or, as he writes, "The master decided to free the slaves without consultation from the slaves."[35] This lack of struggle dooms the former slave to objecthood; he "needs a challenge to his humanity, he wants conflict, a riot."[36] Without this conflict, the black man cannot be more than a body—commodified, objectified, and anatomized. His behavior does not consist of action, only reaction, in which there is "always resentment."[37] Fanon's invocation of Nietzsche's *ressentiment*, which is his term for slave mentality, assigns feelings of inferiority to the Antillean, compounding his feelings of helplessness and passivity. From these statements, it becomes clear why Fanon advocates a violent revolution in 1961 in *Wretched of the Earth*.

The Injury of Modern Identity

In Fanon's despair and unwilling surrender to the label of blackness we gain more than an understanding of the phenomenology of becoming-black: we gain a way to think about the formation of identity. The Antillean man in France in the 1950s experienced his body, his objectification, as suffering. His identity, we can say, was formed traumatically. This dialogue between self and identity, a space that Fanon's narrator describes as experiencing triply, shares with the liberal subject a birth in injury. By drawing this analogy between liberal subjectivity and becoming-black, I seek to highlight the liberal subject's cooptation of the affects of trauma and color blindness. This furthers David Eng's and Jasbir Puar's arguments that the liberal subject is racialized as white because liberal subjectivity is founded on the premise of ascendancy into whiteness.[38] This is another way of looking at the labor of the black body.

In "Wounded Attachments," Wendy Brown argues that contemporary identity is informed by Nietzsche's notion of *ressentiment*. Nietzsche argues that the desire for recognition, which underpins contemporary concepts of subjectivity, is the symptom of a slave mentality. The subject produced not only has no desire for freedom but "loathe[s] it" because his or her power is gained from weakness.[39] The powerless benefit from their victimization because their pain and suffering produce sympathy, which motivates those with power to act on behalf of those without, lest they seem callous. This produces a cycle in which the powerless seek to remain sympathetic in order to have access to some sort of power, or, as Brown writes, "Identity structured by *ressentiment* at the same time becomes invested in its own subjection."[40] This, in turn, naturalizes suffering and moves it from circumstance to a self-defeating identity: "Thus politicized identity that presents itself as a self-affirmation now appears as the opposite, as predicated on and requiring its sustained rejection by a 'hostile external world.'"[41]

In further unpacking the link between suffering and the liberal subject, whom she describes as a "political masochist," Brown turns to Sigmund Freud's "A Child Is Being Beaten" to argue that a cycle of guilt and punishment motivates the liberal subject.[42] Masochism allows Brown to probe the pleasurable components of these negative affects. In this way, she echoes Judith Butler's investment in the subject's "passionate attachment" to subjection.[43]

Indeed, Freud's work makes masochism central to the modern subject. Rather than seeing masochism as a pathologization of the desire to submit or a symbol of what happens when civilization goes awry, Freud transforms it into a universal manifestation of the struggle between Eros and Thanatos and an integral component of a subject's maturation through its linkage with the Oedipus complex. Freud comes to intertwine his modern subject with masochism. Initially the concept perplexes him, but as he does more work toward understanding it, it appeals to him as a way to understand the subject's oscillation between pleasure and pain and how he or she makes sense of irrationality.

In "The Economic Problem of Masochism" (1924), Freud defines three distinct types of masochism: erotogenic, feminine, and moral. He describes erotogenic masochism as receiving pleasure from physical pain and feminine masochism as pleasure in submission.[44] While erotogenic and feminine masochism appear to describe elements of masochism found in *Three Essays* and "A Child Is Being Beaten," moral masochism is an entirely new entity. Freud describes moral masochism as an unconscious desire for punishment that manifests itself clinically as almost paralyzing feelings of guilt. While moral masochism is obviously novel, the other forms are conspicuously revised so as to integrate Freud's belief in Thanatos and his new bimodal (pleasure/pain and life/death) framework. Freud hypothesizes that erotogenic masochism, born out of the struggle and fusion of the libido and the death drive, is at the base of both feminine and moral masochism.[45]

Moral masochism, characterized by an unconscious guilt, is remarkable because it "loosened its connection with what we recognize as sexuality."[46] In saying this, Freud writes that the primary focus in moral masochism is suffering; "Whether it is decreed by someone who is loved or by some-one who is indifferent is of no importance."[47] The explicit sexuality of ero-togenic and feminine masochists is replaced by suffering. This does not mean that the libidinal aspect disappears, however; in moral masochism, guilt houses the libido. To understand this logic, one must remember that Freud theorizes that conscience and morality are functions of the super-ego, which develops through overcoming the Oedipus complex.[48] Once a child processes his or her libidinal attraction to both parents, the par-ents are introjected into the ego and the child seeks other erotic objects. In moral masochism, the ego rather than the superego seeks punishment at the hands of parental power. This desire to be "beaten by the father" signals a resexualization of the Oedipus complex, which causes a regres-sion from morality to the Oedipus complex. In order to achieve the desired punishment, "the masochist must do what is inexpedient, must act against his own interests, must ruin the prospects which open out to him in the real world and must, perhaps, destroy his own real existence."[49] Freud writes that this "turning back of sadism against the self regularly occurs where a *cultural suppression of the instincts* holds back a large part of the subject's destructive instinctual components from being exercised in life."[50] The more the masochist refrains from hurting others, the greater his own suffering and sense of guilt become, but this provides some plea-sure; as Freud writes, "Even the subject's destruction of himself cannot take place without libidinal satisfaction."[51]

In his discussion of moral masochism, Freud rekindles masochism's rela-tionship to pathology by focusing on the individual masochist and his or her relationship to others. The moral masochist wants to submit to and be pun-ished by his or her parents (though Freud was speaking mostly of a paternal figure). This arrangement, however, is not realizable because it takes place in the individual's unconscious where parents (even if living) can never actual-ize their roles as punishers. According to Freud, the impossibility of this per-formance of submission and punishment leads the masochist to consciously act out suffering in nonsexual ways. The moral masochist depends on soci-ety to help him or her enact suffering upon him- or herself.

Suffering, Sympathy, and Race

Labeling the liberal subject masochistic echoes Fanon's comments about the white man's masochism. As I argued in chapter 2, this masochism is born from the guilt produced by the white man's racism. Fanon's coding of guilt and masochism as white offers ways to theorize the guilt of whiteness as the underside to the work of sympathy and empathy. In rendering the black body synonymous with pain, white sentiment and black objectification are activated. To this end, legal scholar Anthony Farley argues that the discourse of race is "a discourse of pleasure-humiliation. In talking about race, we make ourselves white and black—a process which produces pleasure for the former through the humiliation of the latter."[52] Farley argues that the production of the suffering black body "is a process by which whites exorcise their own demons, and is, therefore, a pleasure in itself"; the black body is what the white body is not, and the ability to conceive of both is predicated on the specter of the black body in pain.[53] Race, then, is a social phenomenon born out of the "pleasure of comparison," a pleasure that Farley, channeling the Marquis de Sade, describes as "born of the sight of wretched persons."[54] Race is about power and sentiment. Farley's invocation of Sade is unexpected, but it speaks to a way of understanding racialization as a process not only of Othering but of cruelty. However, Sade's presence is significant for another reason. It further emphasizes our ability to theorize racialization as a process of becoming-biological. Sade, as Beauvoir points out, is a philosopher of the flesh and as such privileges, and even prizes, suffering. In summing up his philosophy, she writes, "Pleasant sensations are too mild; it is when the flesh is torn and bleeding that it is revealed most dramatically as flesh."[55] Since suffering reveals the body to be a body, we can theorize becoming-black as an amalgam of suffering and becoming-biological.

If the biological and suffering can be read as sensations of becoming-black, how do these processes activate white (masochistic) liberal subjectivity? The answer, I argue, lies with the structures of sympathy and empathy, which fuse sentiment with fleshiness and rely on the labor of the black body. Empathy and sympathy are two of racialization's pleasures of comparison.

In *Scenes of Subjection*, Saidiya Hartman illuminates the pernicious undertones of empathy by analyzing the tableaux of suffering that abolitionists presented to garner support for their cause. These pleas for emancipation were largely based on long descriptions of the suffering of slave bodies. Hartman argues that while pain provided the "common language of humanity," it also "required that the white body be positioned in the place of the black body in order to make this suffering visible and intelligible."[56] Empathy functions by asking the listener to imagine him- or herself in the scene of suffering. Seeing the black body as biological facilitates this process, but this substitution, a literal replacement of the white body for the black body, is dangerous both because it threatens to obliterate the suffering of the black body and because, as Hartman writes, it risks "naturalizing the condition of pained embodiment."[57] This, in turn, further entrenches blackness within a biological milieu saturated with pain.

Karen Halttunen links the rise of empathy in the late nineteenth century with the emergence of "the pornography of pain, which represented pain as obscenely titillating precisely because the humanitarian sensibility deemed it unacceptable, taboo."[58] As society became more bourgeois, the desire to inflict or receive pain became a marker of savagery. Pain was redefined as unacceptable and became repulsive.[59] Further, Halttunen argues, this revulsion coincided with an explosion of fantasies of beatings, murder, and flogging, all of which made it into nineteenth-century sexological texts, including Krafft-Ebing's *Psychopathia Sexualis*. One of the text's more infamous case studies wrote that he used Harriet Beecher Stowe's *Uncle Tom's Cabin* as grist for his pornographic fantasies: "Particularly exciting for me was the thought of a man being hitched to a wagon in which another man sat with a whip, driving and whipping him."[60] The explicit eroticization of suffering is striking for its omission of race. The writer does not describe the man being whipped as black, but by invoking *Uncle Tom's Cabin* he does not need to. It is understood that the body that suffers will be black. Therefore, we cannot consider his pleasure in the scene without considering race, especially because his pleasure is derived from the black body in pain. Whiteness, Farley argues, produces a "sadistic pleasure" from the black body in pain, whereas the pleasure of blackness "is a form of humiliation."[61] Hartman argues that the "black performative is inextricably linked with the specter of contented subjection, the torturous display of the captive body, and the ravishing of the body that is the condition of the other's pleasure."[62] What is ambiguous in this fantasy is the narrator's subject position—Is he identifying with the person being whipped, that is to say, has he substituted his own body for the body of the suffering black man, is he the one causing the pain, or is he a voyeur, someone gaining pleasure (corporeal, physical, or psychic) from this scenario through the workings of empathy?

We might also draw parallels between empathy and analogy, which we see most prevalently in rhetoric analogizing interracial and same-sex marriage prohibitions. Siobhan Somerville describes the miscegenation analogy as "obscur[ing] the complicated ways in which race and sexual orientation have been intertwined in US law. Too often the history of interracial heterosexuality in the United States is narrated as if it had nothing to do with the history of homosexuality—except as a precedent."[63] As Somerville makes clear, the connection produced by analogy actually works to naturalize each category and keep them separate. In his own analysis of analogizing same-sex and interracial marriage, David Eng points out that the separateness works with a historical amnesia to produce a rhetoric of color blindness, that is to say, being beyond race.[64] In this invocation of a postracial society, racial difference is theorized as something that no longer structures rights and privileges, thereby writing out the black body in favor of the white body. The intimacy that empathy produces in these situations renders the black body superfluous, made irrelevant by the focus on the present discomfort of the white body.

Sympathy functions according to a different though similar pernicious logic. In *Rule of Sympathy*, Amit Rai argues that in England at the time of the abolitionist movement sympathy "was a paradoxical mode of power" because the differences between object and agent were precisely what needed to be bridged, but "without such differences, which were inequalities of power, sympathy could not function; sympathy produced the very inequality it sought to bridge."[65] Sympathy demonstrated the humanity of blacks while simultaneously othering them. Perversely, those in possession of sympathy were seen as virtuous, thus further distancing themselves from the objects of their pity. Here, again, the black body worked to produce white subjectivity.

We can see more clearly how sympathy operates by looking at a more contemporary example of its failure. Alfred Blumrosen, a civil rights activist, blames the lack of sympathy for the difficulty in increasing civil rights in the 1980s. He writes, "The public sympathy for the plight of black Americans circa 1965 cannot be recreated, because the condition of black American(s) in 1985 is so much improved, as a result of the 1964 legislation. The success of the Civil Rights Act contained the seeds of its loss of public support."[66] By arguing that white Americans no longer feel sympathy for black Americans, Blumrosen makes it clear that sympathy requires the production of distance. According to the logic of sympathy, white Americans supported the 1964 Civil Rights Act because the specter of black suffering was distinct from their own experiences, so that they could objectify and separate blackness and simultaneously produce themselves as virtuous subjects. Blumrosen highlights the dangers of sympathy. As a structure reliant on and mobilized by a power imbalance, it provides shaky ground for a discourse on rights. Ultimately, sympathy does not tend toward equality; rather, it seeks a preservation of an imbalanced status quo. Maintaining a sense of the black body as biological and atemporal is a crucial part of preserving this asymmetry. Further, the place of the biological in this racialized structure produces sympathy as one of the sadistic pleasures of comparison that Farley invokes and foregrounds sympathy's activation of suffering flesh.

When we add race to these structures of sentiment, in addition to objectification, we get white guilt, in particular white liberal guilt. We can add a twist to this, however, when we think about Julie Ellison's analysis of liberal guilt. Though race is at the forefront of her analysis, as a feeling, guilt, she argues, is particular because it is marked by inadequate action, that is to say that it produces action that is "never sufficient to the scale of the problem."[67] Echoing Fanon's claims about white masochism, Ellison argues that "liberal guilt is bound up with the feeling of being implicated in systems of domination and with the subsequent awareness of the emotional instability produced by this ambivalent position."[68] Ultimately, liberal guilt is born from spectatorship: "When those who suffer gaze back at those who do not, guilt is the consequence."[69]

This formulation of liberal guilt offers us a way to theorize it as a racialized performance of passivity. Not only does liberal guilt colonize the suffering of others, but it simulates the powerlessness of circumstance through masochism. Masochism cloaks the fact that one *could* act in the face of another's suffering and produces a discourse of innocence. This innocence is complicated; it is constructed through a focus on the suffering that guilt produces, which, in turn, manifests itself as empathy and analogizes the white body's current guilt to the black body's past (and present) trauma. Through empathy, the substitution of the white body for the black body, current guilt or suffering distracts from the choice of inaction and produces color blindness.[70] Here, we see a sharp distinction between guilt and shame. If Fanon's narrator is flooded with shame, it is because he has suddenly realized that he *cannot* act. This is where we see Sedgwick's colloquial difference between the two at work—guilt attaches to what one does, while shame attaches to who one is.[71]

Temporality, Subjectivity, and Suffering

Shame and inaction characterize Fanon's description of becoming-black, but underlying this is the problem of time. In thinking about temporality, I take up Fanon's revision of Freud because it helps to articulate what precisely is at stake for Fanon when one is rendered atemporal. Freud's emphasis on analyzing masochism as a temporality of stasis and repetition allows us to see more clearly how he theorizes submitting to a regime of progressive temporality as a central component of healthy subjectivity. This, in turn, illuminates the atemporality of the becoming-biological of black bodies.

Even as Freud's analysis of masochism shifted over time, it remained associated with stasis. In "A Child Is Being Beaten" Freud delves further into masochism as a state of arrested development. The essay is a case study of six children that aimed to describe the role of fantasy (particularly of the masochistic variety) in neurosis.[72] Ultimately, Freud argues that the children's desire to see another child punished is a form of masochism that is related to the reactivation of the Oedipus complex. Freud uses the child's sexual impulses for her father, which are manifest as the Oedipus complex, to explain the child's desire for punishment—the child felt first jealous of any attention to another child and then guilty for this emotion because of its sexual root.

In his discussion of moral masochism, Freud again explores masochism as a manifestation of a reactivated Oedipus complex. This allows him to script it as a perversion of stasis and repetition. In moral masochism, Freud argues that the subject is punished by an overactive superego, which Freud later equates with a desire for death (stasis). The masochist wants punishment and repeats his or her performances of "misbehavior" in order to self-punish through guilt. This confuses temporality because the subject seeks to produce a future in the image of the past. Novelty is not the goal; what the masochist wants is a perpetual sameness. This static time echoes the move toward death, which Freud describes as complete inactivity.

Since Freud theorizes masochism as a disruption in the various temporal schemas that organize the subject, his descriptions of masochism are instructive because they offer insight into the way Freud's subject is rooted in time. Freud formulates a subject who is beholden to both individual time and generational time. Masochism suspends that temporality: first, because it signals a moment where the past continually repeats, and second, on a larger scale, because it is intimately connected with the Oedipus complex and with a temporality of generations.

Fanon's Negro offers an arresting counter to Freud's masochist because he also occupies a temporality of stasis. This atemporality, however, is not due to the Oedipus complex; it has to do with the fact that the Negro as a category is associated with the primitive and the biological. The Negro is firmly rooted in the past. In Fanon's narrative, the black man's suffering occurs in the realm of the interior. His emptiness is triggered not by physical blows but by a linguistic act. The affective flows that are opened by interpellation have their roots in the social and historical, not the sensational. The shame that is produced is due to the recognition of the Negro's position in the social field. As Ann Pellegrini notes, "Interpellation proceeds as if through a mirror."[73] The mirror that reveals the Negro's blackness simultaneously acts to negate the coherence of the black subject. Anchoring the mirror in the linguistic, as Pellegrini does, allows us to use Lacan to unpack how Fanon's Negro remains mired in the psychoanalytic despite the nonapplicability of the Oedipus complex. Though Fanon substitutes whiteness and France for the paternal inauguration into the Symbolic, the fact that this assault takes place in the realm of language illustrates one of the ways that Fanon's subject remains in the psychoanalytic fold.

Fanon's subject is also attached to psychoanalysis because, as Daniel Boyarin notes, "Psychoanalysis is *au fond* not so much a Jewish science as a science of the doubled colonized subject."[74] In making this comment Boyarin situates Freud's theories as reflective of Freud's status as an outsider because of his Jewishness. Though Fanon does not speak explicitly about Freud's Jewishness and does not appear to theorize psychoanalysis in this vein, *Black Skin, White Masks* contains many references to the plight of Jewish men and the commonalities between anti-Semitism and Negrophobia. After a lengthy discussion comparing the two, Fanon writes, "Fault, guilt, refusal of guilt, paranoia—one is back in homosexual territory. In sum, what others have described in the case of the Jew applies perfectly in that of the Negro."[75] This is Fanon's attempt to link blackness and Jewishness through the historical and social similarities of oppression. In her analysis of this union, Pellegrini argues that Fanon achieves this cross-racial assimilation through "the fantasy of shared *powerlessness* . . . at the expense of a scapegoated homosexuality."[76] Fanon places homosexuality not alongside but below the black man and the Jewish man in terms of theorizing masculinity and subjectivity, which in Fanon's mind seem to operate synonymously. Pellegrini argues that the figure of the homosexual, which is coded as feminine, also becomes a way for Fanon to differentiate between the black man and the Jewish man. While Fanon fixates on the attacks on the black man's physicality, symbolized through the penis, the Jewish man is described as representative of his race. Pellegrini writes that Fanon "assimilates Jewish men to the feminine" in a "recapitulation" of stereotypes that evoke castration and "effectively deny Jewish men personality and particularity."[77] This reifies the black man as corporeal and masculine.

Aside from Fanon's attempt to parse masculinity racially, what is striking about his words is his invocation of guilt. He does not link the Jewish man and black man through shame, which was an affect that we saw in abundance in his narration of his coming to be a subject; rather, he focuses on guilt, the affect that we can link to sympathy, liberal subjectivity, and the pleasures of comparison. His status as a subject seems to have been bolstered through comparison. It is also interesting to note that he may not invoke shame because the processes of becoming-Jewish and becoming-black diverge. At the time of Fanon's writing (1952), becoming-Jewish operated according to the discourse of confession; the notion of visible Jewishness was largely replaced with a theorization of Jewishness as a potentially hidden identity. Fanon writes, "The Jew can be unknown in his Jewishness."[78] Identification of Jewishness could occur following a disclosure. Becoming-black, on the other hand, was something that one experienced through interpellation. Though there were cases of "confessing" to blackness, Fanon is more invested in those who were deemed black by society.

Indeed, this lack of agency is central to Fanon's argument that the black man cannot be a masochist. Through interpellation, the black man is robbed even of the potential pleasure of inhabiting infelicity. Passivity, which the masochist exhibits through either guilt or performance, is not equivalent to the black man's inability to act. Though Fanon adopts Sartre's outlook on the impossibility of transcendence when one is an object, he does not consider the objectification of the Negro masochistic. This is due to his conflation of masochism with psychoanalysis and the particular way that the Negro is made an object. In contrast to blackness, which is overdetermined from without, masochism is a stance that one has to adopt. Though the Negro's passivity looks similar, he has none of the masochist's powers of transformation. His becoming-a-Negro coincides with the shattering of his previous fantasy of whiteness (thought to be reality) while the masochist remains within the realm of agency and fantasy. While he plays at objecthood and passivity, the Negro cannot escape it.

Yet in that space of slippage between guilt and shame we see Fanon's narrator evoking his own pleasures of comparison vis-à-vis the Jewish man. It is a minor pleasure that is quickly repudiated with "not guilt" and "paranoia," but it does suggest an opening in Fanon's understanding of blackness as a zone of nonbeing. That vulnerability opens a space to bridge this rift between shame and guilt, subjectivity and objectivity, and suffering through pleasure. Yet it is a fraught pleasure because it does not actually move beyond the cycles of sympathy and empathy and sadism and masochism that I have described throughout the chapter. Fanon even notes the fragility of subjectivity founded on comparisons: "The Negro is comparison.... That is, he is constantly preoccupied with self-evaluation and with the ego-ideal. Whenever he comes into contact with someone else, the question of value, of merit, arises. The Antilleans have no inherent values of their own, they are always contingent on the presence of The Other."[79]

In accordance with Fanon's desire to distance the black man from psychoanalytic structures, he turns to history to reject the Oedipus complex, yet he produces a subject who is still mired in psychoanalysis. While Fanon's critique of the Oedipus complex is rooted in the historical realities of Martinique and the absence of a norm of nuclear families, for Fanon the Negro's struggle with becoming-black is deeply bound up with psychoanalysis. Fanon's insistence on focusing on nation instead of family is not minor; it serves as the basis for his counter to the Oedipus complex. Family is central to the Oedipal schema and is the structure that makes sexuality visible. Through taboos against incest, the family structure enacts repressions, which Freud argues are necessary for the advancement of civilization: "The very incapacity of the sexual instinct to yield complete satisfaction as soon as it submits to the first demands of civilization becomes the source, however, of the noblest cultural achievements which are brought into being by ever more extensive sublimation of its instinctual components."[80] It is taken for granted that sexuality is both what causes the family to cohere and what acts as an agent of individual and societal change. Without the familial structure, without Oedipus, sexuality is dethroned as civilization's reigning paradigm and becomes a cultural effect.

Against Oedipus Fanon situates the Negro, whom he defines in terms of lack and desire. The lack of father, the lack of recognition, and the lack of sexuality operate in tandem with the desire for nation and brother-hood. Fanon's Negro is a non-Oedipal subject because of the historical forces of colonialism. His impotence, however, mires him in shame. For Fanon, not being a subject comes at significant cost; it means being a body awash in affect. As an effort to counter the potential isolation of shame, Fanon attempts redemption through a new vision of community, which sidesteps shame by revising kinship and focusing on solidarity.

Fanon's theorization of solidarity provides us with an alternate posi-tion on what it is to exist outside of normative temporality. We have already discussed how his experiential narrative of life outside of Oedi-pus is imbued with shame and bad feeling. This may give us pause, but ultimately Fanon speaks of freedom and possibility—a vision of broth-ers banded together in a common fight. In his elaboration of solidarity, he, too, describes non-normative temporality. Fanon's new nation occu-pies the time of the future (he expresses it as a wish for what is yet to come); the past, while important, does not determine the nation's shape: "I am not the slave of the Slavery that dehumanized my ancestors [mes pères]."[81] We can align Fanon's optimism and interest in the future with that of José Esteban Muñoz, who argues passionately for queer futu-rity: "The future is queerness's domain. . . . The here and now is a prison house. We must strive, in the face of the here and now's totalizing ren-dering of reality, to think and feel a *then and there*."[82] While Fanon, too, speaks of a future that is not determined by the past, it is important to note that his vision of futurity is not ahistorical. Though he speaks of a future nation unburdened by the structures of domination and discrimi-nation that marked his ancestors (and arguably his own) existence, he remains attentive to this past even as he dreams of moving beyond it.

Blackness and Other Sticky Subjects

While it is tempting to read the biologization of blackness against Sim-one de Beauvoir's discussion of women's objectification as a mode of being "shut up in her flesh, her home," there are crucial differences.[83] Though both refer to a scopic form of domination, Beauvoir's under-standing of objectification is based on the premise of disavowed auton-omy while the black man's becoming-biological is understood not only as a form of passivity but as an act of dismemberment. While Beauvoir's woman is shut up in *her* home, the black man is owned by someone else, and it is clear that his body is more valuable than his mind. This biologization of the Negro, then, is anatomical and premised on a particular form of depersonalizing violence. Lee Edelman describes this substitution of the part for the whole as "the master trope of racism that gets deployed in a variety of different ways to reinforce the totalizing logic of identity."[84] Not only is this a violent form of corporeality, but it is a mode of becoming-flesh that is particularly dehumanizing because it reinforces the status of the body as flesh at the cost of personhood.

Returning now to the question of sensation, I want to ask what sensations attend this form of becoming-black. Though Fanon has illuminated the ways that the black man also suffers guilt and shame, we need a new metric for analysis. In contrast to feeling complicit in the pain of others, Fanon's Negro experiences shame at his inability to act. This immobility is yet another manifestation of powerlessness and objectification. Yet the sensations affiliated with this are remarkably different from the coldness that marks complicity; the sensation that Fanon's Negro experiences is what I have described throughout this chapter as a becoming-biological and a particular type of embodiment of temporality. It is the temporality of the stagnant, of the always-already. Though it is tempting to link this to the temporality of suspension and stasis that marks masochism, it is important to see that they differ: the ideal masochistic transformation leads to the emergence of novelty—a new subject—while Fanon's Negro becomes atemporal and essentialized. In becoming-black, particularity is erased, and this loss of individuality, which I describe as becoming-biological, is experienced as a collapse of history into atemporality.

Throughout *Black Skin, White Masks,* we see Fanon grappling with history and agency. At times, he accepts the collapse of history: "Some identified me with ancestors of mine who had been enslaved or lynched: I decided to accept this. It was on the universal level of the intellect that I understood this inner kinship—I was the grandson of slaves in exactly the same way in which President Lebrun was the grandson of tax-paying, hard-working peasants."[85] This is a tentative truce, however, because he is still imagining that there is space for the particular in this connection to his ancestors. By comparing his position to that of France's president, he ignores the deindividualizing aspects of becoming-black. Later, he uses Jung to describe the psychological weight of this transformation: "As I begin to recognize that the Negro is the symbol of sin, I catch myself hating the Negro. But then I recognize that I am a Negro."[86] Fanon seems to sum up the Negro's dilemma thus: "The Negro is aiming for the universal, but on the screen his Negro essence, his Negro 'nature,' is kept intact."[87] Though he wants to *make himself recognized,* essence, nature, biology, and history all collapse onto the figure of the black man.[88]

Darieck Scott provides several ways to read Fanon's interest in temporality. On the one hand, he offers it as an argument for Fanon's interest in the possibility that history offers. If blackness has been shaped in this way historically, it opens doors for change and a new way of being. Scott suggests that "his theory of the historical, his way of thinking of its presence in the ongoing emergency of the now, involves an attempt to organize the information of history along nonlinear axes and in ways that frame its effects as not fully determinative: a reorganization and reframing that the all-questioning revolution which accompanies and grounds the formation of national (as opposed to racial) consciousness permits us to envision."[89] In conjunction with this reading of history and revolution, Scott also reads other moments of Fanon's entanglement with the past as an investment in abjection. To this end, Scott writes, "I am interested in examining the abjection that makes the black past appear to be so useless (and terrifying), and which always has to be surpassed."[90] While we can see aspects of both of these readings in my discussion of Fanon, masochism, and agency, here I am most invested in Scott's discourse on abjection.

Though Fanon does not use this term to describe what it is that the Negro becomes when he becomes black, to speak of becoming-black as becoming-abject or rather encountering abjection feels particularly apt when we reflect back on how Fanon describes the traumatic encounter with blackness. In becoming-black, Fanon's narrator not only becomes a body but becomes a past and a race. This conflation of terms is indicative of what it is to inhabit an essentialized identity. In teasing out the contours of the relationship that Fanon forges between blackness and abjection, Scott, too turns to the body and the metaphor of muscular tension. Scott points to instances throughout *Black Skin, White Masks* and *Wretched of the Earth* where Fanon describes tense bodies as a reaction to being othered through colonialism and racism. Muscle tension has to do with physicality, but importantly it is also the mark of a particular embodiment of temporality.

> This state of muscle tension, resistant *and* terrified, tensely quivering at the juncture of the split by which the black/native subject is

> constituted, is a state which is constantly renewed. Muscle tension is repetitive; and its repetition effects the historical conquest and enslavement that is at the same time its foundation. . . . The repetitive character of the state of muscle tension, and the mimetic quality of its activity—action that does not act in a political sense but nevertheless acts out, a physical mapping of psychic tumult and desires that are repressed, consciousness held back from conscious recognition, trembling with the force of what it corrals but does not contain—gives us Fanon's descriptions of what it is to *live with and in* defeat, to be fully immured in the historically produced consequences of conquest, colonialism, and enslavement: to be black (or native), in other words, before acquiring national consciousness.[91]

Scott describes muscle tension as a marker of inhabiting a defeated past and a present that is mired in the same inability to act. As a metaphor it speaks both to the possibility of change (at an indeterminate time) and to the state of stagnation where past and present blur into a particularly pernicious form of stasis.

I have described Scott's analysis of Fanon's metaphor of muscles, tension, stasis, and abjection so extensively in large part because I think that it works well with my analysis of the sensation of becoming-black as becoming-biological. Here, I turn to the work of Glenn Ligon to articulate the sensation of becoming-black as an encounter with temporal stagnation and stickiness. Given the importance of language and interpellation to Fanon's analysis of becoming-black (here we recall Fanon's most famous line—Look, a Negro), Ligon's text paintings are an apt foil for unpacking the sensations that unfurl in this production of becoming-black. An encounter with Ligon means moving away from representations of the body toward understanding the spaces, sensations, and affects of interpellation. Ligon is a conceptual artist whose text paintings provide us with a glimpse into a space that is unclaimed by the figural. Ligon's body of work is diffuse. Influenced by abstract expressionism, his work evokes corporeality but rarely includes figural representations of bodies. Working with painting, photography, and other material to produce conceptual art, Ligon offers a meditation on identity.

Ligon's 1990 Door series, a collection of twenty-one paintings "eighty inches tall by thirty inches wide [that] repeat texts over and over in black oil stick stenciled first on white-primed, ready made doors and later on canvas," offers insight into the possibility of race without figural representation.⁹² One particularly evocative painting, *Untitled (I Feel Most Colored When I Am Thrown Against a Sharp White Background)*, draws on Zora Neale Hurston's 1928 essay "How It Feels to Be Colored Me." Ligon's painting repeats Hurston's phrase ("I FEEL MOST COLORED WHEN I AM THROWN AGAINST A SHARP WHITE BACKGROUND") over and over again. Beginning with sharp crisp black lettering against a sharp white background, the words gradually become smeared so that the background becomes less sharp and white and the words become less decipherable. Ligon describes this as "the disappearance of language."⁹³

In the catalogue for Ligon's midcareer retrospective in 2011 at the Whitney Museum of American Art, the curator, Scott Rothkopf, writes that this work has "spawned reams of critical exegesis," and indeed there is much to say about Ligon's citation of African American literature, his systematic method of painting, and the way he illuminates the constructedness of race.⁹⁴ However, I am most interested in how Ligon's attention to the text produces "sticky" bodies. The citation and repetition of Hurston's text produce numerous "I"s: Hurston, Ligon, the "I" of the black paint, an abstract black "I," and the viewer are all simultaneously invoked. The viewer is interpellated into the painting by the use of "I" and engages with the other potential "I"s via empathy. While the use of "I" summons the viewer, it also makes him or her aware that others are being hailed in this way. Thus one becomes black with an awareness of the multitude of historical entanglements that that entails.

Darby English describes Ligon's ability to call upon multiple voices as a tactic that "dislodges the strong purchase of the single artistic personality" in favor of emphasizing "individualized reception in order to establish the viewing situation as a site of risk and instability rather than consolidation."⁹⁵ Instead of bringing forth something particular about Ligon's vision, the painting's meaning emerges as a dialogue with the viewer so that it shifts according to any number of affective, environmental, and identitarian factors. Rothkopf argues that the variable experiences one has with the paintings and the various interpretations produce a distinct corporeality. The "I" and the viewer both become-flesh: "The work . . . addresses us physically as a body while it forces us to question our sense of our own bodies and those of others. Taken together, his phrases constitute a densely layered polyphonic response to what it means to be black or white, to be perceived as one or the other, to desire and to frighten, and to be the object of those verbs. Before his endlessly

Glenn Ligon, *Untitled (I Feel Most Colored When I Am Thrown against a Sharp White Background)*, 1990–91. Oil-stick and gesso on panel, 80 x 30 inches. Courtesy of the artist and Luhring Augustine, New York.

babbling paintings, we feel confused, disoriented, a bit off-kilter. The strain of looking and reading extends to our sense of being visible to others and to ourselves."[96] While Rothkopf describes Ligon's work as calling attention to visibility, I argue that it actually calls attention to the affective charge of race. Ligon produces a way for the viewer to inhabit the space of blackness without actually seeing black bodies. This corporeal inhabitation is markedly different from the sympathy or empathy/analogy that the specter of the black body in pain produces. Crucially, it is a space of simultaneity rather than a relation rooted in the past or suspension, though it gestures toward the past through its use of sticky, viscose paint. This multiple presence allows for a multiplicity of affects that extend beyond shame, guilt, and suffering into multiple modes of being. By producing this mode of inhabitation, Ligon also works around the power dynamics of looking—the line between spectator and spectacle does not exist. English describes Ligon's work as "undo[ing] beholding by involving us in an intimacy that is *at one and the same time* a byproduct of the mutual colonization that constitutes viewing a work of art in its fullness, *and* a dramatic two-party staging of 'race-differences in the making.'"[97] The removal of the power of voyeurism allows us to experience racialization in a different way. We see the effects of racialization *and* possibilities for it to be different.

Ligon's mode of producing race consciousness has implications beyond the artistic. Alongside affective inhabitation, we can place Antonio Viego's call for rethinking ethnic-racialized subjects. In *Dead Subjects*, Viego writes that racism depends "on a certain representational capture of the ethnic-racialized subject—rendered as transparent to the signifier, potentially whole and unified."[98] Ethnic-racialized subjects are, in Viego's words, "reduced . . . to whatever can be gleaned from an analysis of the social and cultural forces that affect these subjects."[99] My analysis of blackness as a mode of anatomization speaks to the way black subjectivity has been ignored in favor of the signifying power of the black body in pain. Adopting a Lacanian perspective, Viego argues that disrupting the transparency and unity of this subject, read as a perpetual victim, in order to "insist on the incalculable and indeterminate" is crucial to producing antiracist discourse.[100] In bringing attention to the subject's multiplicity and opacity, Viego calls for further attention to reading these subjects as complex and multiple. Through their emphasis on multiplicity and shifting modes of experiencing both blackness and whiteness, Ligon's paintings offer a path toward rethinking race.

In representing historical modes of racialization through stickiness, Ligon's work also connects to my analysis of blackness as a mode
of inhabiting the biological that ignores black subjectivity in favor of
the signifying power of the black body in pain. We can look at Ligon's
process to see what affective work this mode of racialization does. In the
catalogue for Ligon's Whitney retrospective, Rothkopf describes Ligon's
painting process at length:

> He begins by selecting a phrase from Hurston . . . and then primes
> the surface of a door with gesso slightly doctored with marble dust
> and raw under Tints-All. Once the ground has dried, he covers the
> door from top to bottom with evenly spaced, horizontal pencil rules
> and adds a vertical line at the left to create a margin. . . . Working
> down the surface, Ligon faces countless small decisions that belie
> the systematic nature of his process. Can he squeeze in a full word
> before he reaches the edge of the door? Why leave so much empty
> space after the final COLORED on the tenth line. . . . Once Ligon
> reaches the end of the panel, days after he began, the painting seems
> exhausted, tense, a miasma of stuttering words caught in the act of
> emerging from and receding into one another. He stencils the final
> word, BECAME, so faintly that is it scarcely visible. The E barely
> fits. Ligon's voice—and Hurston's—can almost not be heard.[101]

In Rothkopf's description of Ligon's method, we see a portrait of an artist at work. Ligon toils over each letter, each space, each smudge. This
description is meant to remind the viewer that the paintings' deceptive
simplicity cloaks the artist's physical labor. The painting calls attention
to Ligon's corporeality even as it is not explicitly figured. The unique
quality of each letter testifies to Ligon's mental and physical work. We
can also read this suffering for art as a description of Ligon working
through not only Hurston's words but his own relationship to these
words. Ligon's laborious repetitions call to mind Freud's famous essay
"Remembering, Repeating, and Working Through," where repetition is a
form of reconstructing the past, albeit with a difference.[102] While Freud
sees these forms of repetition as an unconscious way of resisting a move
beyond a particular incident or trauma, I suggest we understand Ligon's
repetition as a process of working through, which Freud describes as "an
arduous task."[103] Through his artistic work, Ligon works through Hurston's words. He uses his body to either invest meaning in the words

or discharge them of meaning. English describes the result as producing "words [that] are very obviously *handled* to the point of dismemberment."[104] At the end of his process, the words are rendered illegible. By working through the words' affective charge, both Ligon and the viewer vanquish the specter of the suffering black body that haunts the word *colored*. Its stickiness, which I argue is a sensation of being-biological and stagnation, remains on the canvas. Ligon illuminates the residue of blackness's atemporality and abjection, but his process of muscle movement (rather than static tension) produces pain, not suffering.

Though the next chapter of this book addresses the question of pain more fully, a short detour here is useful because it allows us to think about the role that gender and agency play in my discussion of atemporality, suffering, and becoming-biological. Audre Lorde provides us with a qualitative and temporal distinction between pain and suffering: "Pain is an event, an experience that must be recognized, named, and then used in some way in order for the experience to change, to be transformed into something else, strength or knowledge or action. Suffering, on the other hand, is the nightmare reliving of unscrutinized and unmetabolized pain."[105] Lorde views pain as something sharp and distinct, while suffering exists as the eternal, "a seemingly inescapable cycle."[106] Through its lack of resolution, suffering essentializes the subject. Pain, on the other hand, is an event. It produces a becoming rather than stasis. Like Ligon's process of painting, it has a beginning and an end. This concreteness of an ending offers the possibility of mutability. Seen in this light, Ligon's paintings offer a record of suffering and its temporality of stagnation and stickiness. In order to resignify becoming-black as a space of positivity, I suggest rereading the painting as an event rather than something that is atemporal. This shift in temporality would also have the effect of removing blackness from the realm of labor. In this way, one can, as Lorde suggests, use that pain to "fuel some movement beyond it." Following Scott and others, this shift could allow pain to move toward pleasure and produce a new way of understanding race, where racialization is not equivalent to victimhood, which as we have seen, plays into a racist imaginary. These, however, are questions to be taken up in the book's conclusion.

In the meantime, we must pause here and ask what has happened to Hurston's voice or, indeed, the voices of black women. While Fanon very much understands the suffering of blackness as a problem of masculinity, Ligon evokes the feminine, as we can see through his use of

Hurston, though this work seems to erase any of the particularities that it might produce. In many ways this is not the task of that painting, but I would like to ask how we can understand these silences. On the one hand, they speak to a habit of equating blackness with masculinity; on the other hand, they also speak to the difficult subject position black women inhabit when speaking of suffering.[107] We might recall *The Story of O*'s or *Venus in Furs*'s rendering of black women as affectively absent or emotionally distant. We might also bring the familiar trope of the angry black woman into the conversation and ask how "anger" works differently from shame or suffering.[108] Here, I am most interested in exploring the difference between the stagnation and stickiness associated with becoming-biological and the affective and sensational force of anger.

As a response to pain, anger correlates with action. I make this statement in connection with the fact that Lorde's meditation on pain and suffering is embedded within an essay on black women and anger. "Eye to Eye" begins with the statement that "every Black woman in America lives her life somewhere along a wide curve of ancient and unexpressed angers."[109] Just as Fanon describes the psychic violence that blackness produces, Lorde has her own response to the pain of being a black woman in America. In contrast to the black man's dismemberment, the anatomization of black women occurs at the level of sisterhood. Lorde mourns the loss of these bonds and describes their undoing as a form of blood shedding: "If I have learned to eat my own flesh in the forest—starving, keening, learning the lesson of the she-wolf who chews off her own paw to leave the trap behind—if I must drink my own blood, thirsting, why should I stop at yours until your dead arms hang like withered garlands upon my breast and I weep for your going, oh my sister, I grieve for our gone."[110] Racism enacts the isolation of black women from each other by mobilizing hatred. Hatred is the affect that Lorde connects to inhabiting a white space, and it is pernicious because it is violent and individuating. Black women "grow up metabolizing hatred like daily bread [which] means that eventually every human interaction becomes tainted with the negative passion and intensity of its by-products—anger and cruelty."[111] Hatred isolates women and breaks the threads that Lorde argues naturally connect them: black women are connected by "a history of the use and sharing of power."[112] Lorde writes, "We have a tradition of closeness and mutual care and support, from the all-woman courts of the Queen Mothers of Benin to the present day Sisterhood of the Good Death."[113] This imagined female community is a provocative inverse of Fanon's postcolonial brotherhood and it is also the site of the greatest violence against black women.

In Lorde's narrative, anger is the result of social injustice; it is "a passion of displeasure that may be excessive or misplaced but not necessarily harmful."[114] That is to say, it is the active response to pain. It speaks not of passivity but of agency. Here we see another key difference between Lorde's response to racism and Fanon's. Her call for change requires anger and outrage and channels agency, not impotence. In this way, we can also read this as a return to the body. We can theorize anger as a different mode of anatomization. In contrast to Scott's descriptions of Fanon's tense muscles, Sara Ahmed describes the unhappiness caused by the angry black woman as producing tension outside of her own body: "It is not just that feelings are 'in tension' but that the tension is located somewhere: in being felt by some bodies, it is attributed as caused by another body, who thus comes to be felt as apart from the group, as getting in the way of its organic enjoyment and solidarity."[115] Anger corporealizes others while simultaneously making the others aware of the subjectivity of the angry agent. Anger produces unruly subjects, who disrupt the passive suffering that sympathy and empathy require; a subject who speaks for herself elicits irritation but not guilt.[116]

Anger is the state that Fanon wants to mobilize toward. It is the emotion that allows for action and agency and, ultimately, solidarity. The cycles of guilt and shame that sympathy and empathy mobilize and the sensations of becoming-biological and atemporal stagnation "vex masculinity."[117] That is to say, this space of abjection exists as what Scott describes as "*not*-masculine," which signals a distance from the presumed masculinity of the liberal subject and a distance from the feminine. Scott explores this other space as a way to illuminate the power in abjection when it is not collapsed with an assumed feminine powerlessness. I call attention to this space because it helps us to see the nuanced corporeal ways that becoming-black (and male) produces a particular mode of objectification. In these last few pages, I have gestured toward possibilities that we might use to rethink these modes of objectification by taking gender into account. This, however, is only the beginning of exploring what happens when we center pain. In the following chapter, I explore more fully what affective and subjective transformations pain enables.

5

Lacerated Breasts: Medicine, Autonomy, Pain

> Of my own free will, I, Bob Flanagan, grant you, Sheree Rose, full ownership and use of my mind and body. I will obey you at all times and will wholeheartedly seek your pleasure and well being above all other considerations. I renounce all rights to my own pleasure, comfort or gratification, except so far as you desire or permit them. I renounce all rights to privacy or concealment from you. I will answer truthfully and completely to the best of my knowledge any and all questions you might ask. I understand and agree that any failure by me to comply fully with your desires shall be regarded as sufficient cause for severe punishment. I otherwise unconditionally accept as your prerogative anything you may choose to do with me whether as punishment for your amusement or for whatever purpose no matter how painful or humiliating to myself.[1]

Viewers hear these words as they watch black-and-white images of a naked man with his legs and arms spread apart and chained to the ceiling and floor of what appears to be a basement recreation room. In the short film *Bob and Sheree's Contract*, which is included in *Sick*, a documentary on performance artist Bob Flanagan's life and death, Flanagan's oath to Sheree Rose plays over footage of them engaged in an S&M scene. Rose wears trousers and a T-shirt; Flanagan is immobilized by the chains. He closes his eyes while she rubs a cotton ball with alcohol over his chest. She sterilizes the blade of an X-Acto knife and carves an S into the side of his chest. Rose then photographs her work, and the film concludes with a close-up of blood beginning to seep from the wound.

On the surface this appears to be a typical S&M scene. Flanagan and Rose are performance artists whose sadomasochistic relationship provides fodder for their art. Flanagan met Rose, whom Dennis Cooper describes as a "housewife turned punk scenester with a master's degree in psychology" and no previous experience with S&M, on Halloween in 1980.[2] They quickly moved in together, and Flanagan declared that he would be content to live chained up in the basement of their home. But, as Chris Kraus writes, "Rose had other plans."³

Bob and Sheree's Contract, the black-and-white video made in 1982, is one of their early collaborations; the central drama is not between Flanagan and Rose however, but between Flanagan and his body. In part this is illuminated by the video, which presents us with a tableau of domination and pain. Flanagan's pale white flesh underscores his (physical) vulnerability in this situation. The frequent close-ups of his eyes squeezed shut testify to the pain that he is enduring, while the beads of blood that we see at the end of the film are evidence of its reality and residence in his body. While Flanagan's words emphasize Rose's pleasure, the video focuses on his pain. In addition to these physical clues, the context of Flanagan's performance—his status as a man with a chronic illness— forces us to think about pain, agency, and subjectivity. Flanagan was diagnosed with cystic fibrosis as a young child and spent much of his life in and out of hospitals suffering from headaches, difficulty breathing, and stomach pain. He lived longer than most others with the disease, but he died on January 4, 1996, at the age of forty-three. His life and his death were marked by pain, much of it chronicled in his writing and performance art. His final published work, *Pain Journal*, gives a portrait of his mental and physical state during the last year of his life. Among his musings on mortality and complaints about his family are descriptions of his pain medications, his difficulty breathing, his nausea, his stomachaches, and his desire to participate in S&M scenes with Sheree Rose. Flanagan's relationship to pain, then, is complicated. He speaks of physical discomfort while he embraces S&M.

This chapter examines the relationship between pain, agency, subjectivity, gender, and race through the prism of illness. Illness, here, becomes a mode to probe powerlessness and becoming-flesh as something that comes from within in the cases of cancer, cystic fibrosis, and chronic debilitation. Flanagan offers one portrait of pain, Gilles Deleuze another, and Audre Lorde and her essays on cancer yet another. As I noted in the previous chapter, Lorde argues that pain produces anger and that that, in turn, leads to survival. In "Uses of Anger," she writes, "My anger has meant pain to me but it has also meant survival, and before I give it up I'm going to be sure that there is something at least as powerful to replace it on the road to clarity."⁴ In the previous chapter, I foregrounded the stagnation and "stickiness" associated with the suffering of becoming-black. Here, I am focusing on the possibilities that pain offers as a site of transformation and how those possibilities are marked by race and gender. This chapter uses pain as an analytic frame to understand how people cope with powerlessness that comes from within, when pain comes from the body because of illness. Beginning with an analysis of Flanagan's S&M play and working through Lorde and Deleuze's meditations on illness, this chapter foregrounds the politics of difference that attaches to the projects of producing subjective cohesion and making sense of bodily disintegration.

Performing Pain, Performing the Self: Bob Flanagan and Masochism

Bob and Sheree's Contract provides a starting point for analyzing the different ways Flanagan performs pain. While Rose sterilizes the blade, Flanagan closes his eyes and appears to steel himself for the impending cut. During the act, we see him looking down at his chest. There is a quick cutaway that shows him with his head arched back and his eyes squeezed shut. In the background, we see his shackled wrist with its venous catheter, a device to facilitate IV insertion. A tight close-up of the wound follows, then an image of Rose documenting her work; finally we see the wound begin to bleed. By arguing that pain is central to this video, I would like to clarify what I see as being at stake in this performance of pain.

In order to do so, I am borrowing from Patrick Anderson's four-point framework for discussing anorexia as a performance in *So Much Wasted*. Anderson argues that anorexia is "durational in character," that is to say, it is not constant but requires work to occur.[5] Anderson writes that it "cannot be named except in reference to its enactment through stretches of time."[6] Further, anorexia is also "an embodiment of predetermined modes of resistance to a given set of alimentary norms."[7] Resistance to societal understandings of nutrition and health is explicitly enacted by an anorexic's refusal to eat. Third, this resistance is increasingly mediated by various representational forms, which is to say that this embodied resistance occupies a recognizable form, though each individual manifestation may be different. Last, "Anorexia is defined by specularity"; it is a visible protest.[8]

Following this definition, I characterize Flanagan's pain in the S&M encounter as a performance. It easily meets Anderson's criteria: it lasts as long as Rose inflicts it upon him; it has been made visible—both by

Flanagan's grimaces and by his blood offering; it is recognizable as part of an established S&M scene; and it refuses societal norms of pleasure and happiness. Anderson's schematic is useful because it emphasizes sources of agency within the performance. In many ways recuperating agency and subversion in Flanagan's pain is akin to doing so in varying modes of anorexia. Flanagan's pain, which occupies a sphere of social undesirability and imagined irrationality similar to that of the anorexic's hunger, is also the way that he subverts norms.[9] Although he is already embedded within an S&M subculture, his embrace and display of pain mark his agency in a different way. Not only does he have control of the scene as a masochist, but he is displaying control over his illness.

Flanagan's performances underscore the fact that his body is where medicine and masochism meet, but they meet on different terms. While we can and, in fact, will consider the impact of these performances on the spectator, first I suggest we examine how Flanagan experiences pain. Medicine and disease transform Flanagan into a passive body; he writes that "it gave him awful stomach aches," a comment that underscores the fact that Flanagan makes cystic fibrosis (and the required medical inter- ventions) into the agents of his pain.[10] In contrast, he experiences S&M's pain as control and power. He narrativizes his masochism as a process that gives him increased control over his body and his pain. In *Sick: Bob Flanagan, Supermasochist*, the documentary about Flanagan's final years, he reflects on finding strength through masochism: "The stereotype of the masochist is sniveling and weak and it's actually not true. The mas- ochist has to know his or her own body perfectly well and be in full con- trol of their body in order to give control to somebody else or to give control to pain so the masochist is actually a very strong person and I think some of that strength is some of what I use to combat the illness."[11] In pitting masochism and cystic fibrosis against each other, Flanagan is describing a binary between activity and passivity. He privileges the active pain of masochism because it signifies knowledge, control, and white masculinity. It is active because it comes from a place of deep cor- poreal intimacy and self-knowledge. It testifies to his status as a survivor.

Flanagan's interest in pain as a productive space of agency and self- making is indicative of the larger history of pain, white masculinity, and the self. As Michel Foucault noted in *Discipline and Punish*, modernity recast the desire to inflict or receive pain as a marker of savagery, which, given my previous discussion of anatomization and the suffering black body, is unsurprising. Foucault related modern forms of punishment to the formation of "the modern soul and a new power to judge."[12] Central to this change was a move away from the corporeal (and the physically painful): "One no longer touched the body, or at least as little as possible, and then only to reach something other than the body itself. . . . From being an art of unbearable sensations punishment has become an economy of suspended rights."[13] It became socially unacceptable to inflict pain because it signaled irrationality. Further, as Talal Asad notes, modern societies became more interested in working to eliminate pain as part of their move toward secularism.[14]

In these statements, however, Foucault and Asad neglect the importance of a discourse on pain for the production of white masculinity. In tracing spectacles of violence and white masculinity in modernity, Kent Brintnall argues that while the ecstasy of sacrifice that characterized premodernity is gone, and while "those entities and bodies that are legitimate targets of violence [are marked] as wholly and completely other," artistic representations can perform this function; the representation, however, "cannot be a watered down, cruelty-free attempt to shock and titillate, nor can it be a scene of brutality with no frame of reference other than its own sadistic frenzy."[15] Through analyses of various tableaux of suffering white male bodies (such as Mel Gibson, Francis Bacon, Robert Mapplethorpe), Brintnall argues that suffering is critical to a certain discourse on white masculinity because it highlights the power and privilege that attend these bodies as they struggle against the assault of pain. Experiencing and getting through pain reifies their status as privileged white males. Brintnall writes, "Although suffering can signify vulnerability, weakness and limitation, enduring pain and injury requires resilience. Similarly, while display of the male body can both render it an object of erotic contemplation and reveal the fabrication of the masculine ideal, it can also mark the body *as* ideal, worthy of attention and admiration. This allure can, at the same time, make the masochistic trial itself appealing."[16] This explicit equation of masculinity and masochism harkens back to my discussion of white masculine domination being couched in terms of masochism in the discourses surrounding colonialism and patriarchy and my previous discussion of the formation of the white liberal subject. In these other formulations, masochism functions as a way to hide the power of the white masculine subject either by inventing a threat of domination (the butch or black man) or by focusing on his own woundedness within an economy of injury. This discussion of white masculinity and masochism differs because it is an attempt to consolidate and make visible the power of white masculinity *through* the spectacle of suffering.[17]

This conglomeration of self-mastery, white masculinity, and suffering is literalized in Flanagan's 1992 installation *Visible Man*. This piece consists of a clear anatomical model that Flanagan has altered so that it more closely reflects his corporeal reality; it is an autobiographical doll meant to mirror Flanagan. In this creation of his new self, his "wishful other self," Flanagan manipulates an extant anatomical model so that white liquid suggestive of sperm drips from the doll's penis, brown liquid, evoking feces, emerges from a hole in its posterior, and green liquid (a substitute for mucous) bubbles from its mouth. He describes his focus on these processes "because cumming and coughing is the only thing I do on a consistent basis these days and also shitting because with cystic fibrosis bad digestion has been with me all my life."[18] We can view this installation as a self-portrait of sorts; while foregrounding suffering, it also emphasizes Flanagan's masculinity and sexuality. Here, Flanagan reinvents himself as a version of the ideal man; suffering leads to reinvention.

Given this, it is not surprising that Flanagan cites Jesus, one of Christianity's master reinventors, to describe masochism: "Certainly Christ is the very first or the most famous masochist."[19] Flanagan's introduction of religion is another way to understand the agency at work in pain. In describing the shift in theorizing pain that secularism produces, Talal Asad argues that Christianity's justification of pain was attacked and replaced with pain that was "objectified, set in the framework of a mechanistic philosophy, and sited within an accumulating knowledge of the living body."[20] Flanagan's desire to seize control of his suffering allows him to return in some ways to an understanding of the self where "pain is not simply a *cause* of action, but can also itself be a *kind* of action."[21] Indeed, Asad argues that S&M allows for a secular conceptualization of agential pain against discourses of victimhood such as those that we examined in the previous chapter.[22] Importantly, as Brintnall describes, these concepts also work to reify certain concepts of masculinity by associating it with active pain and masochism. His performed powerlessness is actually a sign of his masculinity, domination, and whiteness.

Here, we might think about this discourse of white masculinity as residing alongside an erotics of confession, self-production, and pain. This is a relationship that has existed since Krafft-Ebing popularized the term in 1890. Unlike other psychosexual disorders, which some psychiatrists claimed marked the bodies of perverts, often according to the logic of degeneration, masochism could be detected only if one admitted desiring submission. For example, the author of case 50 in the seventh edition of *Psychopathia Sexualis* described himself as physically and mentally normal despite having masochistic desires:

> I must also confess that, in spite of its marked pathological character, masochism is not only incapable of destroying my pleasure in life, but it does not in the least affect my outward life. When not in a masochistic state, as far as feeling and action are concerned, I am a perfectly normal man. During the activity of the masochistic tendencies there is, of course, a great revolution in my feeling, but my outward manner of life suffers no change; I have a calling that makes it necessary for me to move much in public, and I pursue it in the masochistic condition as well as ever.[23]

This description underlines the importance of self-identification to the masochist. Without external symptoms, masochism could be thought of as an invisible pathology, manifest only in fantasies of submission that lurked within the corridors of the psyche until they could be coaxed to the surface if the appropriate opportunity presented itself. Access to the masochist's internal feelings was essential for diagnosis.

Since masochism could not be detected except through confession, the practice was crucial to the diagnosis of masochism. Thinking through confession, however, reveals tension between the medical ability to diagnose and the personal desire for self-knowledge/recognition. It highlights the complex maneuvering of agency between doctor/patient and confessor/confessant. On the one hand, it is easy to situate these confessions within what Michel Foucault terms the "incitement to discourse."[24] Certainly, we can read this impulse toward self-exposure as a method of self-disciplining. We can also see that this practice endows the medical establishment with power and authority, increasing their professional status, fostering the growth of the *scientia sexualis*, and devaluing self-knowledge. On the other hand, these confessions also serve as a method of subject formation and, in the case of masochism, an erotic practice. To this end, Krafft-Ebing was flooded was letters from patients containing confessions of masochism and other sexual desires. These writers wanted to be recognized as subjects and disciplined as perverts, a tension that highlights the erotics of confession.[25]

It is clear, then, that masochism and confession are intimately linked through the performance and the production of the self. In this way it is fitting that the inaugural confession in Rousseau's *Confessions*, which is itself considered an inaugural secular confession, a modern autobiography, and a description of a modern individual, concerns what has become known as masochism. In Rousseau's narration of the incident at Bossey, he describes a moment of transformation (his desires are forever altered by Miss Lambercier's actions), a tapestry of internal life (his guilt and shame at his desire for punishment), and an insistent sense of autonomy (through the very act of confessing).[26] Altogether, we have a portrait of an individual who emerges through masochism. He produces his selfhood both by embracing what he knows will be read as an illogical stance (embrace of pain) and by making that publicly known. In this way, his masochism and manipulation of pain is a technology of the self. It is also important to note that this construction of self is reliant on the stabilization of categories of whiteness and masculinity.

The public nature of this presentation of self and autonomy is also important. Implicit in this discourse of confession, pain, and masochism is the role of the public (real or imagined). We see this vis-à-vis Rousseau's autobiographical performance and Flanagan's art. Flanagan is explicit about inviting the public into his practice of S&M and weaving S&M into his performance of self. In part, his pleasure stems from what is happening to his body, but there is also a pleasure in reaction, a pleasure in subverting expectation, and a pleasure in being watched. We might say, then, that Flanagan's corporeal confessions are an integral part of his masochistic performance. Flanagan challenges the notion of masochism as a private practice by relying on an implicit audience and producing a performance of submission, guilt, or pain. In her review of Lynda Hart's book on S&M, *Between the Body and the Flesh*, Elizabeth Freeman describes witnessing as a central component of S&M. She writes, "The witnesses to an S/M act—the practitioners, the writer, the performance artist, the member of the audience, the voyeur, and, for this book, its writer and reader—are always already participants, both inside and outside the scene they see."[27] S&M's reliance on an economy of witnessing and its status as a "genre of testimony" illuminate the how the control of pain and the demonstration of agency can be thought in conjunction with the production of the individual and white masculinity.[28]

Flanagan and the Disintegration of Man

Against the transformative, self-making potential of active pain lurks another type of corporeal pain, which we might call chronic pain. This is the type of pain brought on by illness; it is pain that Flanagan cannot control, and in large part it works against these self-making efforts by continually revealing the body to be a material object that forces act on. In thinking about the ways that illness produces flesh, I turn to Jean-Paul Sartre. When contemplating the multiple ways that we experience our bodies as objects, he writes: "The psychic object apprehended through pain is illness. This object has all the characteristics of pain, but it is transcendent and passive. It is a reality which has its own time, not the time of the external universe nor that of consciousness, but psychic time. The psychic object can then support evaluations and various determinations. As such it is distinct even from consciousness and appears through it; it remains permanent while consciousness develops, and it is this very permanence which is the condition of the opacity and the passivity of illness."[29] For Sartre, illness is a thing unto itself. It is a condition, marked by pain, which adheres to its own logic (and temporality) that is separate from the influence of both the external world and one's consciousness. Illness, Sartre argues, "is a reality which has its own time." The reality that illness creates is informed not by external objective knowledge but by suffering and pain. Thus illness highlights the corporeality of the body while preying on the mind's inability to enact control: "The body is revealed by the illness and is likewise suffered by consciousness."[30] This fundamental lack of agency produces existential suffering, which offers a reminder that people inhabit bodies, which experience the world through a range of sensations including pain. Sartre describes "pain-consciousness" or the awareness of pain as something that separates consciousness of the external world from the body while simultaneously alienating the self from the body: "Pain-consciousness is an internal negation of the world; but at the same time it exists its pain— i.e., *itself*—as a wrenching away from self."[31] This dual action occurs because pain is a sensation that forces one to think through the body as occupying a space of being-for-others and being-for-itself. Recalling that Sartre's problem with masochism is that it is a preoccupation with being-for-others and objectification, pain also makes clear the uneasy balance between objectification and subjectification. While pain allows one to apprehend one's body as an object, awareness of this objectification is alienating to the subject. In his analysis of Sartre's phenomenology of illness, Fredrik Svenaeus summarizes the dilemma of alienation as "not only the experience of a psychic object, but an experience of the independent life of one's own body."[32] In revealing the object status of the body, illness reveals what it is to be flesh. In this way, it brings forth many of the categories of analysis that I have already used with regard to masochism. Sartre focuses on alienation and the feeling of corporeal otherness, but we should also consider connecting illness to the feeling that one lacks agency, which manifests itself as a distorted temporality and a fascination with one's flesh.

While the catheter in Flanagan's arm is an unremarkable part of the landscape of *Bob and Sheree's Contract*, it marks his body as a body dealing with chronic pain; in this case, it is the pain that comes with cystic fibrosis. The invocation of the temporality of chronic illness provides a sharp contrast to Anderson's criteria for performance as a technique of subversion. The pain caused by S&M is part of a performance, and as such it has a beginning and an end. Masochism's relationship to pain is one of control and subversion; pain is manipulated and enjoyed. The pain caused by cystic fibrosis, on the other hand, is marked by a distinct lack of agency on the part of Flanagan. While he has developed strategies of distraction and transformation (his S&M and masturbation), as evidenced by the ever-present catheter, Flanagan does not know when it will come and go. The experience of this pain is different from Flanagan's willful submission to S&M and, as such, allows us to see what happens when pain is not part of an economy of self-production and white masculinity. Sartre's phenomenology of illness gives us a way to describe the difference between the varieties of pain Flanagan experiences. First, he articulates the feeling of corporeal otherness, which Flanagan translates into eroticism. Second, his discussion of illness as a world where consciousness has no agency makes it easy to understand Flanagan's attachment to masochism as a mode of control and agency. Here we must also think about the helplessness that medical systems can produce. Without medical intervention Flanagan would not have survived beyond infancy, but it is also another structure to which he must submit, and his illness cannot be thought separately from this form of intervention. The frequent hospitalizations and medications are the context within which we come to understand Flanagan's battle with cystic fibrosis. Flanagan's *Pain Journal* offers insight into his attempts to negotiate between active pain, chronic pain, and medicine. This admixture extends to the explanation that Flanagan gives for his masochism. He writes that it developed in response to his childhood medical traumas. He says: "Because of my early, really horrible stomach-aches, I would rub against the sheets and pillows to soothe my stomach and this became more and more erotic—I started to masturbate that way; slowly it all blended together. One way of taking control of the stomach-ache was to turn it into an orgasm."[33] While Flanagan's scientistic understanding of his masochism recalls Freud's early explanation of masochism as an infantile confusion of pleasure and pain, it also rescripts the diseased body as sexual.[34] What is most notable about Flanagan's explanation, however, is the way that he reorients the constellation of affects and sensations that I examined in previous chapters. As we will see, his understanding of his masochism draws on notions of the phallus, cold maternity, and shame in very different ways.

On April 27, Flanagan describes a desire for masochistic pleasure because he has managed to silence the pain from cystic fibrosis: "Last call for Demerol (I wish). Don't need pain killers now. I'm a masochist again! Thirteen alligator chips after last nights [sic] entry. Wasn't as turned on as I was the previous night, but the discipline is still there."[35] In August, he describes getting excited by sadomasochistic thoughts but being unable to fathom the notion of the pain because of a headache: "It all looks good and makes me feel wistful, and it even makes my dick jump a little, but I just don't have the lungs for it. My head is throbbing like a gong. What other kind of pain do I need?"[36] Flanagan is aware of the irony of his situation and comments on it at length in a September entry:

> That's funny: I used to talk about *using* pain to reach an altered state: *I'm high as a kite on a drug called pain.* Well this kite has had all the wind knocked out of it. Some part of me is still a masochist, but I can't fight the shortness of breath, well I can fight it, but in order to do that I have to surrender to it and that means move slowly, sit still, and do absolutely nothing. SM requires a certain amount of running around and a lot of mind over matter. Fuck it, I'm tired. I don't mean tired tonight and I want to go to sleep, I mean life tired.[37]

From Flanagan, then, we see that there are depths of pain that S&M does not penetrate, that one needs to already have control over one's body in order to submit. Flanagan frequently frames his enjoyment of masochistic pain in terms of strength and endurance; he feels closer to his body, but more specifically he feels closer to his masculinity. As part of their sadomasochistic exchange, Flanagan's devotion to Rose comes through in the physical acts that he performs as her slave. He wonders if he and Rose "can get our mistress/slave thing back" in the absence of his physical prowess: "How can it work with me barely able to stand anything or do anything?"[38] For example, he describes seeing a friend help Rose mount curtain rods, a fact that "embarrasses [him]" and leads him to feel as though he has failed in his masochistic role: "I'm a long way from the slave I was."[39] The pain of cystic fibrosis leaves him fatigued and alienated from his body and masculinity.

Flanagan's statements speak to his frustration with his lack of control over what is happening in his body. Not only does Flanagan lack the ability to access his conscious method of coping with pain—S&M—but as his illness progresses his self-knowledge becomes outmoded and his body becomes more of an obstacle than an instrument. The palpable way that Flanagan experiences his body as an object complicates the spectatorial dimension of his performances of S&M. While this internal tension manifests itself as alienation, it plays out in myriad ways among his spectators. The becoming-flesh that illness produces disrupts the S&M scene. Though it appears only in the background of the scene, the catheter in Flanagan's arm not only forces us to confront his illness but deepens our understanding of Flanagan's body as flesh.

Flanagan plays with this objectification to a certain extent. Many of his later performances explicitly draw on medical themes in order to underscore the idea that Flanagan has already lost control of his body. Often, however, Flanagan subverts the expectations of submission through performance. His installation *Visiting Hours* is one such example. The show transforms a museum space into a simulation of a medical clinic with a waiting room and a hospital room. Flanagan plays the patient and is occasionally hoisted up by his feet toward the ceiling. In his discussion of the piece, Ralph Rugoff writes, "Perhaps the most disconcerting element of *Visiting Hours* is the underlying implication that desire and disease share a common principle of contagion."[40] In this instance, Flanagan's body is at once riddled with illness and objectified by medicine, but it remains a canvas for his art. Flanagan's participation in this alternative narrative of patienthood represents his submission to medicine (as a patient) and illness while making those terms signify differently. Rugoff writes, "Ironically, by subverting the clinical aura of the exhibition space, Flanagan was able to remind us of art's potentially therapeutic side effects."[41] This play between objectification and resignification illuminates the way that the chronic (pain, illness, temporality) forms a context for Flanagan's work.

If, however, we are *seeing* Flanagan's body made flesh, what does this mean? Flanagan's pain and objectification are made visible through both his facial gestures and his blood. While he could fake his response, we assume that the bodily fluids (tears, blood) offer a testament of his pain's realness. As Lynda Hart points out, pain is imagined to reveal the corporeal, what is thought of as the real thing, and in masochism "getting beyond words seems to be the thing, the point, the 'real thing.'"[42] Flanagan's visible illness also works to make his pain real. The audience does not have difficulty imagining that he is perpetually in pain. This realness has several effects, which Hart argues mark Flanagan's performances as queer. Queer performances, for Hart, are characterized by "a near collapse between the sign and referent": that is, they are not read as performances but taken to be a form of unmediated reality.[43] I argue that this willingness to imagine that there is no distance between what is being seen and what is felt by the performer replaces the critical impulse with empathy. If Flanagan's pain is real, the audience responds by recalling their own experiences of pain and grafting it onto his performance. On the one hand, this misrecognition allows spectators to imagine that acts are more painful than they actually are. As an example of this Hart describes the extreme audience reactions to Flanagan nailing his scrotum to a wooden board, "a procedure that he knows does not really hurt, but that appears to the audience to be excruciatingly painful."[44] Flanagan receives "a kind of gleeful (sadistic?) pleasure" from the audience reaction and repeats the act privately, deriving pleasure from the "*sight* of his scrotum splayed out and nailed down, so one might surmise that he places himself in the spectator's role when he performs this act in private."[45] This leads Hart to describe Flanagan as shamelessly shameless, in reference to Flanagan's excitement at making the public feel shame at their witnessing of his body and pain and shame at Flanagan's lack of shame. Hart writes, "It is credible that Flanagan would have begun to perform his masochistic sexuality in public in order to introduce an element (the spectators) that might have recharged his shame."[46] On the other hand, this discourse of realness allows the audience to imagine that they are enjoying a certain type of intimacy with Flanagan and that because they have access to his flesh his psyche is similarly transparent.

In an interview with Deborah Dreier, Rose dispels that idea: "We're playing with the idea of what's real. People say, 'This is so real, this is really Bob,' but it isn't exactly. When people see Bob in a hospital bed, it's Bob Flanagan they're seeing, but it's also Bob Flanagan playing Bob Flanagan. And it's only part of him that he's revealing at that moment, not the totality. . . . He's a real person, but at the same time he's also this object hanging there, and playing with that concept makes people really uncomfortable."[47] While this discourse of realness activates circuits of empathy because it allows people to imagine their bodies in place of Flanagan's suffering body, it also emphasizes Flanagan's singularity. As Amelia Jones argues, Flanagan's performances allow him to externalize his pain, but his "flamboyantly performed relationship to pain" has a distancing effect.[48] Jones writes that "Flanagan seduces us only to make us more aware of his singularity in pain."[49] Namely, what we become aware of is Flanagan's pain in illness. While we witness Flanagan's performance of pain, we cannot help but be reminded of the pain he cannot control. There is a perceived gap between the performer, "Bob Flanagan," who controls his pain, and Bob Flanagan, chronic sufferer of cystic fibrosis, and in that gap we become aware of Flanagan's vulnerability. This, Jones argues, illuminates the vulnerability of the white masculinity that Flanagan inhabits: "There is no essential 'male subject' here (wielder of the phallus, as confirmed through the veiling of his anatomical penis); rather, through medicine as well as the masochistic acts of mutilation, not to mention death, the (male) body in all of its vulnerabilities and contingencies is made evident."[50] The visibility of Flanagan's chronic pain hinders our reading of the pain that he sustains in his S&M performances as entirely voluntary. The viewer is always aware of the potential excess of pain caused by either Flanagan's cystic fibrosis or the medical treatments for it, which threatens to overwhelm any voluntary pain that he submits to. This disrupts the connection between masochism and white masculinity. If we are witnessing a body that suffers rather than a body in control of his own suffering, Flanagan's authority and domination over the scene are compromised, as is his masculine bravado. In return, however, we are given ways to queer white masculinity.[51]

Along these lines, Linda Kauffman reads Flanagan's performance of suffering as a deconstruction of masculinity. Further, she argues that Flanagan offers insight into the posthuman, "for he illustrates step by step how the human senses—taste, touch, smell, hearing, and sight—have been utterly reorganized by medical technology."[52]

In reading Flanagan's singular suffering as indicative of a larger discourse on the limits of humanity, Kauffman's understanding of Flanagan's performance of fleshiness, which she describes as having "no interiority, no transcendence—only the ills that flesh is heir to," has a certain resonance with the biological flesh that I argued the suffering black body connotes.[53] One of the primary differences between these ideologies, however, is Flanagan's embeddedness in technology and medicine. If Flanagan is posthuman, it is because his dependence on technology is clear. Rather than signifying a body that is primitive or historic, Flanagan's body can be read as a symbol of humanity's collective future.

This suggestion of futurity is also facilitated by the dynamic between Rose and Flanagan. In many ways their relationship appears to adhere to the model of maternal dominant and submissive masochist that Gilles Deleuze discusses in "Coldness and Cruelty."[54] In *Bob and Sheree's Contract*, Flanagan verbally cedes control of his body to Rose. Physically, his willing surrender is marked by the fact that he initiates the encounter by chaining his arms to the ceiling. As I have already discussed, Flanagan has set the terms of the contract. He gives Rose control over his pleasure *and* his pain. The realm of his corporeality is to be ruled by her. The film makes this manifestly clear by having her carve an S (for Sheree, perhaps) into his chest; his flesh belongs to her. This process of initializing also serves as Rose's agreement to the terms of the contract. Theirs is a relationship that is explicitly formalized by a contract and consent. Rose's collaboration, however, can and should be read as maternal. Even as it is at odds with the coldness that Deleuze ascribes to the dominant, the closeness between Flanagan and Rose is palpable. When Rose places her hands on his body and carves the S, it is a performance of tenderness. In a statement that echoes Deleuze's analysis of masochism as adhering to a power structure where paternal law is replaced by maternal law, Rose likens her role as a dominant to that of a mother: "A lot of the skills that you use in dealing with a submissive are very motherly skills. You have to be a very strict mother, you can't let them get away with anything."[55] Her invocation of maternity speaks to a relationship governed by contract, care, and performance.

Even as I have emphasized the drama between Flanagan and his flesh, it is easy to see that Rose's participation is necessary to maintaining Flanagan's agency. It is what allows for his transformation and rebirth. When Rose enters the room, her casual, calm demeanor contrasts with Flanagan's intensity. Her T-shirt and trousers do not indicate that this is an event of any kind. She methodologically goes about her tasks of sterilization, carving, and documenting, but she is on the periphery of the film's literal borders, often with her back toward the camera. In many ways Rose is a secondary character in this drama. We hear Flanagan's words, but never hers. At moments she appears to be somewhat of a glorified handmaiden, charged with producing Flanagan's pain and pleasure. I have previously discussed the difficulty of theorizing the feminine dominant role, and here, too, we are left with questions about how we should understand Rose, her agency, and the space of the maternal in the context of Flanagan's white masculinity.

Audre Lorde and the Reclamation of the Feminine

"Woman, a black lesbian feminist mother lover poet."[56] These are the words that Audre Lorde uses to describe herself in *The Cancer Journals*. These terms connote identities, desires, actions, emotions, and sensations that speak to a world beyond that of cancer and pain. Since Lorde sees herself as "not only a casualty [but] . . . also a warrior," these words help to articulate the contours of her response to cancer.[57] Against cancer's assault from the interior, which Lorde frames as a product of sociocultural factors, Lorde turns to language, writing, and femininity as a guard against the silence that pain and illness threaten to produce. Through these pathways, she produces a reclamation of self and an attempt at a new form of cohesion and agency.

Lorde's discussions of objectification, femininity, race, and community provide an arresting counterpoint to Flanagan's meditations on masculinity, pain, and the dissolution of self. *The Cancer Journals*, written in the late 1970s, is a combination of essays, poetry, and journal entries in which she processes her breast cancer diagnosis and her mastectomy. Lorde reflects on women's relationship to their breasts, the difficulty of navigating the health care system, the types of love that have sustained her throughout the ordeal, and her own physical pain. Here I am dwelling on Lorde's discussion of pain because her reflections offer insight into the ways that the objectification of pain and illness is compounded by racism and sexism.

1/26/79

> I'm not feeling very hopeful these days, about selfhood or anything
> else. I handle the outward motions of each day while pain fills me
> like a puspocket and every touch threatens to breech [*sic*] the taut
> membrane that keeps it from flowing through and poisoning my
> whole existence. Sometimes despair sweeps across my conscious-
> ness like luna winds across a barren moon-scape. Ironshod horses
> rage back and forth over every nerve. Oh Seboulisa ma, help me
> remember what I have paid so much to learn. I could die of differ-
> ence, or live—myriad selves.[58]

In this passage, we cannot help but notice Lorde's fixation on her physical pain and the ways it affects her perception of the world around her.
In particular, Lorde describes a tentative grasp on selfhood ("I'm not
feeling very hopeful these days, about selfhood or anything else"), a consciousness of the particularities of her body ("Ironshod horses rage back
and forth over every nerve"), a temporality of the internal ("I handle the
outward motions of each day while pain fills me like a puspocket"), and
the possibility of transformation ("I could die of difference, or live—
myriad selves"). Ultimately, what Lorde is describing is how her cancer
has made her aware of her body as an object and the consequences of its
raced and gendered fleshiness.

Indeed, Lorde's writing on coping with cancer is rife with descriptions of alienation and the feeling that she has lost agency. On October
10, 1978, Lorde writes, "I want to write of the pain I am feeling right
now, of the lukewarm tears that will not stop coming into my eyes—for
what? For my lost breast? For the lost me? And which me was that again
anyway? For the death I don't know how to postpone? Or how to meet
elegantly?"[59] Reflecting on this moment of despair, Lorde later writes,
"And all the time as a background of pain and terror and disbelief, a thin
high voice was screaming that none of this was true. . . . Another part of
me flew like a big bird to the ceiling of whatever place I was in, observ-
ing my actions and providing a running commentary, complete with
suggestions of factors forgotten, new possibilities of movement, and rib-
ald remarks. I felt as if I was always listening to a concert of voices from
inside myself, all with something slightly different to say, all of which
were quite insistent and none of which would let me rest."[60] Despair produces multiplicity for Lorde, but it is the multiplicity born of alienation.

It is what allows her to see herself from a distance as though she were another. To argue that the totality of Lorde's experience with cancer can be summed up as objectification, despair, and misery would be misleading, but meditating on it vis-à-vis Sartre provides us with a way to mark the impact that chronic pain produces on the body and Lorde's understanding of her relationship to it.

Lorde's relationship to illness is also defined by modern medicine. In *The Cancer Journals*, she describes how diagnosis, mastectomy, and aftercare have profoundly altered her relationship to her body. She enters into the category of the unhealthy and is told that her body is unruly. This comes across most clearly when Lorde narrates her feelings after her first biopsy, which occurred a year before the biopsy that found cancer and resulted in her mastectomy. Lorde writes, "Less than two months ago, I was told by two doctors, one female and one male, that I would have to have breast surgery, and that there was a 60 to 80 percent chance that the tumor was malignant. Between that telling and the actual surgery, there was a three week period of the agony of an involuntary reorganization of my entire life. The surgery was completed, and the growth was benign."[61] Later, after her masectomy, the hospital insists on providing her with a breast prosthesis, thereby attempting to shape her physicality in accordance with a feminine norm so that her treatment follows a certain form and she appears to be a model patient. In Lorde's narrative of pain, objectification, and the medical system, categories such as autonomy and dissolution of self emerge as distinctly gendered and racialized terms.

William Major considers Lorde's writings on cancer a form of autopathography in which autonomony and agency are "useful to the auto pathographer attempting to resist not only the somatic eruption of a serious illness, for instance, but also its coding within the social world."[62] Writing, according to Major, is Lorde's way of coping with the loss of agency. Indeed, there are many ways to discuss what happens when Lorde writes. Margaret Kissam Morris argues that Lorde "refuses absolutely to confine herself, even temporarily, to any one aspect of her heterogeneous identity, whether to support a political program or to make others feel comfortable. And each part of the self she constructs is based on a sense of corporeal materiality that she attempts to render in both her prose and poetry."[63] Elizabeth Alexander writes that Lorde "works the science and logic of her own hybridity. . . . She must make a physical space for herself in a hybrid language, a composite, a creation of new language to make space for the 'new' of the self-invented body."[64] Further, Alexander compares *The Cancer Journals* to *Zami*, Lorde's bio-mythography, arguing that both "are autobiographies of Lorde's body. Both books are also erotic autobiographies, with *Zami* in particular describing Lorde's sensual life in intricate detail. The African-American woman's body in Lorde's work—specifically, her own body—becomes a map of lived experience and a way of printing suffering as well as joy upon the flesh."[65] Jeanne Perreault argues that this link between Lorde's writing and her production of self is strong enough that Lorde fears that "recreating the time in words may recreate it in her body."[66] Lorde writes to produce a new self. In this regard it is telling that Lorde titles the first essay in *The Cancer Journals* "The Transformation of Silence into Language and Action" and writes about the activism that her diagnosis spurs. She argues forcefully for the power of words to combat not just the lack of agency that she faces as someone with cancer but also the lack of agency that she has as a black woman in America.

While the relationship between the production of self and the desire to control pain is something that I have explored throughout this chapter, I am most interested in the particular ways that Lorde navigates cancer as a threat to her femininity and the strategies that she produces to recuperate it. In many ways, I am reading her writing of *The Cancer Journals* as a parallel narrative to Flanagan's use of S&M to reassert and to queer his own masculinity. Here I want to stress that while the act of writing gives Lorde a voice as an activist (and income to live off of), it also gives us a glimpse at Lorde's major innovation—the plural female subject. To get a sense of this, let us examine a portion of "The Transformation of Silence into Language and Action." Lorde writes, "That visibility [produced by language] which makes us most vulnerable is that which also is the source of our greatest strength. Because the machine will try to grind you into dust anyway, whether or not we speak. We can sit in our corners mute forever while our sisters and our selves are wasted, while our children are distorted and destroyed, while our earth is poisoned, we can sit in our safe corners mute as bottles, and we still will be no less afraid."[67] While Lorde is the one doing the writing, she invokes a plural female subject as both her audience and part of her expanded sense of self. These "sisters and our selves" are bound not only through interpellation but through socioeconomic oppression (the machine). This plural subject is one born from racism and sexism, but Lorde aims not only to rouse a sense of self in them but to work with them for a different future.

Given that many of Lorde's identities are woman centered and that she aims to form a community from individual oppressed women, the fact that she is dealing with breast cancer and the surgical removal of her right breast gives her the opportunity to reflect on her femininity in relation to her corporeality and pain. In the immediate aftermath of her surgery, Lorde writes about this difficulty in terms of her identity: "Off and on I kept thinking. I have cancer. I'm a black lesbian feminist poet, how am I going to do this now? Where are the models for what I'm supposed to be in this situation? But there were none. This is it, Audre. You're on your own."[68]

Not surprisingly, many of Lorde's reflections center on her relationship to her breasts. Initially, she describes anger at the alientation from her body that the initial lump and biopsy produced: "I had grown angry at my right breast because I felt as if it had in some unexpected way betrayed me, as if it had become already separate from me and had turned against me by creating this tumor which might be malignant. My beloved breast had suddenly departed from the rules we had agreed upon to function by all these years."[69] The following year, however, when she faces the actual removal of her breast, she feels grateful for the extra time that she had with her right breast. She writes, "I sure am glad that I had this extra year to learn to love me in a different way. . . . Since it is my life that I am gambling with, and my life is worth even more than the sensual delights of my breast, I certainly can't take that chance."[70] However, Lorde's sober decision to choose surgery knowing that it would extend her life despite costing her one of her breasts does not mean that she does not mourn.

In the same entry, she writes, "7:30 p.m. And yet if I cried for a hundred years I couldn't possibly express the sorrow I feel right now, the sadness and the loss. How did the Amazons 2 of Dahomey feel? They were only little girls. But they did this willingly, for something they believed in. I suppose I am too but I can't feel that now."[71] This particular passage of mourning is intriguing because Lorde uses her connection to her breasts and the loss of one of them to insert herself within an African lineage. By connecting herself with the Amazons of Dahomey, the women warriors of West Africa, Lorde places herself into a narrative beyond the individual. The invocation of these women, who were called Mino, or "our mothers," in the Fon language, also speaks to the connection that Lorde draws between the breasts and the maternal.[72] There are several places within the text where Lorde equates the loss of her breast with the loss of her mother. She writes, "The pain of separation from my breast was at least as sharp as the pain of separating from my mother. But I made it once before, so I know I can make it again."[73] Later, she compares the shock and grief after her surgery to facing the death of one's mother, saying, "Throughout that period, I kept feeling that I couldn't think straight, that there was something wrong with my brain I couldn't remember. Part of this was shock. . . . But a friend of mine recently told me that for six months after her mother died, she felt she couldn't think or remember, and I was struck by the similarity of the sensations."[74]

In scripting the removal of her breast as a loss of the maternal, Lorde underscores the importance of establishing the maternal for her identity as an African American woman, whose community is already infused with the aura of a lost mother. We might, in fact, think about the way that the idea of African American communities is already built on a complicated combination of absent mother and omnipresent mothering. Hortense Spillers writes, "In effect, under conditions of captivity, the offspring of the female does not 'belong' to the Mother, nor is s/he 'related' to the 'owner,' though the latter 'possess' it, and in the African American instance, often fathered it, *and*, as often, without benefit of patrimony. . . . The offspring of the enslaved, 'being unrelated both to their begetters and to their owners . . . find themselves in the situation of being orphans.'"[75] Spillers connects this to a larger structural problematization of theorizing kinship and family within African American contexts, but it is this loss of the maternal that links Lorde to her ancestry. Lorde's connection to her breasts is not only about a link to the past, however; it is also about a link to the future. Lorde mourns being a part of a general community of women. She does this by voicing her daughter's sadness at the loss of her maternal breast. "My daughter Beth cried in the waiting room after I told her I was going to have a mastectomy. She said she was sentimentally attached to my breasts. Adrienne comforted her, somehow making Beth understand that hard as this was, it was different for me from if I had been her age, and that our experiences were different."[76]

The breasts, then, are material objects that Lorde points to when she articulates her connection to the larger community of women. Here, their meaning beyond the maternal is also important. Lorde also theorizes them as a potent source of sensuality. We see this most sharply when she discusses her reaction to being fitted for a prosthesis. Lorde interprets the volunteer from Reach for Recovery's message as "You are just as good as you were before because you can look exactly the same. Lambswool now, then a good prosthesis as soon as possible, and nobody'll ever know the difference. But what she said was, 'You'll never know the difference,' and she lost me right there, because I knew sure as hell I'd know the difference."[77] While the volunteer is speaking about the inability of observers to detect the absence of a breast once the bra has been filled with a lambswool pouch, Lorde thinks about the potential difference that the absence of a breast will make in her lovemaking:

> I was thinking, "What is it like to be making love to a woman and have only one breast brushing against her?"
>
> I thought, "How will we fit so perfectly together ever again?"
>
> I thought, "I wonder if our love-making had anything to do with it?"
>
> I thought, "What will it be like making love to me? Will she still find my body delicious?"
>
> And for the first time deeply and fleetingly a ground-swell of sadness rolled up over me that filled my mouth and eyes almost to drowning. My right breast represented such an area of feeling and pleasure for me, how could I bear never to feel that again?[78]

Lorde fears that the loss of her breast will represent the loss of a sensual arena for connecting to women and experiencing her own sexuality. Ultimately, Lorde's recovery is marked by a return to loving herself via an affirmation that she makes in the moment that she rejects the prosthesis: "I would love my body one-breasted now, or remain forever alien to myself."[79]

Much of *The Cancer Journals*, then, is filled with Lorde's chronicle of refinding that connection to others and enacting a plural subjectivity. This is why Elizabeth Alexander discusses it as an "erotic autobiography," but the terms of its eroticism are different from those that fill *Zami*. Here, she describes masturbation as something that heals her because it allows her to learn how to love herself: "November 2, 1978 How do you spend your time, she said. Reading, mostly, I said. I couldn't tell her that mostly I sat staring at blank walls, or getting stoned into my heart, and then, one day when I found I could finally masturbate again, making love to myself for hours at a time. The flame was dim and flickering, but it was a welcome relief to the long coldness."[80] The most persistent thread of the erotic, however, comes with Lorde's invocation of "the joy, the lightness, the laughter so vital to my living and my health" and her discussion of the women who have supported her throughout.[81] Lorde writes, "My work kept me alive this past year, my work and the love of women."[82] She elaborates on this further by saying, "And it was the concern and caring of all those women which gave me strength and enabled me to scrutinize the essentials of my living. The women who sustained me through that period were black and white, old and young, lesbian, bisexual, and heterosexual, and we all shared a war against the tyrannies of silence."[83] Indeed, in Lorde's essays and journal entries, we find references to her friends, her lover, her children, her nurses. This community of women provides Lorde with the power to resist the difficulties of survival, and Lorde herself sees her participation in this economy of femininity as vital to other women. She frames her writing as both a project of self-creation and a step toward increasing feminine cohesion:

> I have found that battling despair does not mean closing my eyes to the enormity of the tasks of effecting change, nor ignoring the strength and the barbarity of the forces aligned against us. It means teaching, surviving and fighting with the most important resource I have, myself, and taking joy in that battle. It means, for me, recognizing the enemy outside and the enemy within, and knowing that my work is part of a continuum of women's work, of reclaiming this earth and our power, and knowing that this work did not begin with my birth nor will it end with my death. And it means knowing that within this continuum, my life and my love and my work has particular power and meaning relative to others.[84]

Lorde's version of femininity evokes her discussion of the erotic as a subjectivity of plurality. In contrast to Flanagan's drive toward autonomy and singularity, Lorde seeks connection and multiplicity. Importantly, she does so because of the politics of her subject position. By affirming her place among a lineage of women who have been oppressed because of racism and sexism, Lorde positions her illness not as singular but as a manifestation of these systems of oppression. She is working against the temptation to dismiss her illness because it is hers alone. Writing a plural subjectivity spreads the responsibility for transformation and envisions health, not as belonging to the individual, but as a mark of politics. In doing this, she is reclaiming bodies that were never seen as autonomous and giving them power and agency.

The Affective Politics of Disintegration

One of the more evocative elements of Flanagan's performances is seeing him confront his body as a body. Underlying the discourses of realism, posthumanism, and spectatorship is the fact that we witness Flanagan grappling with his own corporeal limitations. We see him submitting not only to pain but to his body's materiality. In this space we witness Flanagan gain another type of knowledge. As Fredrik Svenaeus argues, illness is not only alienation but "an experience of the in-itself of *the body*."[85] That is, it produces alienation that is itself an experience of corporeality: "It reveals the body to us in different ways, through making it heavy, stiff, hot, nauseated, plagued by pain, twists, jerks, shivers, etc. This facticity of the body is the result neither of the gaze of the other, nor of the reflection adopting the outer perspective of the other in an indirect way, but of the very otherness of one's own body which *makes itself known* (addresses itself) to us as a for-itself of the in-itself."[86] The knowledge that comes from illness is something that can be produced only from experiencing the body. The other modes of becoming-flesh that we have examined have focused on how external agents call attention to the body's flesh—whether this is desired or not—but illness is not exactly an external agent. It can render the body powerless, but the body and illness are not entirely separable, so that when one surrenders to illness one is also surrendering to one's own body and not something strictly definable as outside.

Though Flanagan does not discuss this experience of self-annihilation as anything other than a form of alienation, I suggest that we use Lorde and Deleuze to unpack the forms of self-knowledge that come from attending to the disintegrating body. Both articulate this space of subjective incoherence as producing a politics of illness in which bodies and subjects come together in novel ways.

Stricken with a recurring respiratory ailment in his twenties, Deleuze rarely traveled, had to give up drinking, and was dependent on many medications to maintain his health. Deleuze's illness, I argue, made him attentive to the body and corporeal sensations, as we see in his analysis of masochism and the BwO.[87] His illness was rarely discussed, however, and his statements on it are confined to a 1989 interview with Claire Parnet. In the interview, which was conducted over several days and was filmed and edited into an eight-hour television event, *L'Abécédaire de Gilles Deleuze*, to be broadcast after Deleuze's death, Deleuze's ill health is obvious, and the conversation circles back to his health in expected (the entry "Maladie," for example) and unexpected (discussions of drinking) ways. In one of the interview segments, Deleuze describes his hospitalization for tuberculosis and his reliance on doctors and machines (which he detested), but he does not dwell on pain or discomfort. Instead, Deleuze argues that illness brings a certain type of freedom because it allows one to "listen" (s'écoute) to life. This "listening to life," Deleuze argues, facilitates thought because the state of illness, of feeling fragile and overwhelmed, amplifies life's situations by illuminating and augmenting the impressions, sensations, and affects that they produce. As Charles Stivale writes, "So for Deleuze the question is clear: illness sharpens a kind of vision of life or a sense of life. He emphasizes that when he says vision, vision of life, life, it's in the sense of him saying 'to see life,' these difficulties that sharpen, that give life a vision of life, illness, life in all its force, in all its beauty."[88]

For Deleuze, says Stivale, illness offers freedom through constraint; it offers him an opportunity to meditate on his body and its limitations "free . . . from things that one cannot be free from in ordinary life."[89] Illness is an affirmative process for Deleuze; it offers the possibility of new realms of pleasure through sensation. Even its primary side effect, fatigue in Deleuze's case, produces freedom. Deleuze interprets fatigue as a sign that "the day is done," one is not able "to draw anything further from oneself," so one is free to just be.[90] Illness "releases" one from societal norms through sensation and a reorganization of temporality. Fatigue, for example, is an illustration of the limits of the body. Deleuze conceives of it as a biological limit. With fatigue come slowness and immobility. Immobility allows Deleuze to travel emotionally within "immobile systems, like music, like philosophy."[91] Though Deleuze does not desire slowness of the mind, slowness of the body, as a temporal mode, is not undesirable. Slowness signifies a "receptivity toward affect," an anticipatory mode that is marked by attention to the past, and caution.[92] Slowness is a way of being that is grounded in the real, in what really happened, in how one is experiencing every moment; it is a state of vigilance and attention.

In Deleuze's conversations about illness, he emphasizes creativity and freedom, themes that are familiar from his analysis of masochism. In this iteration, however, they are created through an extra-ordinary relationship with the body in contrast to masochism's emphasis on control. Deleuze argues that it is his body's constraints—lack of antibodies, lack of energy—that allow the mind freedom through the augmentation of perception. Illness, for Deleuze, alters temporality and sensation, and in this way he forges an unspoken link between his own body and that of the masochist, which he describes in terms of suspended time and pain. In this interpretation of pain as providing a type of freedom through submission, Deleuze articulates a stance that Susan Wendell describes as transcendence through disembodiment.[93] Drawing on Wendell, we can situate Deleuze's statements within a vein of disability studies; he is grateful to be excluded from the norms of the able-bodied because his exclusion allows him a type of social freedom.

Further, we can link these statements about illness to Deleuze's discussion of masochism as a practice of desubjectification. Deleuze, writing in collaboration with Félix Guattari, turns to masochism as a way of producing the Body without Organs (BwO), an alternative to the Oedipal sphere of organization.[94] They argue that Sigmund Freud's insistence on the universality of the child's infantile desire for the parent of the opposite sex forecloses other paths of desire by repressing them or rendering them illegible. The singularity of the Oedipal circuit of desire coupled with its presumed universality is problematic because it prevents the productivity of desire, which Deleuze and Guattari understand as the mechanism that creates reality. The BwO is a body in which desire flows freely without being restricted by established patterns of organization. These flows allow for a multiplicity of desires. Deleuze and Guattari position the BwO in opposition to Man, the stable privileged knower.

"November 28, 1947: How Do You Make Yourself a Body without Organs?" is the essay that describes the creation of the BwO, the site of resistance and freedom that Deleuze and Guattari prize. The title contains the date of Antoine Artaud's infamous radio broadcast. Between November 22 and 29, Artaud, a French playwright, poet, and director, produced a radio show, "Pour en finir avec le jugement de Dieu" ("To Have Done with the Judgment of God"), which was a mishmash of sounds and antireligious and anti-American rants. The show, which was incomprehensible, was not publicly broadcast until 1978. In the midst of this schizophrenic cacophony, Artaud introduced the idea of the body without organs. In a poem that preceded broadcast, Artaud wrote, "The body is the body, / alone it stands / and in need of no organs, / organism it never is, / organisms are enemies of the body . . . // Reality is yet unconstructed for the / legitimate organs of the human body / are still to be composed and set."[95] Following Artaud's privileging of disorganization and shock, Deleuze and Guattari describe the body without organs in *A Thousand Plateaus* as the body of the masochist, a body that is filled with waves of pain.

By invoking Artaud, Deleuze and Guattari emphasize the importance of the body and its sensations over any notion of the unconscious. The body in shock, after all, is overwhelmed. In this state, there are only sensations; there is no process of internalizing senses. Deleuze and Guattari understand masochism as a process of transformation; pain becomes pleasurable and man becomes animal. Importantly, the masochist's transformation is rooted in the corporeal: "It has its sadist or whore sew it up; the eyes, anus, urethra, breasts, and nose are sewn shut. It has itself strung up to stop the organs from working, flayed, as if the organs clung to the skin; sodomized, smothered, to make sure everything is sealed tight."[96]

This masochistic program allows for pain to flow freely: "What is certain is that the masochist has made himself a BwO under such conditions that the BwO can no longer be populated by anything but intensities of pain, pain waves."[97] These flows of pain are important not because of the specificity of pain but because they signal an empty body. The emptiness of the body means that disorganization has been achieved; that is to say, the body can be understood to be operating in opposition to the hegemony of the organism ("a phenomenon of accumulation, coagulation, and sedimentation that, in order to extract useful labor from the BwO, imposes upon it forms, functions, bonds, dominant and hierarchized organizations, organized transcendences"),[98] which, we might understand, following Foucault, as related to biopolitics. In resisting these diffuse modalities of regulation, the masochist becomes a way for Deleuze and Guattari to think about activity and affirmation in a concrete way.

This is most concretely seen in relation to Deleuze and Guattari's concept of masochism as a form of becoming-animal. In *A Thousand Plateaus*, they move beyond the specter of pain to examine what masochism produces (aside from a BwO). In the quest for immanence, the masochist reimagines humanity and, in the words of Deleuze and Guattari, starts to become-animal. I will quote extensively from Deleuze and Guattari in order to illustrate what they mean by this becoming-animal:

Take a masochist who did not undergo psychoanalysis: "program ... At night, put on the bridle and attach my hands more tightly, either to the bit with the chain, or to the big belt right after returning from the bath. Put on the entire harness right away also . . . Ride the reins for two hours during the day, and in the evening as the master wishes. . . . The master will never approach her horse without the crop, and without using it. If the animal should display impatience or rebelliousness, the reins will be drawn tighter, the master will grab them and give the beast a good thrashing."[99]

Starting with Roger Dupouy's case studies, Deleuze and Guattari describe the masochist's desire to be ridden like a horse, not as imitation, but as becoming-animal, in this case becoming a horse. Deleuze and Guattari write, "The masochist presents it this way: Training axiom—destroy the instinctive forces in order to replace them with transmitted forces."[100] The masochist is training his own instincts to be the instincts of a horse, using the mistress as the force of conversion. The masochist aims to construct a new assemblage of horse, self, and mistress.[101] This assemblage is a new form of organization, but it offers the appeal of multiplicity and becoming rather than stasis and stratification. Masochism becomes important to Deleuze and Guattari's notion of freedom because it symbolizes both the production of a BwO where desire could circulate freely and the possibility of reorganization into a zone of becoming-animal, which Deleuze and Guattari advocate because it decenters man. Man, in this case, is presented as the stable privileged knower, and becoming requires mobility of thought and freedom from the fixed boundaries of man as subject; this can be achieved through becoming-animal or becoming-woman. Masochism is a process that acts as an affront to the subject.

The link that I am making between Deleuze's mode of embodiment and those that he ascribes to the masochist forms the bedrock of a politics of nonidentity by illuminating a way to be attentive to the flesh while not reifying a connection between experience and subjectivity. This is affinity through sensation, a mode of relationality and methodology in which Deleuze considers himself embedded. Deleuze writes: "What do my relations with gays, alcoholics, and drug-users matter, if I can obtain similar effects by different means? . . . The question's nothing to do with the character of this or that exclusive group, it's to do with the transversal relations that ensure that any effects produced in some particular way (through homosexuality, drugs, and so on) *can always be produced by other means*."[102] Deleuze's emphasis on sensation and affect speaks to experience, but this experience is not legible as identity, nor is it subject-forming. Given Deleuze's antipathy toward subjectivity, this is not surprising. Deleuze argues that subjectivity is pernicious and should be unraveled: "It's not a question of being this or that sort of human, but of becoming inhuman, of a universal animal becoming—not seeing yourself as some dumb animal, but unraveling your body's human organization, exploring this or that zone of bodily intensity, with everyone discovering their own particular zones, and the groups, populations, species that inhabit them."[103] This state of hypercorporeality exists in tension with the disembodied freedom of disability. Deleuze helps us to consider the ways that illness produces a state that oscillates between an intense being-in-the body and disembodiment. In other words, it produces a form of self-annihilation, which, though associated with masochism, is actually distinct from it. By submitting to the corporeal, illness annihilates the subject and enacts desubjectification or impersonality, which is akin to the state of freedom that Deleuze and Guattari describe with regard to the BwO. Rather than the subject, however, the sensations produced by illness are the agents of transformation.

Lorde produces an arresting comparison to Deleuze's theorization of transformation and desubjectification in her discussion of the erotic vis-à-vis the plural subject and its political implications. Lorde begins her "Uses of the Erotic: The Erotic as Power" by positing that "the erotic is a resource within each of us that lies in a deeply female and spiritual plane firmly rooted in the power of our unexpressed or unrecognized feeling."[104] Toward the conclusion of the essay, which was first delivered as a paper at the Berkshires Conference on the History of Women in 1978 (six months before Lorde's mastectomy, but after her initial breast cancer biopsy), Lorde provides an extended description of how to find the erotic within one's self. She writes: "When we begin to live from within outward, in touch with the power of the erotic within ourselves, and allowing that power to inform and illuminate our actions upon the world around us, then we begin to be responsible to ourselves in the deepest sense. For as we begin to recognize our deepest feelings, we begin to give up, of necessity, being satisfied with suffering and self-negation, and with the numbness which so often seems like their only alternative in our society. Our acts against oppression become integral with self, motivated and empowered from within."[105] Here, Lorde equates the erotic with realizing oneself as a coherent subject. The project of selfhood, as Lorde describes it, is one of empowerment through affective transformation. Against suffering and self-negation, Lorde situates responsibility, selfhood, and feeling.

While Lorde emphasizes the importance of individual selfhood, her version of the erotic is not merely about reinforcing subjectivity but about a space where community is formed. In this way it is similar to Deleuze's description of affinity through sensation. We see this explicitly in "Uses of the Erotic" when Lorde emphasizes the importance that individual empowerment will make for the community at large: "The aim of each thing which we do is to make our lives and the lives of our children richer and more possible."[106] From this statement we see that the individual is important only insofar as she serves to buoy the rest of the community. In addition to this emphasis on community, Lorde posits the erotic, not as something that is created in an intersubjective space but as something that exceeds it. Even in a statement that appears to describe the importance of the erotic for self-actualization, there is an excess of feeling: "The erotic is a measure between the beginnings of our sense of self and the chaos of our strongest feelings"; it is this feeling that builds community.[107] The erotic, then, is "an assertion of the lifeforce of women; of that creative energy empowered"; it is both something that belongs to individuals and something that cannot be contained by them.[108] Lorde's discussion of the erotic belongs to the realm of affect.

Talking about affect helps displace identity as the basis for community formation and opens political possibilities. Lorde's discussion of the erotic touches on this potential because the most central component of the erotic, after all, is its creation of an affective community. Lorde describes the erotic as a space of mutuality and collaboration; the erotic "provid[es] the power which comes from sharing deeply any pursuit with another person."[109] Importantly, the erotic is based on communal affective bonds—specifically joy—outside of the parameters of identity: "The sharing of joy, whether physical, emotional, psychic, or intellectual, forms a bridge between the sharers which can be the basis for understanding much of what is not shared between them, and lessens the threat of their difference."[110] This formation of community through affective flows is one of the hallmarks of the plural subject.

Lorde's politics of the erotic can be understood as a response to the traumas of racism and discrimination that prevent the formation of community among African American women. Indeed, Lorde produces an extended meditation on the anguish of being part of a dislocated community. As we saw in her identification with the Amazons of Dahomey,

Lorde posits blackness as an identity that crosses geographic and historical boundaries. Lorde writes in *The Cancer Journals* that this community supports her, but it is also a place of great vulnerability because of racism and patriarchy. This vulnerability, however, is something that Lorde must contend with whether she is part of a community or not. The community simply furthers her desire for a new politics. Initially Lorde responds to this vulnerability with anger, but while anger acts, it also separates individuals. The erotic and its politics of solidarity and affirmation are vital to the production of a black female community and to its survival. This message comes through most saliently in the conclusion of "Eye to Eye": Lorde writes, "And it is empowerment—our strengthening in the service of ourselves and each other, in the service of our work and our future—that will be the result of this pursuit. . . . I have to learn to love myself before I can love you or accept your loving."[111] Though Lorde is not using the term *the erotic*, her emphasis on community, self-empowerment, and feeling makes it clear that this step away from anger toward action is infused by the same currents that inform the erotic. The erotic is a politics for black women because it is a move away from anger toward the formation of a new community. The erotic, for Lorde, is a space for women to form bonds with each other to repair the damage done by patriarchy and racism and to formulate ways of moving beyond those systems by enacting the plural subject.

Lorde shares a great deal in common with Deleuze in this imagined affective solidarity. While Deleuze understands illness and masochism as processes that decenter the individual and privilege a reorganization of corporeality so as to highlight new forms of affinity, Lorde focuses on the community of women who are formed by and help to unleash the erotic. The erotic decenters the individual in order to produce an alternate form of kinship between women. The erotic is also a space where women can learn to find joy and feeling in life. This parallel, though instructive in helping us to reread both theories through a new lens, breaks down in one major difference. While Deleuze is explicit in extolling the virtues of masochism for producing new forms of being, Lorde is critical of the practice.

In opposition to the erotic, Lorde positions sensation and pornography. First, she writes that "the erotic offers a well of replenishing and provocative force to the woman who does not fear its revelation, nor succumb to the belief that sensation is enough."[112] Later, she writes that pornography "represents the suppression of true feeling. . . . [It] emphasizes sensation without feeling."[113] Further, she argues that this "world of flattened affect," defined by the "ascetic who aspires to feel nothing," is ruled by "self-abnegation."[114] Lorde writes that when she is in touch with the erotic she "become[s] less willing to accept powerlessness, or those other supplied states of being which are not native to [her], such as resignation, despair, self-effacement, depression, self-denial."[115] Sensation, what we might think of as sensory pleasure, is the opposite of the erotic.

While it is easy to assign Lorde's characterization of the erotic as feminine and her distrust of pornography to the radical feminist milieu from which she emerged, seeing how Lorde separates feeling from sensation opens another dimension to reading "The Uses of the Erotic" by fleshing out what it is to experience "a racist, patriarchal, and anti-erotic society."[116] Without an affective connection, the feelings of others are not shared but used, "and use without consent of the used is abuse."[117] Additionally Lorde classifies this *use* of the feelings of others as a form of objectification, which "is to deny a large part of the experience, and to allow ourselves to be reduced to the pornographic, the abused, and the absurd."[118] These statements allow us to understand Lorde's division of feelings from sensations—feelings can be shared, while sensation (and pleasure without emotion) is individuating. Sensation, then, is not only a province of the individual but something cultivated by an inappropriate relationship to the other. This separation of feeling from sensation and the equation of sensation with various modes of self-annihilation and patriarchy allow us to explore what the linkage of sensation, self-annihilation, and patriarchy means.

Lorde's investment in emphasizing sensation's trappings stems from a structural perspective on inequality. She focuses on the conceptual dangers of sensation without feeling rather than the immediate issues of participation. Lorde worries that the focus on sensation emphasizes a turn away from others; it advocates a mode of antisociality. This can be read as a braiding together of looking and distancing, where these actions become modes of performing antisociality. The problem with antisociality, according to Lorde, is that it prevents communities from forming, thereby eliminating bonds between women and avenues for nurturing and collaboration.

While I believe that the affective affinities that I use to link Deleuze and Lorde provide us with ways to politicize this particular form of objectification—indeed, Lorde frequently invokes the political dimensions of her illness—this difference between the two theorists over the matter of masochism is something that fuels the next chapter. In large part, their disagreement comes down to the possibilities afforded to various identities. Does Lorde experience less leeway than Deleuze when it comes to theorizing desubjectification because she is a black lesbian woman? The next chapter discusses the difficulty of thinking black women in tandem with masochism as a way to examine the limits of the flesh.

Conclusion: Making Flesh Matter

A nearby label reads "Kara Walker, American, b. 1969. The End of Uncle Tom and the Grand Allegorical Tableau of Eva in Heaven, 1995. Cut paper and adhesive on wall." Stepping back to consider again the silhouetted scene, reading from left to right, we are met with several challenges, one after another. We see a young woman with stereotypically black facial features, seated with her back against a tree and legs raised onto the shoulders of a younger white boy who dangles a toy sword in front of her vagina, while being egged on by a female playmate. Nearby, three women dressed in domestic workers' garb form a chain of suckling, mouths to breasts, as if to mimic the action of the baby resting on one of their laps. These women appear to be unaware of the events surrounding them, so engaged are they with one another. Elsewhere, without necessary connection to the preceding, a newborn emerges from a man's anus, just to the right of a one-legged man—with a little girl's body inserted partway into his own anus—who leans on a sword upon which a small child has been impaled. The only solitary figure in the scene is an impish baby whose placement separates the above scenarios from a central event. Traipsing before us, the baby leaves his mark in mounds of shit that draw an arc around a three-figure grouping, thus demarcating its place as a plinth does a monument's. This group comprises a menacing girl who wields an axe, backward, over the head of a small child with a pronouncedly "Negroid" physiognomy, while behind her an adolescent figure aims a huge splinter at her buttocks.[1]

When read from left to right, *The End of Uncle Tom* comprises four groupings of silhouette characters involved in nightmarish acts. The first scene contains a group of three slave women and a child involved in a moment of mutual nursing. This is followed by a larger arrangement of three small slave children, one holding a basket, another a spike, and the third a tambourine. Their young mistress, who raises an axe high above her head, stands in the center of the grouping. The third scene is dominated by the character of a corpulent and crippled master who rests his belly on the back of a pubescent slave whom he is sodomizing. He counterbalances his girth with the aid of a saber that is thrust into the body of an infant beneath him. The final scene centers on a balding male slave who, knees bent and hands clasped in prayer, is connected by a cord dangling from his anus to a baby lying on the ground. The tableau concludes with two partially obscured women.[2]

The work of art that Darby English (the first quote) and Gwendolyn DuBois Shaw (the second) describe is one of Kara Walker's most well-known and more controversial pieces—*The End of Uncle Tom and the Grand Allegorical Tableau of Eva in Heaven*. Produced in 1995 and composed of black paper cutouts stuck to a white gallery wall, the work is compelling both for its subject matter and for its effect on the viewer. The black shapes and the work's title make it clear that it is a tableau about slavery; more specifically, it is a re-visioning of Harriet Beecher Stowe's seminal abolitionist work *Uncle Tom's Cabin*. The tufts of trees and houses that dot the background evoke a plantation, while the large images in the foreground are familiar as stereotypical renditions of black and white bodies engaged in a variety of violent and erotic acts. We see, or I should say, I see, a trio of women (and an infant) nursing, a boy defecating, a girl wielding an ax, an old man sodomizing a young slave, a man with his hands raised to the sky in prayer as a fetus lies on the ground near him. Walker's tableau is graphically specific and yet open to multiple readings and interpretations. While there are commonalities between these descriptions, I am most interested in the differences. Either a pubescent slave is sodomized by her master or a little girl emerges from a one-legged man's anus; Shaw notes that the "balding male slave" is praying even as he is connected by a cord from his anus to a baby on the ground; English describes the solitary baby who leaves a trail of excrement around the group of figures; English opens with a rape scene but omits the partially obscured women that Shaw describes. The list could go on, but highlighting these examples illustrates the mobility of Walker's work. By foregrounding the multiplicity inherent in one image, an image whose own complicated relationship to masochism will be explored, Walker calls attention to the frames that figure these

Kara Walker, *The End of Uncle Tom and the Grand Allegorical Tableau of Eva in Heaven*, 1995. Cut paper on wall, 156 x 420 inches, 396.2 x 1066.8 cm. Installation view: *Kara Walker: My Complement, My Enemy, My Oppressor, My Love*. Hammer Museum, Los Angeles, 2008. Photo: Joshua White.

possibilities. In this way, the work operates at an arresting angle to the histories of masochism that fill this book.

Throughout this book I have used empathetic reading to flesh out multiple relationships to power by focusing on sensations correlated with masochism. While this methodology has enlarged our concepts of masochism and foregrounded how power can be embodied, there are still further questions to be explored. Lurking at the heart of these narratives are particular relationships between subjectivity, sexuality, and agency. Masochism provides insight into this nexus because it forces us to attend to all three at once. In making this claim, I argue that the discussions on masochism tend to fall into two camps—those who see masochism as functioning as a tool that masks agency and eroticizes powerlessness and those who see masochism as offering a parallel narrative to other processes of desubjectification and alienation. In the former group I place the characterization of patriarchy as alienating and abusive, complicity as linked to coldness, and liberal subjectivity as laced with guilt. In these three narratives, masochism allows for the illusion of powerlessness while simultaneously coding for other forms of agency. In the latter group I place colonialism, becoming-black, and illness. Here, tropes of masochism are activated so as to indicate the actual lack of agency in these structures of power. This divides subjects into those who have agency and those who do not because of structural constraints. Sexuality, then, enters these narratives in multiple, complex ways, often cloaked by the language of love and authenticity. While *love* and *sexuality* are not interchangeable terms, the possibility of sexuality has been framed by these narratives as akin to the possibility of giving and receiving love. Here, let us recall Frantz Fanon, Simone de Beauvoir, O, and even Audre Lorde. The relationship between sexuality, subjectivity, and agency is often phrased thus: Can subjects who do not possess agency love? Do they possess sexuality? These debates about false consciousness matter because they speak to the assumption that one must have agency and subjectivity in order to have sexuality and vice versa.

In this concluding chapter, I turn to Walker's *The End of Uncle Tom and the Grand Allegorical Tableau of Eva in Heaven* as a way of interrogating these questions. Because it opens onto many readings and offers multiple points of entry, this work of art focuses our attention on sexuality, agency, and subjectivity for black women, who, as we have seen, occupy a particularly fraught space within these configurations of power, agency, and subjectivity. This chapter asks whether they can have agency and whether they can have sexuality. Put another way, can the possibilities of masochism as sexual exceptionalism/subversion (which I explored in the introduction) extend to black women?

In addition to opening us up to think about the myriad ways that the tableau can be read, I begin this chapter with descriptions from English and Shaw in order to emphasize the interactive practices of viewing that *The End of Uncle Tom and the Grand Allegorical Tableau of Eva in Heaven* encourages. The viewer must insert him- or herself into the tableau to give it meaning. Thus Walker's art allows us see how the silhouette works as a device that flattens depth into a two- dimensional shape; complexly racialized bodies are morphed into black shapes that we might think of as skins. Popular throughout the seventeenth, eighteenth, and nineteenth centuries for capturing likeness, silhouettes solicit imagination and attention through their flatness. In Walker's work, we experience the affective result of the transition from paper to skin in several ways. Shaw writes, "With their elegant, albeit negative, form, Walker's silhouettes express a void: an unknowable black hole, a kind of blank darkness, which is signified by an outer contour line.... This delineation produces an extraordinary space of psychological projection."[3] As Joan Copjec notes, this process renders all bodies black, leaving marks of difference visible through stereotype: "Composed of black paper, all the human figures are, technically, black, though we are able to distinguish the diegetically white 'folk' from the diegetically black on the basis of their stereotypical profiles, postures, and clothing."[4] By allowing viewers to latch onto stereotypes as part of their practice of reading the image, the silhouettes invite viewers to construct the narrative according to their own relationships to history, identity, and race. This process of projection and the dynamic meaning of the tableau highlight the constructedness of identity in general, as David Joselit points out, and the fantasies that surround our relationship to the past.[5] English writes, "Beginning to square with the difficult possibility that slavery may be no more real—for us, now—than it can become within the terms of this 'play,' means curbing the urge to restore the tableaux to the realistic mode that they evacuate precisely in order to distinguish themselves."[6] Walker's use of the silhouette (a play of surfaces), then, produces a space for various interiorities—viewer, history, and fantasy—to mingle, thereby illuminating the work of the frame.

In unpacking the collision between surface and depth, I have structured this conclusion so that it echoes the process of viewing Walker's piece. If we first notice the black figures and their flatness, I equate this to the reduction of the black female body into a homogeneous signifier for the flesh. Walker's images become part of a lineage of representations of woundedness. This results in a meditation on the way Walker's images play with history and this concept of black female flesh. Recognizing Walker's work as a space of historical play sets the stage for a larger reflection on history and the viewer's place within it. Here, that is manifest as a discussion of masochism, race, and history and the possibility of black female masochism. Finally, I step back to discuss the framing of Walker's work, which opens into questions of thinking subjectivity, agency, and sexuality.

Black Women and the Flesh

In thinking about the flattened black figures of Walker's silhouettes, I want to pause for us to dwell on what this circuit of viewing and feeling does. In many ways these silhouettes evoke affective currents similar to those of Glenn Ligon's *I Feel Most Colored When I Am Thrown against a Sharp White Background*, which I discussed in an earlier chapter, because they activate processes of identification within the viewer (it should be stated that these may become manifest in any number of ways, including nonidentification and alienation). While Ligon's piece forces the viewer to experience the simultaneity of identifying with the colored "I" and/or the sharp white background, the points of potential identification in Walker's piece are figural. This is an important difference from Ligon's abstract and inclusive "I" because Walker's figures are weighty. Despite being flat surfaces, they come bearing their own matter; they are gendered and raced and embedded in a particular historical context. I argue, in fact, that by calling attention to bodies in this way, Walker makes visible the ways that certain bodies—those of black women—are associated with the flesh. This is not just any flesh, however: it is flesh that resists theory, and it is flesh that does not possess agency.

The linkage of black female bodies with untheorized corporeality has been a thread throughout this book. In this way it works alongside Sharon Holland's argument in *The Erotic Life of Racism* that the black female queer body remains unthinkable in contemporary theory. She writes, "Black.Colored.Female.Queer. marks an undisciplined sector of the discipline: the representations of her have shifted from the dangerous and volatile to the abject and weak; S.H.E. (Singular. Historical. Exogenous) is both protector and protected. Her status continually reminds us that we have not yet accomplished our lofty goal of politically efficacious and practiced theory."[7] The failure to grapple with the ways in which she has not been theorized is something that I have traced throughout this book. In each chapter, women of color have served as an underside to the discussions about masochism and sensation. Audre Lorde's discussion of the erotic provided an alternate model for processes of desubjectification and masochism; the angry black woman contrasted with the passive ahistoric, biological black man; the dominance of Norah and the black handmaidens in *The Story of O* reminded us of the line between complicity and economic necessity; and the figure of the black butch illuminated the hollow nature of the phallus. This concluding chapter centers the persistent connection between black femininity and the flesh by working through the historical frames that create this vision.

There are several layers of dealing with the historical embeddedness at work in these figurations of black women as untheorized flesh. Most important, however, is the removal of these bodies from theory because they have been deemed historical. Even in progressive projects, which aim to invigorate theory with the bodies of black women, a temporal flattening occurs. We see this most clearly in the history of intersectionality, where the initial desire to be attentive to black female difference ends up perversely reifying the black female body as a site of woundedness.

Intersectionality began as a mode of inquiry to draw attention to the force of multiple marginalizations. In proto-intersectional texts such as those written by the Combahee River Collective, black feminists argued that black women's lives are structured according to multiple forms of domination; their task was to create a movement to examine and challenge the "manifold and simultaneous oppressions that all women of color face."[8] These oppressions included race, gender, class, and sexuality and led to the consolidation of intersectional theory in black feminism. As intersectionality gained institutional traction it focused more narrowly on the intersection of race and gender than on sexuality and class. As Jennifer Nash argues, "Sexuality and class would become largely erased by black feminist work on multiple marginalization, suggesting that black women's lived experiences were constituted solely by the interplay—or intersection—of race and gender."[9] This focus on race and gender and the particular figure of the black woman has had several important consequences. As Nash notes, it "neglects the heterogeneity of 'black woman' as a category" and equates black feminism almost exclusively with this intersection, thereby foreclosing "explorations of other intersections to a range of related activist-intellectual projects."[10] That is to say, black women became *the* sign of marginalization; they were invoked as a trope to consider the multiplicity of marginalization, but the category's own multitudes were seldom interrogated.

The erasure of heterogeneity from the category of black woman is the mechanism that works to produce black women as the fleshy (yet flat) other. The consolidation of the category "black women" into a singular entity who becomes emblematic of a series of historical and structural oppressions marks the black body as irreducible flesh, the limit of theory and agency. In her own analysis, Holland argues that the black queer woman has become the position to describe various exclusions, but while that fact leads to critique, it has not led to the incorporation of her body into theory: "But the categories 'black,' 'colored,' female, queer point to a persistent problem in queer theorizing—how to have our queer theory and our feminism while still seeing the colored body or how to have our colored criticism while still seeing the female and the queer body and so on."[11] As Jasbir Puar notes, intersectionality both reifies difference and situates the woman of color (we might consider the black woman a subset of this category) as an always marginal subject: "But what the method of intersectionality is most predominantly used to qualify is the specific 'difference' of 'women of color,' a category that has now become, I would argue, simultaneously emptied of specific meaning on the one hand and overdetermined in its deployment on the other. In this usage, intersectionality always produces an Other, and that Other is always a Woman Of Color (WOC), who must invariably be shown to be resistant, subversive, or articulating a grievance."[12] Intersectionality has produced a vision of the woman of color subject as emblematic of oppression at the hands of patriarchy, capitalism, and racism, a subject who is defined by both her difference and her marginalization. The omission of other potential axes of identification and the assumption that women of color are persistently marginalized regardless of context are some of the by-products of attempting to account for the woman of color as a situation who is thought most insistently as wounded flesh. In this way, structural and historical violence becomes interchangeable with the specter of female bodies of color. The most marginal theoretical position becomes visible as the woman of color's body. Not only does this form of centering the woman of color render her opaque and undertheorized, but it marks her as passé. According to Holland, "Her figuration at this point in our critical history looks profoundly like that of . . . a dead zone (think 'impasse')."[13] By this Holland means that she is a reminder of historical wrongs but is not assimilated into a political future.

This link between black femininity and historicity provides us with one frame for reading Walker's tableau. From this perspective, the tableau illustrates the perpetual and enduring wound of slavery. Following Carol E. Henderson, I use the trope of the wound to invoke the way this traumatic history manifests itself in visible corporeal form.[14] In keeping with this reading, we might argue that Walker illuminates both the woundedness of black women by figuring the atrocities of slavery and the flattening effect of this woundedness through her use of silhouette. These processes are described at length in Hortense Spillers's essay, "Mama's Baby, Papa's Maybe: An American Grammar Book." Here, Spillers traces how black women become flesh through the Atlantic slave trade. While all black bodies become flesh through the process of enslavement—"Under these conditions, we lose at least gender difference in the outcome, and the female body and the male body become a territory of cultural and political maneuver, not at all gender-related, gender specific"—there is still a particularly gendered dimension to the experience.[15] This happens because sexuality is the frame for interacting with racialized flesh, the broad contours of which Spillers outlines: "1) The captive body becomes the source of an irresistible, destructive sensuality; 2) at the same time—in stunning contradiction—the captive body reduces to a thing, becoming being for the captor; 3) in this absence *from* a subject position, the captured sexualities provide a physical and biological expression of 'otherness'; 4) As a category of 'otherness,' the captive body translates into a potential for pornotroping and embodies sheer physical powerlessness that slides into a more general 'powerlessness,' resonating through various centers of human and social meaning."[16] What we see in Spillers's articulation of how gender and sexuality shape the modes of fleshiness is the explicit link between violence, sexuality, and powerlessness. While these factors also clearly work in the production of black masculine flesh, Spillers is more concerned with articulating how this wounds black women.[17] Here, Spillers focuses on the reordering of kinship through the separation of mothers from children and the inability for a woman to elect whether to reproduce and with whom. This denial of motherhood and removal of the paternal function produces a web of contradictions that, Spillers argues, are unique to the black female subject and render her flesh in a particular way: "In this play of paradox, only the female stands *in the flesh*, both mother and mother-dispossessed."[18] Spillers is insistent that the black woman's equation with the flesh is distinct from other forms of becoming-flesh. Indeed, it is clear that this form of objectification is different from the becoming-flesh that Beauvoir discusses because the terms of objectification do not veer into narcissism. It is also different from the becoming-flesh that Fanon describes because this formulation of becoming-flesh is linked to the particular historical moment of slavery rather than the sticky temporality of animality and becoming-biological. Nor is this mode of the flesh equivalent to the pain produced by illness or the dominating gaze of patriarchy or colonialism. While it shares some things with these forms of embodiment, this fleshiness is marked by a particular conglomeration of sexuality, violence, and objectification. This is flesh that has been caught in the perpetual wound of slavery, so that agency cannot even be illusory: it has already been foreclosed.

Through this emphasis on objectification, we begin to see the particular processes of flattening at work. In addition to reading this flattening into flesh as a mode of inhabiting historicity, the politics of slavery enable us to read this flattening as part of a circuit that uses black women's bodies and absents their sexuality. Spillers, here, is adamant that the flesh that black women inhabit is one that does not allow her access to her own sexuality but renders her available for the use of others. The black woman functions, Spillers argues, not only as a marker of difference but as a route for others to experience that difference. In "Interstices," she writes, "[The black woman] became instead the principal point of passage between the human and the non-human world. Her issue became the focus of a cunning difference—visually, psychologically, ontologically—as the route by which the dominant male decided the distinction between humanity and 'other.'"[19] Further, she adds, "While there are numerous references to the black woman in the universe of signs, many of them perverted, the prerogatives of sexuality are refused her because the concept of sexuality originates in, stays with, the dominative mode of culture and its elaborate strategies of thought and expression."[20] Even as black female bodies are sexualized because of their relationship to difference (as it is produced by various hierarchies of domination), sexuality is foreclosed for black women, just as motherhood is.[21] I will return to thinking about this linkage between sexuality and maternity later in the text, but what I want to emphasize in this discussion of Spillers is the way black women's alterity becomes coded as sexually available flesh, what Spillers calls "pornotroping." This is the wound and flattening that slavery produces.

Through this process, however, representation also becomes its own wound.[22] The assumption of marginalization works in tandem with the very structures of oppression that it is attempting to highlight and subvert. This produces a double bind in which subjects attempt to avoid these flattening processes but end up with a different set of constrained behavioral choices. Most notably, we can see this tension in Patricia Hill Collins's critique of "controlling images." Controlling images are representations of black women that hew to "racial-sexual mythologies."[23] Varying widely in scope, they depict black women as "licentious, animalistic, libidinous Jezebels; as asexual, comical, masculinized Mammies; or as tough, detached, 'strongblackwomen.'"[24] Collins argues that these images proliferate because they justify the continued disciplining of black women and black female sexuality as linked to the "moral and fiscal 'deterioration of the state.'"[25] In her critique of the various forms of marginalization that these images enact, Collins seeks to distance representations of black female subjects and sexuality from them, which is to say that she ends up advocating for self-discipline in order to prevent disciplining from the outside.

Walker's emphasis on flatness, then, plays both with and against these tensions. She calls attention to the processes that fix and flatten black female sexuality, but her relationship to these images is ambiguous. Is her tableau a critique of this process, or do these representations reinscribe them? These are central questions in thinking about the reception of Walker's art and the production of her fame. In 1997, the year that Walker was awarded the MacArthur Grant, Betye Saar, an artist known for exploring how cultural images circulate, began a letter-writing campaign against her work. Saar's letter asked: "Are African-Americans being betrayed under the guise of art?"[26] Responding in support of Saar's campaign, another critic, Michael Harris, writes, "When we become artists who use Pickaninnies as a means to develop notoriety and artistic success, there's no need for a Klan. There's no need for any kind of racist opposition because they are so Stockholmed to the point where we will begin to oppress ourselves if we're not careful."[27] In addition to voicing anxiety that representations of the past might cloud the present and further reify notions of black flesh as other, these criticisms speak to the policing of representations of blackness so as to avoid the problem of injury. These critics view Walker as trafficking in woundedness. As English argues, their critiques suggest that "the motivation behind work like Walker's is perceived to be anachronistic *in itself*, like a fragment of slavery carried over unmodified into the present."[28] Further, English makes clear the link between representation, historic wounds, and present injury when he writes, "In order to be communicable, the notion that Walker's work virtually reimplements slavery, or its operative psychologizations, requires a contemporary perceiver who enjoys an unbroken view of the institution and its mechanisms, who can *picture* them."[29]

Given the fraught nature of representation, it is clear why Walker's silhouettes have ignited firestorms. Since black female subjectivity has been reduced to flatness either because of the process of othering or as a tactic of self-disciplining, Walker's silhouettes carry a lot of representational weight. Since they do not conform to idealized models of blackness, they ask the viewer to look more closely, thus making their opacity and dependence on the viewer's projection more overt.

Playing with History, Playing with Race

In thinking about the relationships between history and identity that her tableaux stir within the viewer, Walker provides her own insight into the affective historical games that she is playing. In an interview with Jerry Saltz, Walker says, "Afro-Am or African-American artists are always espousing the horrors of slavery and Gen-Afro Apartheid. . . . But the horrors are always tolerable to repressed individuals to whom they may occur. This allows for a stronger sense of masochism in future generations, makes for riots, very colorful."[30] In his discussion of this comment, English interprets Walker's invocation of masochism as having to do with an attachment to a scripted role of submission: "Indeed, the endless reproduction of rhetorics and images about slavery's 'direct' impress upon our time, insofar as they minimize or eliminate the inscription of mediation, *will* strengthen masochism, one version of which depends on an attachment to scripted roles and a submission to the restrictions they imply."[31] Underlying English's analysis of Walker's invocation of masochism is the idea that the passage of time renders the horrors of slavery more abstract and produces a different relationship to them. Masochism, then, stems from an alienation and attachment to this history. While I agree with English's understanding that history plays a large part of thinking through what masochism might mean in this context, I think it is important to emphasize the affective attachments to history that are taking place. In her statement to Saltz, Walker not only emphasizes pleasure in remembering history but suggests that pleasure may have been part of slavery in and of itself. Walker's investment, then, might also be understood as using history to play with the different types of identification that she wishes to facilitate, identifications that may or may not have to do with masochism.

In this section, I take up English's claims that Walker's work operates according to a distance from history and attachment to it by focusing on one section of *The End of Uncle Tom*—the cluster of four figures (three women and a baby) engaged in mutual nursing. In addition to illuminating Walker's play with history, this portion of the tableau situates the black woman at the center and asks us to heed her claims or lack thereof on history, subjectivity, agency, and sexuality. In making his claim that Walker plays with history, English argues that Walker's tableaux resist the facile readings that Saar and Harris wish to graft onto them. Instead, English argues, they illuminate multiplicity and produce an array of strong contradictions: "The tension itself comprises a laundry list of dynamic oppositional entanglements, between black and white, obviously; but also between violence and pleasure, death and birth, orality and anality, documentation and fantasy, art and nonart, seeing and imagining, and so on."[32] *The End of Uncle Tom* in particular "depicts the force of desire as capable of stressing nearly every boundary required for the order of 'civilized society' to hold: human and animal, old and young, safe and unsafe, powerful and subjected, consensual and forced."[33] It is in these affective chasms that subjectivity (both that of the viewer and that of Walker) is located. Walker writes, "In order to have a real connection with my history, I had to be somebody's slave. But I was in control: that's the difference."[34] Despite the historical foreclosures that I have already outlined, Walker is invested in allowing for agency, not only her own, but that of her viewers to identify as they wish.

Indeed, at the heart of the detail from *The End of Uncle Tom* we see women who appear to be taking control. Shaw describes this scene as "an unsettling arrangement of four silhouetted characters, three bare-breasted slave women and an infant child, who are engaged in a chain of mutual nursing. All three women essentially look alike: they are young, they have kerchiefs on their heads, their dresses are pulled down about their waists, their backs arch forward, and their rear ends press outward."[35] Shaw argues that this image subversively represents "female sexual reflexivity" because it alters the script for the idea of black women nursing.[36] Though the representation of bare-breasted women recalls the inability of black women to own their bodies during slavery, these women depart from that imagery. They are not figured as mammies, and their engrossment in the activity of mutual nursing suggests that they are neglecting their duties both as women sexually available to their masters and as caretakers. Shaw writes, "The child, instinctively knowing that it must obtain the breast in order to be satiated, in order to survive, strains hopelessly to get a teat within its grasp. However, the women have lost all desire to placate it. With the attention they give to their erotic activity, they all but forget the infant."[37] Further, the enjoyment that Shaw reads into this scene is one of explicit subversion: "This orgiastic carnality speaks of a racialized transgression of sexual and gender roles. No longer are their bodies to be used by others, by men or by babies; now they are to be enjoyed by the self and one's own kind, now they are in themselves the objects of desire as they consume the bodies of their analogues."[38]

In Shaw's reading, Walker has taken a historically harmful trope and inverted it, so that these women, though they may be legible as slaves, are subverting the social order by not performing the prescribed script. Instead of nursing white infants, they nurture each other. Instead of making their bodies available for white men, they seek comfort within the realm of women. This reading of this grouping endows them with individuality by linking their activity with pleasure and resistance. This process of rescripting grants them a form of liberal subjectivity in which resignification produces agency and subjectivity.[39]

There is more to this historical play, however. Since the piece is a dialogue between representation and identity, we are also asked what it means to see this as an image of history. That is to say, what is at stake in producing this image of the non-Mammy suckling? Shaw's pleasure in the image's subversive potential is clear, but when Walker was asked what this vignette was about, her response hit upon different notes: "History. My constant need or, in general, a constant need to suckle from history, as though history could be seen as a seemingly endless supply of mother's milk represented by the big black mammy of old. For myself, I have this constant battle—this fear of weaning. It's really a battle that I apply to the black community as well, because all of our progress is predicated on having a very tactile link to a brutal past."[40] Seen in this light, it would be easy to view Walker's explanation as an extension of Audre Lorde's discussion of the erotic in which women are connected historically through their blackness and historical marginalization. This would link Walker's reading with Shaw's and work toward a recuperation of history through agency. Christina Sharpe's reading adds to this through her attention to the fact that it is not mother's milk but mammy's milk that the women are consuming. This is a mode of nonbiological community: "What is most extraordinary about Walker's reading of the portrait (which is not, I think specifically about the portrait itself) is that what she analogizes is the mammy-as-history-as mother's milk."[41] The connection between milk as a nurturing substance and the "orgiastic carnality" that Shaw reads into the image adds to this interpretation. Indeed, even Spillers's linkage of maternity and sexuality as foreclosed sites of experience and pleasure for black women can be mapped onto this type of recuperative reading of the image.

On the other hand, we might read Walker's comments about historical connectedness as further entrenching these figures within a milieu without agency. Rather than recuperate the image, Sharpe's comments actually veer toward this direction. The image, then, traffics in historical hurt in several arenas. First, it references the historical reality that black women were made to care for white children at the expense of their children; Sharpe reads the child who is unable to suckle as part of this cycle of foreclosed maternity. Playing off of history in this way highlights the simultaneously absent and omnipresent maternal at work in thinking about black women. Second, these images force the viewer to confront the ways that these histories play into contemporary black women's lives and understandings of themselves. Sharpe argues that the images are "an attempt to look at shame itself, in order to try to account for its eruption into the present."[42] Sharpe comes to this conclusion by foregrounding what is invoked but absent in the image—the white suckling child. That is to say, the ties that bind these women are not actually produced by their own machinations but have been structured by their collective exclusion from agency. Sharpe writes that the women are "held together by their emphasis on reproduction, on passing on evidence, on making the horrors of slavery as 'visible as the blood,' and in reproducing *for* and reproducing the desires *of* the slave owner."[43] This image can be read, then, not as subversive, but as an illustration of the continued shame that this historical form of objectification produces from our contemporary vantage point. Sharpe reads this image as the "*animation* of shame (as the opposite of pride, black pride in particular)."[44]

Shaw's insistence on seeing pleasure and on reading it as a site of resistance that offers the possibility of a heroic recuperation of agency and subjectivity from the dehumanization produced by slavery is at odds with Sharpe's vision of shame, but Walker also asks us to consider another possibility—the middle ground where pleasure and shame mingle. We are invited to ask if there can indeed be happiness in slavery.

In *Extravagant Abjection*, Darieck Scott considers the question of pleasure vis-à-vis the production of black power in abjection. He asks, "Would such a pleasure [in abjection] be a form of the (black) *power* that we are investigating—which is to say, would such pleasure be a way to resist, or work with or work through, the challenges presented by a process of racialization through sexual degradation?"[45] In parsing out the possibility of this formulation of pleasure, Scott makes clear that the primary barrier is that which separates the present viewer/reader from the past. Understanding whether pleasure was possible in these situations is impossible because our understandings of pleasure rely on contemporary notions of individuality and personhood, which cannot be grafted onto the historical reality of slavery.

The only thing that we have access to is a projection (literalized by Walker's silhouettes) that tends to perpetuate the idea of blackness and femininity as "total objecthood," "complete abjection."[46] This projection, however, has a flattening effect on understanding the multiple possibilities of subjectivity and experience, reducing them to a stance of victimization. Representations of pleasure in abjection, however, grant us access to the *possibility* of pleasure even as they may not have an exact correlation to reality. Scott argues that the illumination of these pleasures is "at once a suturing of the past to present and a declaration of independence from that history."[47] Even as the past is inaccessible in the present moment, we can imagine pleasure as possible because we are not actually in the past. Scott writes, "We *can* name our reimagination and even our reenactment of what they experienced as pleasure (just as we could name it as pain or anything else, even, however morally or ethically bankrupt it might be to do so, as boredom). We can do so because we are not them *and* because they did suffer, because our legacy is both their suffering and their achievement of recovery from suffering (or, perhaps more accurately, their achievement of living-with-suffering) and the (relative) political advantages brought thereby. To represent blackness as/in abjection in such scenes is a way of working with the legacy of history."[48] These representations, then, are about one's *relationship* to history rather than a statement about reality. While playing with history is a way of connecting to the past and affirming the idea that it is important to connect to these ancestors, this distance between the past and present is crucial. As Scott writes, "This removal is key: it depends on a connection to a history in which people really were violated, people who, because of the effectiveness of racialization, are presumably of intimate (though at the same time far distant) relation to oneself."[49] In part, identification with this past means that these projections of history are operating on a circuit of sympathy and empathy similar to the one I described in the fourth chapter. However, as Scott makes clear, our participation in these circuits is "not *fully* a choice, since we are all of us, as participants in a culture that like all cultures recycles and revises and repeats the narratives that have given it life and shape, the unwilling, unasked inheritors of that culture's terrors and suffering."[50] This absence of choice means that we must "work *with* the material of history bequeathed to us."[51]

We can easily map Scott's analysis onto Walker's image. The pleasure that we might excavate from this detail of the nursing women is symptomatic of our own connections to the past. By calling forth violence, history, and sexuality in silhouetted form, Walker, I argue, invites us to consider our own relationship to this history and how we have made our own identities vis-à-vis this image. More specifically, the complex identifications that the silhouettes produce invite us to think about masochism and how racialization, shame, and pleasure coalesce through agency and subjectivity.

Attending to Race and Masochism

Since I have argued throughout *Sensational Flesh* that masochism is a mobile entity whose meanings shift depending on context, I am not invested in producing a fixed idea of masochism around Walker's images, but I am interested in how masochism hovers around these discussions of pleasure and racialization. Though I have previously discussed masochism as it applies to the formation of white masculine subjectivity and the suffering black body, complicity in the objectification of female bodies, and an individual project of corporeal integrity in the face of illness, different sensations attach to these usages of the term. This form of masochism has to do with history and one's relationship to it and the forms of identification produced with historical figures. To put it another way, why do we think about masochism, either Walker's or our own, when we see her images?

Precisely because of the difficulty of thinking about agency, subjectivity, and sexuality, these forms of identification are often figured as fraught when one is talking about the history of African Americans. To this end, both Elizabeth Freeman and Christina Sharpe are drawn to Isaac Julien's film *The Attendant* because it makes these difficulties clear by explicitly thematizing S&M because of its exploration of black history. *The Attendant* features a black museum guard who has an after-hours sexual encounter with a white museum visitor in one of the museum's galleries. The encounter, however, appears modeled on a painting depicting the transatlantic slave trade. Reality and fantasy begin to mix at this point, and the film becomes a series of tableaux vivants depicting the black man's domination by the white man. These images invoke the transatlantic slave trade and the historical oppression of black people, but the atmosphere is suffused with eroticism and pleasure.

In her analysis of the film, Freeman draws on its use of S&M to analyze the reparative possibilities that this queer temporality produces. She writes that "it is inescapably true that the body as sadomasochistic ritual becomes a means of invoking history—personal pasts, collective sufferings, and quotidian forms of injustice—in an idiom of pleasure."[52] In this S&M scene, the histories that are embodied are recognizable as historical traumas—they are responsible for producing the *imago* of the suffering black body that I discussed in the fourth chapter, "Time, Race, and Biology." However, Freeman argues that Julien, by drawing on race play, enacts a critique of this model of blackness. Julien's film uses history in a way that "relentlessly physicalizes the encounter with history and thereby contributes to a reparative criticism that takes up the materials of a traumatic past and remixes them in the interests of new possibilities for being and knowing."[53] In this way S&M functions as a therapeutic repetition of the past in order to open possibilities in the present.

The scene's corporeality is important because it suggests that S&M in this instance is functioning not as a mode of mere repetition but as a mode of temporal disruption that brings the flesh to the surface. Flesh, in turn, introduces difference and multiplicity. More specifically, Freeman argues, it sutures queerness and blackness: "His *tableau vivant* of the slave trade insists that the sufferings of black people are in the first instance fleshy—and thereby not fully reducible to the heterosexist, sentimentalist account that the violation of their family ties constitutes the worst offense against them. Conversely, the *tableau vivant* also offers a queer image of aliveness, of sheer animacy unfettered by the narrative drives of biography or history, and in so doing conjures up the possibility of a future beyond both reproduction and writing."[54] This flesh, which is brought to the fore through historical embodiment, disrupts heteronormativity by illuminating flesh in a nonreproductive mode and as a space of possibility. It is this critique, along with the forced encounter with the historical material conditions of slavery, that leads Freeman to discuss the film as belonging to the genre of queer of color critiques. As Freeman writes, "S/m might be a way of feeling historical that exposes the limits of bourgeois-sentimental, emotional reactions to historical events."[55] Through its reliance on embodied temporality and the unruliness of sensation and affect, the film offers the possibility of contingency and therefore different futures.

Freeman argues that Julien's film uses S&M to "bring the body to a kind of somatized historical knowledge, one that does not demand or correct information about an original experience of past events, nor even engender legibly cognitive understandings of one's space in a historically

specific structure."[56] This form of embodied history "enacts the oscillation between historically specific forms of time (or between a historically specific form of time and its constructed or fantasized opposite)
and illuminates some past consequences and futural possibilities of this
movement."[57] This emphasis on multiplicity and embodiment leads to
new formations of belonging in history; different possibilities for orient-
ing oneself toward the past and future have been introduced. Indeed,
following on Walter Johnson's discussion of the different temporalities
of African Americans and the potential subversive spaces they offered
during slavery, we can read this form of historical play as reinvigorating a
sense of the multiple temporalities that black bodies could occupy and as
an attempt to subvert the dominant narratives surrounding blackness.[58]

Sharpe's reading of the film differs from Freeman's in that she argues
that it illuminates the "sadomasochism of everyday black life."[59] Sharpe
is not invested in reading S&M as a rewriting of the past. Rather, she
sees it as emblematic of the unspeakable tensions that occupy the present. She writes, "The uncanny juxtaposition of *Slaves on the West Coast
of Africa*, s/m, and daily museum work shifts the look of slavery and the
viewer's relationships to it from the past to the present, from the way the
history of slavery is archived in the museum, narrativized in film, and
presented in museological practices to the way it is worked out in everyday relations."[60] S&M mobilizes the unspeakable because it refuses to be
reduced to something simple; in conjunction with history and complicity, it works to undermine simple readings of the film. This multiplicity
ruptures what Sharpe calls the "proper affective responses to slavery"
because "through them [Julien] turns the viewer's attention back to the
production of post-slavery subjectivity itself, to the ways that post-slavery subjects continue to occupy these abjected bodies in their postures
of submission and mastery and the ways that this occupation in the present is a source of (ambivalently experienced) pleasure."[61] Here, Sharpe is
quick to point to the pleasure that we see on both men's faces as well as
the pleasure that is produced by witnessing the scene.

In Sharpe's reading of the film, it is not just black pleasure that is at
stake but pleasure in understanding how the present is a continuation
of the past. While it is important to see that this is not a simple repetition of the past, it calls attention to our interest in the abject and our
investment in understanding blackness as abject. Sharpe argues that this
manifests itself in the film as a "compulsion for white and black viewers
to 'play the slave a little bit,' to occupy and then disavow the occupation

of an abject, subjugated position."[62] Though this plays out differently for different bodies, it emphasizes the fact that "*it is black bodies* that continue to be the port of entry or point of access into any number of physical, spiritual, or subjective states."[63] The representation of black flesh, then, is embedded within various circuits of masochism, producing guilt and shame either through identification or, as I discussed earlier in the book, through sympathy.

This terrain of masochism through identification is complicated, however, when we return to Darieck Scott's examination of the reimagined pleasure in scenes of subjection. His own analysis talks around the question of masochism. Though many of masochism's key terms (*pleasure, power, subjection, objectification*) are at work in his analysis, he is leery of collapsing black power with masochism. He writes that he is describing something analogous to masochism: "And is this possible pleasure or power a window to, an access granted to, a *constitutive* masochism in human sexuality, as we could see Fanon's muscle tension as such an access to an anonymous or amorphous existence inhering in the body as it existed by consciousness? Or is this power/pleasure distinct from that masochism, perhaps analogous to it but different?"[64] Later he creates more distance between his discussion and masochism, writing, "That such masochistic pleasure and its confusions might become the ground, the material, or even the expression, for the abilities or powers I am attempting to locate in blackness's abjection . . . does not mean that this is a study in black masochism, however."[65] He rejects the idea that he is talking about erotogenic masochism in the Freudian sense, and he does not discuss moral masochism: "Though such familiar terms as *masochism* and *castration* overlay, overlap, and even partly describe this power, they do not fully encompass it, adequately name it, or exhaust it."[66] Scott's anxiety about using *masochism* to describe this relation points both to the difficulty in attaching masochism to anything in particular and to the baggage that the term has when applied to black bodies.

As difficult as it has been for critics to merge discussions of masochism with race, the problem is compounded when one is speaking of black women. Here, I believe it is worth pointing out that these attempts to discuss race and masochism have been articulated by working through black masculinity. The discourse on black female masochism has been dominated by voices from 1980s debates on sexuality. Critics such as Alice Walker and Audre Lorde revile the practice for dismissing the historical record. In contrast to many of the articulations of masochism as offering the potential to understand the history in new ways, these critics argue that S&M is emblematic of a problem within society. I am not attempting a prescriptive statement about S&M, but working through these tensions illuminates a great deal about how individual practices of subversion, suspension, or therapy can be read as conservative, regressive, and harmful for society by critics of S&M.

Walker's critique of S&M in "Can This Sadomasochism Be Saved?" is that individual choices of submission are read as potential reinscriptions of slavery, which is to say that they will produce a collapse between the past and the present. Her short story produces a debate between students in the fictional classroom. A pro-S&M student in Walker's class argues for the individuality of the practice: "It is all fantasy, she said. No harm done. Slavery, real slavery is over, after all."[67] Walker's retort, which she voices as a black female student, describes these fantasies as regressive and harmful because they cannot be contained by the individual and threaten to reproduce historical violences against black women: "I feel abused. I feel my privacy as a black woman has been invaded. Whoever saw that television program can now look at me standing on the corner waiting for a bus and not see *me* at all, but see instead a slave, a creature who *would* wear a chain and lock around my neck for a white person— in 1980!—and accept it. *Enjoy* it."[68] In addition to recalling the specter of the suffering black body, Walker articulates a slippery line between fantasy and reality and individuals and society. In this rescripting of history, the particular historical suffering of black women is used as grist for other people's erotic benefit and threatens their contemporary freedom. Indeed, as I have already argued, tableaux of suffering were circulated both for generating sympathy and for the explicit purposes of erotic practice.

The fear that Walker describes is that social order will slip away. It is a fear not only of temporal suspension but of reversion to a prior time. In an interview with Susan Leigh Star for the volume *Against Sadomasochism*, Audre Lorde expresses a similar fear about S&M. She argues that it is this timeless quality that is most pernicious; she describes it as feeding "the belief that domination is inevitable."[69] "Sadomasochism," Lorde says, "is an institutionalized celebration of dominant/ subordinate relationships. And, it *prepares* us either to accept subordination or to enforce dominance. *Even in play*, to affirm that the exertion of power over powerlessness is erotic, is empowering, is to set the emotional and social stage for the continuation of that relationship, politically, socially, and economically."[70] This articulation of suspension is one that suspends subversion and extends the status quo of oppression. Lorde argues that sadomasochism is perceived to operate on the level of the individual but is actually about the manipulation of society. Further, Lorde uses the feminist mantra of "The personal is political" to think about the implications of sadomasochism. She says, "I do not believe that sexuality is separate from living. As a minority woman, I know dominance and subordination are not bedroom issues. In the same way that rape is not about sex, s/m is not about sex but about how we use power. If it were only about personal sexual exchange or private taste, why would it be presented as a political issue?"[71] Lorde's description of the politics of sadomasochism is part tautology—calling on the feminist debates regarding S&M to argue for its politics beyond individuals—and part reminder of the contingency of the very concept of individuality. Her statement, like Fanon's argument that the black man cannot be a masochist, illuminates the structuring of individuality by forces such as capitalism and is articulated through notions of privacy. In effect, Lorde argues that black women are seen as representatives of their race and as such do not have the luxury to partake in individual projects that suspend time because they are already assumed to be living in the past.

In many ways this problem of an impossibly individual black woman is signified by the collapse of black women into not only the flesh but the most objectified, most abject sign of fleshiness. In their refusal to allow for individual agency, Walker's and Lorde's criticisms of S&M speak to the way that sexuality has been foreclosed as a space for black women. Thus they enact Spillers's argument that black women are discursively outside of sexuality and individuality. This reading also collapses racialization with masochism, forgetting that masochism, as we have seen through the book—despite the forms it takes—is elected.

Race Play: Choosing Powerlessness

By way of thinking through black female masochism, I turn toward Mollena Williams, an African American BDSM practitioner and educator who has emerged as a spokesperson of sorts for S&M. While Williams's status as an individual who practices S&M would seem to foreclose questions regarding its possibility for black women, I am interested in reading her own statements on S&M and other people's writing on her

in order to analyze the ways that she navigates the collapse of subjectivity, agency, and sexuality in a system where one would assume she does
not have access to these things. Williams has been interviewed extensively about S&M and her attraction to it. This, in large part, is because
she favors S&M play that revolves around historical racially charged situations—race play. She defines race play as "any type of play that openly
embraces and explores the (either 'real' or assumed) racial identity of
the players within the context of a BDSM scene. The prime motive in a
'Race Play' scene is to underscore and investigate the challenges of racial
or cultural differences."[72] Though there are numerous possible ways to
enact race play, the explicit foregrounding of historical circumstances of
oppression remains constant.[73]

Williams argues that race play serves a therapeutic function. In this
way, we can read it as another version of Freud's repetition compulsion
in which people are compelled to repeat the trauma of the past in order
to come to terms with it. She says, "It is not blasphemy to want to touch
that wound. You can't heal something in your soul by letting it remain in
its original state of pain. It HAS to be touched. Otherwise it will never
heal."[74] She also emphasizes the importance of trust in race play. This
reopening of the wound, as she describes it, requires particularly attentive participants so that the therapeutic function is preserved. Race play,
according to Williams, demands commitment and consent because it is
emotional and physical labor: "Doing race play is HARD. It isn't some
walk in the fucking park. And finding people I trust enough to do it with
is almost impossible because it is hard, and they are at risk. . . . The one
thing—the *only* thing—that separates BDSM from abuse is consent.
Now, there is implied consent. However, at no point is [there] not [*sic*]
control. Never."[75]

Here, we see that Freeman's analysis of *The Attendant* as a form of
reparative historiography could also be applied to Williams's performances of race play. In her published writing on race play, she describes
playing the part of a virginal slave who is raped by her master. While
Williams scripts her character, Molly, as a reluctant participant in the
scene, she describes small ways that her body yields to the Admiral's
touch. She writes, "I felt horribly ashamed and yet . . . as he pulled his
hand away, my hips lifted every so slightly toward him."[76] Though it does
not subvert historical scripts, Williams's fantasy, like Julien's film, speaks
to a mode of inhabiting an oppressive history with hints of pleasure. This
reading of Williams's work foregrounds the pleasure that she gains by

experiencing a different affective connection to the past and can be read alongside Shaw's recuperation of pleasure and agency in Kara Walker's depiction of the quartet of nursing bodies.

By way of thinking about electing pleasure as a way of recuperating sexuality for black women on both the individual and the collective level, I turn toward the work of Jennifer Nash, who foregrounds the possibility of finding pleasure in racialization in her readings of black women in pornography. Nash's methodology is racial iconography, "a critical hermeneutic, attentive to the nonracist meaning-making work that black women's bodies perform in pornography and to the historical contingency of racialized pornographic texts," in order to rescript agency and sexuality onto black female bodies.[77] Through a reading of *Sexworld*, a pornographic film from 1978 that features many interracial couplings, Nash illustrates how one can take pleasure in blackness. She describes an encounter between Roger, a white man who initially describes his disgust at blackness and mistakes Jill, his black scene partner, for a maid when she first appears in his room. Undeterred, Jill seduces him, and Roger ultimately gives himself over to his desire for black women. Conventional readings of this scene position Jill as a stereotypical "hyperlibidinous black woman for the pleasurable consumption of both the white male protagonist and the ostensibly white male spectator."[78] Instead, Nash reads the scene as articulating the way that "blackness is represented as a pleasurable site for the black protagonist."[79] Nash does this by reading Jill's seduction as an attempt to transform racism into pleasure in racial difference. Jill, Nash argues, is "emphatically present . . . insisting on the potential pleasures of interracial sex *and* the pleasures she takes in her black body."[80]

Is there a way to perform this sort of reading on race play? This is where the difficulties of S&M come in. While Freeman offers us tools to read race play as producing pleasure from historical oppression, the pleasure that Williams describes is very different from the pleasure that Nash reads from Jill's body. Williams takes pleasure, not in her blackness, but rather in the seductive aspects of whiteness and debasement. She describes how as a child watching *Roots*, the television miniseries on slavery, she began to fantasize about the master: "I wondered if, possibly . . . just maybe . . . it wouldn't be so bad if your master was . . . nice. . . . And if he was handsome, then that would be kind of neat, too!"[81] This admiration of the Other manifests itself in her other fantasies as well, yet it is always mixed with bad feelings on her part. In

her description of her fantasy with the Admiral, she finds herself trans-
fixed and terrified by his penis: "I could not take my gaze from his hand
wrapped around the enormous shaft thrusting aggressively from his
lap. . . . I was sickened."[82] This admixture of interracial eroticism and
humiliation constitutes Williams's experience of race play. She is not
playing with her race as much as she is playing with the racial assumptions that *she* assumes others bring to the table. This much is made clear
when she voices her difficulties with race play: "Playing with real-time
fears and hatreds is hot for precisely the same reason it is risky: danger.
Danger of slipping into a bad headspace. Danger of believing that your
top is really a racist. Danger of believing that your bottom really is your
inferior and has no intrinsic value, is less than human, because of their
race."[83] These statements indicate Williams's interest in S&M as a form
of objectification and humiliation. She wants to play at powerlessness
without actually inhabiting that position. The danger is that because
of race and gender her subjectivity may become flattened, so that her
desires are read not as desires particular to her but as a collapse of the
historical script. For Williams, race play is not only about blackness but
about power. She wants to retain her individual desire to submit and to
play. The scripts of her racial and gender identity, however, are things
that she cannot avoid; and so, Williams writes, "I do 'race play' whether
or not I want to."[84]

We might profitably think about race play as a form of disidentification. Like racial iconography, disidentification is another hermeneutic
that helps us read difference. According to José Esteban Muñoz, "Disidentification can be understood as a way of shuffling back and forth
between reception and production."[85] Disidentification is useful in this
scenario because it captures the interplay between an external assign-
ment of identity and an internal response to that identity formation.
The term captures the affective dissonance that comes with forms of
partial identification. In describing the work of various queer minority
performance artists, Muñoz uses *disidentification* to describe modes of
agency that subjects who "are hailed by more than one minority identity component . . . [and] encounter obstacles in enacting identifications"
possess.[86] This space of conflict is where "discourses of essentialism and
constructivism short-circuit."[87] If race play for Williams is where racial
essence meets sadomasochistic sexual preferences, we can identify it as
a mode of disidentification. Williams's blackness and interest in S&M
are identities at odds with each other, yet race play allows her to bring

them together in order to complicate the experience of both. What S&M means is changed by her participation because the racial element is inescapable. Likewise, her relationship to race is complicated by her attachment to a performance of powerlessness.

Not only does the frame of disidentification help us to see how Williams's performances of S&M are constrained by her legibility as a black woman, but it allows us to focus on the ways that her identity is considered a public matter.[88] The public nature of the black body is something that Nash considers at length in her discussion of racial iconography: "The regulation of the black female body has rendered it a public site, a space onto which social debates and collective anxieties about morality, religion, policy, and the state are inscribed."[89] Nash goes on to describe the confluence of antipornography feminism and black feminism as manifesting itself in unpacking this public black body as overexposed and subject to racial fetishization. Race play mobilizes the visibility of Williams's body and channels it into a different type of public performance. At the same time, race play may allow her to enact a certain freedom vis-à-vis race, a freedom that Muñoz might describe as the ability to imagine transformative politics and counterpublics.

Disidentification is also precarious. The stigma surrounding race play is such that although Williams is producing an act of radical resignification, she is read as adhering to particular essential categories. This reading of Williams as performing not disidentification but false consciousness is precisely the difficulty that we encountered when discussing the problem that radical feminists have with lesbian S&M in general and what Alice Walker and Audre Lorde describe with regard to race play in particular. In this reading, we return to the flattening of the black female subject into the fleshy limit of theory. Williams's status as a black woman shapes the ways that she is perceived and how she interacts with others. Most pressingly, it produces her as a member of a category, which limits her ability to be read as possessing individual agency. This is the other side to disidentification. If S&M is Williams's mode of performing the self, it can also be read as symptomatic of her identity as a black woman. The opacity of her subject position produces this confusion and renders her (and race play) threatening.

There, is, however, another aspect of critique in Williams's performance of race play: even as her performances of self may be difficult to disentangle from marginalization, she uses the practice to illuminate the workings of racialization in general. In her analysis of "play with racial, ethnic, and national themes," Margot Weiss argues that Williams's play with race is as much about her own pleasure as it is about "mak[ing] visible, and thus available for reimagining, the normally invisible construction of racialized belonging."[90] In describing Williams's wish to add realism to the slave auctions staged by the Society of Janus, Weiss underscores the link between slavery, S&M culture, and race that Williams wishes to trouble. She writes, "For her, the realism of the scene—dragging in unwilling slaves, stripping, and inspecting them while they scream not to be separated from their children—would 'rock people's worlds': intervene in the social world by smacking it 'upside the head.'"[91] Here, we see that Williams's intervention into history, pleasure, and violence is akin to but different from Kara Walker's. While Walker troubles identification with slavery and our reading of the past, Williams wants to make visible the ways that race and racial histories structure domination and submission and the pleasures that they might provide. Weiss writes, "By dramatizing, often spectacularly, the social meanings of race, the invisibility of whiteness (as race), and the trace of a US history of slavery, this play provides an opportunity to challenge the colorblind white social logics that produce and justify the community."[92] Ultimately, race play calls attention to the larger framing of blackness.

Framing Race

In this way, Mollena's SM is less about sex-desire as a personal, private, affective relation and more about sexual performance as a social, cultural, and public dramatization of power, a dramatization that forces SM practitioners to reflect on their eroticization of and reliance on racialized national belonging. Making the referents of a scene public and generating an affective response can, she hopes, be educational; her desire is to create scenes that demand a public recognition of what is normally unspoken or unseen, by making people connect what they do in a scene with their own history, a larger national history.[93]

But if we accept, as I think we must, that part of what Walker's work takes on is the transmission and effects of profound interracial (sexual) violence (as well as intraracial violence) in, for example, *The End of Uncle Tom and The Grand Allegorical Tableau of Eva in Heaven*, from which the vignette of the four women/girls is drawn, how are we to read these scenes as scenes of slavery (and its traumatic return) without those white characters who are its primary agents (master, mistress, young master, young mistress) and their agents (driver, overseer)? . . . Without the white characters we see nonchalance and not horror in these black performances; without the white characters and with no memory of the conditions under which such acts are compelled, the excessive sex and violence that we see might well be described as that phenomenon called "black-on-black crime."[94]

I begin this final section with these two extended discussions of Mollena Williams and Kara Walker because they both illuminate the ways that playing with race and playing with history extend beyond the purview of an examination of blackness. In the first, Weiss describes Williams's commitment to S&M as a form of political play in which she aims to make visible the connection between simulations of domination and histories of race. In the second, Sharpe draws attention to the white figures in Walker's tableaux to illuminate the fact that her portrayals of the violence of slavery are not complete without a consideration of the interracial dynamics at work in the institution. This fact, which is frequently forgotten, alters readings of the images as merely performances of degradation and shows them to illuminate the monstrosity of slavery as an institution. In both of these narratives, masochism (both in its S&M incarnation and in its looser sense) functions as a way to draw attention to the framing of race more broadly. It attempts to show how everyone, not just black women, is embedded in the historical narrative put forth by slavery.

While this reading of masochism is politically salient, it arguably produces an erasure of black female subjectivity and agency. Weiss goes so far as to remove Williams's performance of S&M from the realm of "sex-desire as a personal, private, affective relation," and Sharpe's attention to the white figures in Walker's work illuminates the black figures' lack of agency. Rather than see this as furthering Spillers's discussion of the impossibility of black female sexuality, however, I will take this opportunity to look at the conditions that produce that impossibility. By doing this, I examine the frame that surrounds both the black and white figures. In this way, I am taking up Chandan Reddy's argument that landscape "is a social space constituted through and against the complex networks and webs of social relations that characterize the racialized industrial mode of production."[95]

Here, I am talking about the background for these performances of masochism. In Walker's case, this means examining the stray houses and tufts of nature that dot the background of the tableaux as well as the white gallery walls that they are mounted on. Both offer ways for us to interpret how masochism is functioning in this context. In his examination of Walker's paintings, English foregrounds Walker's use of landscape, which he argues is "a type of representational enactment, an interested act of social vision."[96] English argues that Walker's images participate in the "picturings and erasures, desires and violences that are endemic to culture formation."[97] Walker's works achieve this, English argues, by illuminating the artifice of the tableaux that they are meant to represent. They commemorate violence, which "point[s] to the capaciousness of landscape, as an idiom, to absorb and amplify the power of rhetorical, political, and historical representations."[98] That is to say, Walker's tableaux reveal the failures at the heart of America; they show that the underside is actually constitutive of the ideology. In this way, Walker's play with landscape reinforces the message that her figures send, but what of the white gallery walls?

Most literally, the gallery walls provide the conditions of visibility for Walker's work. The galleries, as arms of the artistic establishment, have deemed Walker's art to have artistic merit and to be worthy of display, backing up that commitment with physical space, financial support, and cultural approval. What this institutionalization of the work calls forth, however, is a longer, larger history of the representation of race, gender, and sexuality in America. While that topic is far too large to be broached here, the way it intersects with the backdrop of S&M is one of the larger stakes of this project. As I have worked through various local histories of S&M and masochism, the terms shift and the underlying sensations change, but there is one constant—its embeddedness in a discourse that tethers subjectivity, sexuality, and agency. Masochism cannot be theorized outside of this frame.

Whether masochism is connected to colonialism, patriarchy, racialization, or constructions of the self, it relies on a logic that makes sexuality, subjectivity, and agency almost interchangeable terms. While I discussed this conflation briefly at the beginning of this chapter, here I would like to argue that masochism is bound up in this nexus of subjectivity, agency, and sexuality because of its formation through the sciences of sexuality. As Michel Foucault points out in *History of Sexuality*, overlapping ideologies linking the construction of sexuality with the discourse on the self and the management of populations with racialized hierarchies are emblematic of our contemporary investments in sexuality as a nexus of power. The sciences of sexuality are one of the instruments by which this power is reified. We see this most clearly in the first chapter's history of reading masochism as an exceptional and subversive practice, but all of the local histories of masochism that fill these pages also offer testament to these commitments by illuminating how these discourses are attached to particular iterations of masochism and particular sensations.

In the historical trajectories that I have traced, masochism does not emerge prior to sexology or psychoanalysis, and in each of the local histories we can see the imprint of this relationship between these sciences and the concept. While these connections are overt in the relationships between Sigmund Freud and Frantz Fanon, Richard von Krafft-Ebing and radical feminist arguments against S&M, and Bob Flanagan's casual use of psychoanalysis, they also underlie the formations of masochism at work in *The Story of O*, *The Second Sex*, and Gilles Deleuze's theories of masochism. Both Pauline Réage and Simone de Beauvoir write against the conventional scientific scripting of female passivity as natural and female masochism as an aberration, but they simultaneously fuse sexuality with agency and subjectivity. As I argued earlier, O submits so that she gains recognition as a subject, and Beauvoir argues that a woman's path to transcendence (autonomous subjectivity) is economic independence or an authentic (mutual) sexuality. Deleuze formulates his early theories on masochism explicitly against Freudian ideas by putting women in the position of power; these narratives culminate in the "new man," a persona in which sexuality, agency, and subjectivity are fused to the degree that he emerges as almost sadistic. Deleuze's later theorization of masochism as a mode of desubjectification differs from this, but I will deal with it separately.

We might, then, ask how we might begin to shift frames of knowledge so that it is possible to think about black female masochism and produce an agential black female sexuality. In some ways, however, I wonder if asking that question tethers us further to a biopolitical logic. We would still be stuck in a world where some are marked by surfaces and flatness. Alternatively, we might ask how else to think about sexuality, thereby truly engaging Foucault's project to find resistance in "bodies and pleasures." We have several options for theorizing agency outside of sexuality and subjectivity. One of them is Deleuze and Guattari's concept of assemblages, and the other is Audre Lorde's formulation of the erotic. In the previous chapter I discuss both of these concepts at length, and both have appeal for several reasons. Deleuze and Guattari's portrait of power as diffuse and spread around various components of an assemblage (recalling here that they describe the masochist as a form of becoming-animal in which masochist, mistress, saddle, and whip collaboratively desire to become-horse) opens us to thinking about desire in an alternate vocabulary to that of subjectivity and sexuality. But it is an uncontrollable entity; these processes of opening desire can easily be attached to any number of political projects and can work to obscure black female sexuality on other terms. Indeed, my usage of assemblages as part of my practice of empathetic reading speaks precisely to this openness. This leaves us with Lorde's formulation of the erotic, which, as I argued previously has resonances with Deleuze and Guattari's concept of the assemblage. The notable differences are that Lorde's erotic destabilizes subjectivity by introducing the plural subject, who is explicitly political and agential. Bound through affect, this subject is often reduced to a homogenous, flat, public subject, but this does not have to be the case. We could consider the plural subject, hailed by the erotic on the register of multiplicity. While Lorde does not delve into this possibility because she is invested in the erotic as a space for black women, I conclude this book by asking what it would take to maintain the multiplicity of the erotic.[99] To produce an erotic multiplicity that could enliven not only black female bodies but others, I suggest we shift sensational registers and, to this end, think of the erotic as a polyphony of voices, thereby activating Lorde's description of erotic connection as "stretch[ing my body] to music and open[ing] into response, hearkening to its deepest rhythms."[100]

Here, I turn to Nina Simone's song "I Ain't Got No, I Got Life." Recorded for her 1970 album *Black Gold*, it is a medley of two different songs from Galt MacDermot's 1968 musical *Hair*, suturing them together to form a narrative arc of pain and empowerment. The fast tempo drives the listener through the track while Simone's low voice registers the emotional rollercoaster that she takes us on.

> I ain't got no home, ain't got no shoes
> Ain't got no money, ain't got no class
> Ain't got no skirts, ain't got no sweater
> Ain't got no perfume, ain't got no bed

Ain't got no mind

Ain't got no mother, ain't got no culture
Ain't got no friends, ain't got no schooling
Ain't got no love, ain't got no name
Ain't got no ticket, ain't got no token
Ain't got no God

And what have I got?
Why am I alive anyway?
Yeah, what have I got
Nobody can take away?

Got my hair, got my head
Got my brains, got my ears
Got my eyes, got my nose
Got my mouth, I got my smile
I got my tongue, got my chin
Got my neck, got my boobs
Got my heart, got my soul
Got my back, I got my sex

I got my arms, got my hands
Got my fingers, got my legs
Got my feet, got my toes
Got my liver, got my blood

I've got life, I've got my freedom
I've got the life

I've got the life
And I'm gonna keep it
I've got the life
And nobody's gonna take it away
I've got the life

First, Simone sings of material lack—lack of clothes, money, and home. Digging deeper, she sings of a lack of mother, love, and religion. Instead of despairing, however, she turns inward to find that what she has left is her body, her flesh. Most notably she has her heart, her soul, her sex, and her freedom. In this instance Simone reterritorializes her flesh. She takes back her body from a landscape of lack and flatness. She enacts what Fred Moten describes as "an erotics of the cut," which is "blurred, dying life; liberatory, improvisatory, damaged love; freedom drive."[101] She's got the life and we have her voice, a voice that breathes life, subjectivity, and possibility into the frame. When she sings we can hear how flesh and sensation matter.

Notes

Notes to Chapter 1

1. For an example from another field we might turn to Stanley Lieberson's sociological analysis of changing patterns in children's names (*Matter of Taste*). While Lieberson is not speaking about sensation, his analysis points to an external structure, taste, that is both shared and individual. This is an argument similar to the one I would like to make about sensation.

2. Krafft-Ebing, *Psychopathia Sexualis, Translation*, 91. Using a translation to understand theoretical concepts is undeniably problematic. Bauer's insightful article "Not a Translation but a Mutilation" traces the subtle differences between the English and German editions of *Psychopathia Sexualis*. She argues that the translations produced not only language differences but also cultural ones, portraying Krafft-Ebing as judgmental toward his subjects and their pathologies and thereby damaging his reputation in English-speaking countries. With this caveat in mind, the English translation can still be used to assess Krafft-Ebing's concept of masochism. Unless otherwise noted, all quotations will be from this edition of the text. If the German deviates substantially from the English translation, I will make a note of it.

3. Krafft-Ebing argued that masochists experienced a "feminine" desire to please one's partner. He argued that masochism was an extreme form of the "passive" (feminine) role: "[It] represents a pathological degeneration of the character (really belonging to woman) of the instinct of subordination, physiological in woman." Krafft-Ebing, *Psychopathia Sexualis with Especial Reference* [trans. Rebman], 203.

4. Krafft-Ebing, *Psychopathia Sexualis, Translation*, 194.

5. I am drawing my notion of exceptionalism from Puar, *Terrorist Assemblages*, 3–5.

6. This social anxiety materialized itself in a multitude of ways at the turn of the century; the increasing popularity of sciences such as criminology, anthropology, and medicine, all of which struggled to define difference in essentialized biological terms, spawned changes in literature, law, architecture, and other organs of the social and political body.

7. Krafft-Ebing, *Psychopathia Sexualis, Translation*, 223.

8. Ibid., 225.

9. Ibid.

10. Nancy Cott, in "Passionlessness," makes this argument with regard to the ideology of passionlessness, which flourished in the mid- to late 1800s. According to this ideology, women were not naturally sexually aggressive or desirous of sexual encounters. Laqueur, in *Solitary Sex*, links this to the problematic figure of the female masturbator, whose autonomy is threatening to the social order. For more on the specter of the lesbian, see M. Gibson, "Clitoral Corruption."

11. Freud, *Three Essays*, 59.

12. When Jean Jacques Rousseau was eight years old, he was sent to Bossey, a village near Geneva, to board with Minister Lambercier for educational purposes. Miss Lambercier, Rousseau's nursemaid, was given the task of disciplining his brother and him. If unruly, the boys were spanked. Rousseau found that the punishment was "much less terrible in the event than it had been in anticipation, and what is even more bizarre, that this punishment made [him] even fonder of the woman who administered it" (*Confessions*, 14). He grew to crave being beaten: "I had found in the pain inflicted, and even in the shame that accompanied it, an element of sensuality which left me with more desire than fear at the prospect of experiencing it again" (14). He did fear Miss Lambercier's wrath enough to avoid further actual beatings; however, he began to fantasize about a woman who would treat him in the same despotic manner. Rousseau wrote, "To lie at the feet of an imperious mistress, obey her commands, to be obliged to beg for forgiveness, these were sweet pleasures, and the more my inflamed imagination roused my blood, the more I played the bashful lover" (15). These ideas filled Rousseau with humiliation and excitation; they formed the substance of his first confession and laid the groundwork for the rest of the *Confessions*, which would become celebrated in the nineteenth century as one of the first modern autobiographies. See F. Hart, "Notes for an Anatomy"; De Man, "Autobiography as De-Facement."

Reading Rousseau over a hundred years later in Austria, Krafft-Ebing labeled him a masochist. While noting Rousseau's interest in flagellation, Krafft-Ebing followed Alfred Binet in describing Rousseau's yearning for "the frowning eyebrow, the raised hand, the severe glance, the imperious attitude" as noteworthy sexological symptoms. While Binet took them as a marker of fetishism, under Krafft-Ebing's gaze Rousseau's desire for punishment became a paradigmatic example of masochism. According to Krafft-Ebing, the main marker of Rousseau's masochism was "the consciousness of subjection to and humiliation by the woman"; Rousseau "like[d] the haughty, disdainful woman, crushing him under her feet with the weight of her regal anger" (*Psychopathia Sexualis, Translation*, 194).

13. Freud writes, "The real-life performances of masochistic perverts tally completely with these phantasies. . . . In both cases—for the performances are,

after all, only a carrying-out of the phantasies in play—the manifest content is of being gagged, bound, painfully beaten, whipped, in some way maltreated, forced unto unconditional obedience, dirtied and debased" ("Economic Problem," 162). Freud's description of the perversion both as one occurring primarily among men and as one concerning performances of pain and submission resonates strongly with Krafft-Ebing's descriptions of masochists.

14. While Foucault would take umbrage at my decision to put his discussion of S&M in conversation with Freud's, there are many compelling reasons to do so. We can, for example, find echoes of Freud's discussion of the death drive in Foucault's conception of power as diffuse and pervasive. Gearhart, for example, performs this reading of Foucault when she discusses him in relation to Freud. She argues (and I agree) that Freud's psychoanalytic theorization of sadomasochism edges toward an understanding of repression as productive of creativity, which, read alongside Foucault, opens possibilities for understanding the relationship between power and the self. She writes, "It is true that the term sadomasochism was rarely, if ever, used by Foucault in his discussion of political power. But even if it remains implicit in his work, a concept of sadomasochism is nonetheless central to both the social and psychological dimension of Foucault's theory" ("Foucault's Response," 389). In Foucault's *Use of Pleasure*, this productive potential, Gearhart argues, is manifest in art: "Through his sadomasochistic mastery of his own sexuality, the Greek becomes the ultimate expression of his will to power and his own self-created work of art" (394). Art becomes the signal of freedom, but sadomasochism the means of liberation. Indeed, while Gearhart is attached to an essential idea of S&M, her reading of the Freudian aspects of Foucault is useful, and it is with this eye that I turn toward Foucault and his concept of S&M, which I read as a form of embodied subversion.

15. Foucault, *Will to Knowledge*, 157.

16. Ibid., 57.

17. Foucault, "Sex, Power," 167.

18. Ibid., 163.

19. Ibid., 165.

20. Ibid.

21. Rubin, "Miracle Mile," "Leather Times," and "Sites, Settlements."

22. Foucault, "Sex, Power," 170.

23. This occurs despite the fact that Foucault acknowledges Krafft-Ebing's inclusion of masochism in *Psychopathia Sexualis*.

24. Seidman, "AIDS," 377.

25. Ibid., 376.

26. Ibid.

27. Here, we might turn to Jasbir Puar's analysis of homonationalism in *Terrorist Assemblages*.

28. Bersani, "Is the Rectum a Grave?," 222.
29. Ibid.
30. Bersani, *Freudian Body*, 51.
31. Bersani, *Homos*, 82.
32. Ibid., 83.
33. Ibid., 95.
34. Ibid., 99.
35. Ibid., 100.
36. Ibid., 101.
37. Ibid., 7.
38. In *Intimacies*, Bersani articulates a more far-ranging mode of relationality through self-annihilation, which he terms *impersonal narcissism*. Self-shattering allows the self to relate to the other in a way that does not depend on the ego. Bersani writes, "The self the subject sees reflected in the other is not the unique personality vital to modern notions of individualism" (85) but rather "a kind of reciprocal self-recognition in which the very opposition between sameness and difference becomes irrelevant as a structuring category of being" (86). Bersani expresses hope for impersonal narcissism's ability to ameliorate violence in the world: "The experience of belonging to a family of singularity without national, ethnic, racial, or gendered borders might make us sensitive to the ontological status of difference itself as what I called the nonthreatening supplement of sameness in *Homos*" (86). In Bersani's vision, self-annihilation is capable of producing a new world order.
39. Bersani, *Freudian Body*.
40. Edelman, *No Future*, 25.
41. Ibid., 9.
42. Ibid., 31.
43. Butler, "Critically Queer," 228.
44. Halberstam, "Anti-social Turn"; E. Freeman, *Time Binds*; Berlant, "Neither Monstrous nor Pastoral"; Muñoz, *Cruising Utopia*.
45. Muñoz, *Cruising Utopia*, 11.
46. Reddy, *Freedom with Violence*, 20.
47. I would like to acknowledge the vibrant work being done under the rubric of black queer studies and queer of color critique. While these projects do take on the intersections of race and sexuality, I am speaking of work that does not explicitly fall into these categories and that therefore tends to ignore race while discussing sexuality.
48. Reddy, *Freedom with Violence*, 176.
49. Beauvoir, *Second Sex*, 598.
50. Spillers, "Mama's Baby," 67.
51. Ibid.
52. Bray and Colebrook, "Haunted Flesh," 35.

53. Colebrook describes queer theory as "an enquiry into the emergence of terms and relations. . . . The theory would set as its task the notion of the Idea as a problem: how have such relations and terms emerged, what—given effected relations—might have occurred otherwise; what are the forces of potentiality hidden in our experienced encounters?" "How Queer Can You Go?," 31.

54. E. Freeman, *Time Binds*, 141.

55. Smith's history of artisanal knowledge in *Body of the Artisan* offers an example of this trend toward highlighting the importance of the body and embodied knowledge. Against the rapid intellectual shifts of the scientific revolution Smith describes the way, for example, that artisans would show their apprentices how to feel for clay that was suitable for pots; this was information that could be transmitted only experientially.

56. Deleuze, *Francis Bacon*, 15.

57. Ibid., 16.

58. Ibid., 37.

59. Deleuze, "Letter to a Harsh Critic," 8–9.

60. Deleuze, "On Anti-Oedipus," 23.

61. Dinshaw, *Getting Medieval*, 50, 53.

62. E. Freeman, *Time Binds*, 120.

63. Hartman, *Scenes of Subjection*, 19–20.

64. In this I am drawing on Cheng's discussion of Anna Deavere Smith's performance of *Twilight*. Cheng argues that Smith "dramatizes [Elin] Diamond's insight that 'the borders of identity, the wholeness and consistency of identity, is [sic] transgressed by the very act of identification.' . . . Anyone who has witnessed Smith's performances understands the discomfort of being made to watch the fine lines separating the speaking *for*, speaking *as*, and speaking *against*" (*Melancholy of Race*, 188).

65. Diamond, "Violence of 'We.'"

66. Cixous and Clément, *Newly Born Woman*, 99, quoted in Diamond, "Violence of 'We,'" 403.

67. Diamond, "Violence of 'We,'" 411.

68. Gerhard's *Desiring Revolution* describes the relationship between radical feminism and sexology.

69. Activists such as Paula Caplan pushed for a revaluation of these theories and proposed ideas that would prevent women from falling into cycles of self-abuse because they believed that it was inevitable (Caplan, *Myth of Women's Masochism*; Shainess, *Sweet Suffering*).

70. Jagose, *Orgasmology*, 182.

71. Ibid., 196–97.

72. Berlant, *Cruel Optimism*, 43.

73. Ferguson, *Aberrations in Black*, 4.

74. Ibid.

75. Chen, *Animacies*, 3.

Notes to Chapter 2

1. Rich, "Meaning of Our Love," 225.

2. Wilson, "Context," 38.

3. Ibid.

4. Gerhard, *Desiring Revolution*.

5. Ibid., 153.

6. Ibid., 158.

7. Ibid., 176.

8. Rich, "Compulsory Heterosexuality," 632.

9. Ibid., 641.

10. Linden, "Introduction," 4.

11. MacKinnon, "Francis Biddle's Sister," 176.

12. Jonel, "Letter," 18.

13. Ibid., 20, 21.

14. Foucault, *Discipline and Punish* and *Birth of the Clinic*.

15. Here we might consider the lineage that Martin Jay, in *Downcast Eyes*, traces of the prominence (and eventual decline) of vision in twentieth-century French thought.

16. Harris, "Sadomasochism," 94–95.

17. Metz, "Imaginary Signifier," 48.

18. Ibid., 51.

19. Ibid., 59–60.

20. Ibid., 48.

21. Mulvey, "Visual Pleasure," 7.

22. Interestingly, this echoes Richard von Krafft-Ebing's equation of domination, sexual agency, patriarchy, and masculinity.

23. For an example of popular stances against sadomasochism, see Coalition for a Feminist Sexuality, "Notes and Letters," 180. Gayle Rubin and Pat Califia wrote extensively about the prejudice surrounding S&M; see Rubin, "Leather Menace," and Califia, "Among Us, Against Us."

24. Butler, "Against Proper Objects," 7.

25. This has been described in many places, but for more detail see Halberstam, *Female Masculinity*.

26. Terry provides a good overview of this in *American Obsession*.

27. See Halberstam, *Female Masculinity*, and Cvetkovich, *Archive of Feelings*.

28. Findlay, "Freud's 'Fetishism,'" 564.

29. Lamos, "Postmodern Lesbian Position," 93.

30. Ibid.

31. Ibid., 90.

32. Butler, *Bodies That Matter*, 86.

33. Ibid., 88.

34. L. Hart, "Doing It Anyway," 91.

35. L. Hart, *Between the Body*, 106.

36. Ibid., 95.

37. Linden, "Introduction," 7.

38. Hoagland, "Sadism, Masochism," 157.

39. Morgan, "Politics of Sado-Masochistic Fantasies," 109.

40. In "Strange Bedfellows," Jennifer Nash has already called attention to how antipornography feminism and black feminisms came together against pornography. Nash argues that antipornography feminists frequently equated racism with sexism and that black feminists' efforts to work against histories of racialized oppression colluded to produce a black female subject who was separate from the pornographic imaginary.

41. Walker, "Letter of the Times," 207.

42. Ibid.

43. See Nash, "Strange Bedfellows" and "Re-thinking Intersectionality."

44. Fanon, *Black Skin*, 8 [*Peau noire*, 6]. The Markmann translation is known to elide certain particularities in Fanon's original, so where relevant I have included the French text and have also provided the corresponding citations in the French original.

45. Ibid., 174 [*Peau noire*, 142].

46. Ibid., 176 [*Peau noire*, 143].

47. Ibid., 178 [*Peau noire*, 143].

48. Ibid. [*Peau noire*, 143].

49. Despite Fanon's protests regarding the lack of a Negro unconscious, Lauretis, in "Difference Embodied," provides a symptomatic reading of *Black Skin, White Masks* in which she uncovers Fanon's own neurosis surrounding gender and sexuality.

50. Fanon, *Black Skin*, 178 [*Peau noire*, 144].

51. Ibid., 179 [*Peau noire*, 145].

52. Ibid., 178 [*Peau noire*, 144].

53. Ibid., 179 [*Peau noire*, 145].

54. Pellegrini, *Performance Anxieties*, 121.

55. Boyarin reads Fanon with Freud to argue that the hypermasculinity that Fanon describes can be read as the case of a phallus that is possessed, but also not entirely. In discussing Fanon's account of Negrophobia, he argues that "the internalized self-contempt that the colonized male feels for his disempowered situation . . . powerfully determines the colonial misogyny and homophobia. The situation of both Jew and Negro is misrecognized as feminine" ("What Does the Jew Want?," 37). Boyarin reads Fanon's homophobia as the result of his discomfort with the Negro's feminization. His reading of Freud and Fanon

helped me make this connection, as did Butler's reading of the impossibility of the lesbian phallus in "Lesbian Phallus."

56. Fuss, *Identification Papers*, 31.

57. Fanon, *Black Skin*, 152 [*Peau noire*, 123–24].

58. Macey, *Frantz Fanon*, 32–49.

59. Hall, "After-Life of Frantz Fanon."

60. Spillers, "Mama's Baby," 66.

61. Fanon, *Black Skin*, 136 [*Peau noire*, 110].

62. Ibid., 149 [*Peau noire*, 121].

63. Ibid., 191 [*Peau noire*, 154].

64. Pellegrini writes that Fanon "adds another, no less fundamental distinction to Freud's primary distinction between having or not-having the penis (a distinction Lacan reformulates as having or being the phallus): a distinction between being or not-being white" (*Performance Anxieties*, 118).

65. Fanon, *Black Skin*, 8 [*Peau noire*, 6].

66. Ibid., 8 [*Peau noire*, 6].

67. Ibid., 112 [*Peau noire*, 88].

68. Ibid. [*Peau noire*, 88].

69. Ibid., 177 [*Peau noire*, 143].

70. Chafe, *Unfinished Journey*, 141.

71. Interestingly, the images of Till's mutilated corpse, published in magazines such as *Jet* and *Look*, were catalysts for the civil rights movement. The publicity surrounding the case turned attention to Mississippi: "Mississippi became in the eyes of the nation the epitome of racism and the citadel of white supremacy. From this time on, the slightest racial incident anywhere in the state was spotlighted and magnified. To the Negro race throughout the South and to some extent in other parts of the country, this verdict indicated an end to the system of noblesse oblige. The faith in the white power structure waned rapidly. Negro faith in legalism declined, and the revolt officially began on December 1, 1955, with the Montgomery, Alabama, bus boycott" (Whitaker, "Case Study").

72. Pellegrini, *Performance Anxieties*, 90.

73. Mirzoeff, "Right to Look," 476.

74. Higginbotham, "African-American Women's History."

75. Somerville, *Queering the Colorline*, 35.

76. Hart, *Between the Body*, 93.

77. Lorde, *Zami*, 224.

78. Ibid., 181.

79. Ibid., 224.

80. Ibid.

81. Halberstam, *Female Masculinities*, 132.

82. Lorde, *Zami*, 151.

Notes to Chapter 3

1. Réage, *Story of O*, 1.

2. The *New York Times* obituary for Aury notes that "French censors forbade any publicity for the novel when it appeared in 1954 under the pseudonym Pauline Réage. . . . But the book sold millions of copies and in 1955 it won the Deux-Magots prize, an important French literary award" ("Dominique Aury," 90).

3. Réage was revealed to be Dominique Aury, née Anne Desclos, in 1994. Dominique Aury was a well-known translator and Paulhan's lover (De St. Jorre, "Unmasking of O," 42).

4. Paulhan, "Happiness in Slavery," xxv.

5. Ibid.

6. Ibid.

7. Ibid.

8. Ibid.

9. Gearhart, for example, performs this reading of Foucault; she writes, "It is true that the term sadomasochism was rarely, if ever, used by Foucault in his discussion of political power. But even if it remains implicit in his work, a concept of sadomasochism is nonetheless central to both the social and psychological dimension of Foucault's theory" ("Foucault's Response," 389).

10. See Dworkin, "Woman as Victim," and Griffin, "Sadomasochism."

11. Réage, *Story of O*, 14.

12. Ibid., 15.

13. Griffin, "Sadomasochism," 190.

14. Barthes, *Mythologies*, 51.

15. Ibid.

16. Griffin, "Sadomasochism," 190.

17. Réage, *Story of O*, 95.

18. Ibid., 96.

19. Ibid., 98.

20. Griffin, "Sadomasochism," 188–89.

21. Réage, *Story of O*, 7.

22. Foucault, "Technologies of the Self," 18.

23. Foucault writes that technologies of power "determine the conduct of individuals and submit them to certain ends or domination, an objectivizing of the subject" (ibid.).

24. Sandra Lee Bartky, "Foucault, Femininity."

25. Unfortunately, this rush to get the book to an American audience led to the production of a truncated version of Beauvoir's two-volume opus. The translator of the American version, Howard Parshley, a biologist by training, has been much maligned for failing to accurately translate Beauvoir's

philosophical language. There are many discussions of the translation's failings; see Moi, "While We Wait," and Simons, "Silencing of Simone."

26. For a direct comparison between Beauvoir's and Sartre's concepts of transcendence, see Lundgren-Gothlin, "Simone de Beauvoir's Notions."

27. Given the extensive literature on the limitations of Parshley's translation, I will give the citation for his version of the text and the original French. If there is a particular issue in the translation, I will address it. Beauvoir, *Second Sex*, 399 [*Deuxième sexe*, 1:474].

28. Ibid., 400 [*Deuxième sexe*, 1:474].

29. Moi states, "When Beauvoir writes that the body is a not a thing, but a situation, she means that the body-in-the-world that we are, is an embodied intentional relationship to the world. Understood as a situation in its own right, the body places us in the middle of many other situations. Our subjectivity is always embodied, but our bodies do not always bear the mark of sex." That is to say, it is not because of biology that women were faced with this predicament; rather, what it means to be a woman is defined by how society views the role of women in that given space and time. Moi, *What Is a Woman?*, 67.

30. Beauvoir, *Second Sex*, 615: "Il veut qu'elle soit l'*Autre*; mais tout existant, si éperdument qu'il se renie, demeure sujet; il la veut objet: elle *se fait* objet; dans le moment où elle se fait etre, elle exerce une libre activité; c'est là sa trahison originelle; la plus docile, la plus passive est encore conscience" [*Deuxième sexe*, 2:332].

31. Ibid., 598 [*Deuxième sexe*, 2:307].

32. Ibid., 598 [*Deuxième sexe*, 2:307].

33. Here we can see the resonance with Audre Lorde's description of the erotic as a potent form of mutuality.

34. Ibid., 401 [*Deuxième sexe*, 1:476].

35. The Marquis de Sade (Donatien Alphonse-François de Sade) was an eighteenth-century French aristocrat who was notorious for his violent, pornographic writings and unconventional lifestyle. He was imprisoned for his writings and died in prison. For centuries, his name was synonymous with perversion and deviance. In the early twentieth century, however, he was resurrected as a philosopher of freedom. The Marquis de Sade was hailed as a hero for his thinking outside of the paradigm of the Enlightenment; existentialists admired his authenticity as signaled by his radical freedom, and surrealists applauded his ability to think outside of the confines of the prevailing system. This rereading of Sade as a philosopher rather than a pervert was made possible in part because of Freud's depathologization of the pervert and the universalization of sadism and masochism. Dean, *Self and Its Pleasures*, covers this period of Sade's rediscovery.

36. Steintrager, "Liberating Sade."

37. Bergoffen, *Philosophy of Simone de Beauvoir*, 131.

38. Beauvoir, *Marquis de Sade*, 37.

39. Butler, "Beauvoir on Sade," 176.

40. I am aware that my focus on the erotic elides the importance of violence for Beauvoir's philosophy. For an interpretation of Beauvoir's examination of violence, see Murphy, "Between Generosity and Violence."

41. Beauvoir, *Second Sex*, 692 [*Deuxième sexe*, 2:449].

42. Ibid., 400 [*Deuxième sexe*, 1:475].

43. Ibid., 393 [*Deuxième sexe*, 1:470].

44. Moore, "Frigidity, Gender," 335.

45. Beauvoir, *Second Sex*, 598 [*Deuxième sexe*, 2:307].

46. Beauvoir's use of biology problematizes her notion of transcendence, whose space is in large measure crafted out of the ambiguity between the limits of woman's physiology and her unlimited potential. The materiality with which Beauvoir discusses women's bodies (and their horrors) contradicts the existentialism of transcendence. Moi uncovers this problem in her essay "Existentialism and Feminism." In analyzing Beauvoir's description of the female body, Moi writes, "It is as if women's bodies produce a negative, monstrous and immensely powerful discourse of their own, one which always intrinsically threatens to undermine the very same women's emancipatory project" (90). Against the trappings of the body, woman cannot reach transcendence. Moi further writes, "By this logic, then, the 'woman' to be liberated must first and foremost be freed from that which makes her a woman in the first place: her own body" (90). Moi wishes to suggest that this dilemma is a productive one and underscores a tension that many feminists face: "As a feminist she could hardly argue either that woman can be reduced to their physiology or that women have nothing at all to do with the female body" (90). Though I agree with Moi's analysis of the inconsistency between Beauvoir's theory of transcendence and her scrutiny of the female body, her examination of Beauvoir's use of biology is lacking. Beauvoir's analysis of the science is provocative, regardless of the consequences for her theory, which are, as Moi discusses, detrimental. Beauvoir's relationship to biology is complex and often contradictory; she employs a multitude of diverse strategies to combat ideas of female inferiority, yet her description of the female body's biological victimization marks the discourse an oppressive one (Moi, "Ambiguity and Alienation").

47. Beauvoir, *Second Sex*, 22 [*Deuxième sexe*, 1:59].

48. Ibid., 23 [*Deuxième sexe*, 1:61].

49. Beauvoir's description of menopause underscores this idea of corporeal entrapment. Menopause brings slight feminine relief because "woman is now delivered from the servitude imposed by her female nature, but she is not likened to a eunuch, for her vitality is unimpaired. . . . Often, indeed, this release from female physiology is expressed in a health, a balance, a vigor [the woman] lacked before." Ibid., 31 [*Deuxième sexe*, 1:71].

50. Deleuze, "Coldness and Cruelty," 20.

51. Ibid., 33.

52. Ibid., 101.

53. Ibid., 47.

54. Ibid., 51.

55. Ibid., 52.

56. L. Sacher-Masoch, *Venus in Furs*, 246.

57. Wolff links Sacher-Masoch's emphasis on furs to his attachment to the Hasidic Jews in Galicia (introduction, vii–xxviii).

58. Janos, "Politics of Backwardness."

59. Wolff, introduction.

60. For more on female vampires in literature, see Gladwell and Havoc, "Erogenous Disease"; McNally, *In Search of Dracula*; Twitchell, *Living Dead*; Whitehead, "Vampire in Nineteenth-Century Literature."

61. L. Sacher-Masoch, *Venus in Furs*, 148.

62. For more on feminine symbols of domination, see Dijkstra, *Idols of Perversity*.

63. Krafft-Ebing, *Psychopathia Sexualis, Translation*, 96. Another man wrote, "A person hired by me could never take the place in my imagination of a 'cruel mistress.' I doubt whether there are sadistically constituted women like Sacher-Masoch's heroines." Krafft-Ebing, *Psychopathia Sexualis with especial Reference* [trans. Rebman], 136.

64. Ibid., 126.

65. Krafft-Ebing, *Psychopathia Sexualis, Translation*, 92.

66. Ibid., 93.

67. The following is one such passage of banter:

> "To be the slave of a woman, a beautiful woman whom I love and worship."
>
> "And who in return ill-treats you!" laughed Wanda.
>
> "Yes, who fetters me, whips me and kicks me and who all the while belongs to another."
>
> "And who has the impudence, after driving you mad with jealousy, to confront you with your happy rival, to hand you over to his brutality. Why not? Or does the final picture appeal to you less?" (L. Sacher-Masoch, *Venus in Furs*, 180)

68. Djikstra, *Idols of Perversity*, 374.

69. Wanda changed her name from Aurora von Römelin in order to better resemble the character in the book.

70. W. Sacher-Masoch, *Confessions*, i.

71. Ibid., 119.

72. Drawing on Modleski's work (*Feminism without Women*), Stewart, in *Sublime Surrender*, argues that masochism is "feminism without women."

73. L. Sacher-Masoch, *Venus in Furs*, 258.

74. Djikstra, *Idols of Perversity*.

75. Deleuze, "Coldness and Cruelty," 61, 61, 60.

76. Ibid., 63.

77. Ibid., 66.

78. Ibid., 68.

79. Deleuze, "On Philosophy," 144.

80. James, in "Complicity and Slavery," describes Beauvoir's understanding of complicity not as bad faith but as "a condition of an embodied self whose abilities, and therefore options, have been formed by its social circumstance" (152).

81. In an intriguing harmony with Deleuze, Sontag describes O's trajectory toward becoming an object as "becom[ing] more what she is, a process identical with the emptying out of herself" ("Pornographic Imagination," 55). Sontag reads O's masochism as a form of liberation. In this, O fulfills the promise of desubjectification that Deleuze describes. Further, Sontag describes O's desire for objectification not "as a by-product of her enslavement . . . but as the point of her situation, something she seeks and eventually attains" (55). Sontag's reading of *The Story of O* removes O from the patriarchal milieu and focuses on her agency, which she describes as her own desire to annihilate herself in order to reach sexual fulfillment. Sontag writes, "O's quest is neatly summed up in the expressive letter which serves her for a name. 'O' suggests a cartoon of her sex, not her individual sex but simply woman; it also stands for a nothing" (55). Sontag brings focus to O's desires, which she understands as occurring in a separate sphere from the desires of the men around her. O, she argues, uses her agency to become an object and transcend her humanity. That this goal directly opposes Beauvoir's (and existentialism's) valorization of subjectivity complexifies our notion of agency.

Sontag's description of O's selflessness introduces a way of reading *The Story of O* as a love story. She writes, "My own view is that 'Pauline Réage' wrote an erotic book. The notion implicit in *Story of O* that eros is a sacrament is not the 'truth' behind the literal (erotic) sense of the book . . . but, exactly, a metaphor for it" (68–69). Sontag's invocation of the erotic, though different from Beauvoir's and Lorde's, nevertheless leads us toward looking at intersubjectivity in the context of the novel. What does it mean to look at eros as a sacrament rather than an affective exchange?

82. Réage, *Story of O*, 193.

83. Ibid., 199.

84. Benjamin, *Bonds of Love*, 52.

85. Ibid., 52.

86. Ibid., 53.

87. Ibid., 55.

88. Ibid., 56.

89. Sartre, *Being and Nothingness*, 378.

90. Ibid., 379.

91. Ibid., 376.

92. In this way love is different from Hegel's master-slave dialectic, which is premised on the desire to annihilate the Other despite the need for recognition from him or her. Sartre writes, "What the Hegelian Master is for the Slave, the lover wants to be for the beloved. But the analogy stops here, for with Hegel, the master demands the Slave's freedom only laterally and, so to speak, implicitly, while the lover wants the beloved's freedom *first* and *foremost*." Ibid., 370.

93. Ibid., 378.

94. Ibid.

95. Réage, *Story of O*, 187.

96. Ibid.

97. Sartre, *Being and Nothingness*, 378.

98. Ibid., 379.

99. Ibid.

100. Ibid.

101. Dean, "Productive Hypothesis," 287.

102. Beauvoir, *Second Sex*, 642 [*Deuxième sexe*, 2:477].

103. Ibid., 643 [*Deuxième sexe*, 2:478].

104. Ibid., 650 [*Deuxième sexe*, 2:489].

105. Ibid., 669 [*Deuxième sexe*, 2:507].

106. Severin, the Austrian protagonist of *Venus in Furs*, is a man from privilege; he is wealthy and well educated, and he wants to be Wanda's slave. Larry Wolff describes *Venus in Furs* as having "a perverse nostalgia for slavery" (introduction, xvii). He singles out Wanda's statement "I want to be *alone in having a slave*" as an illustration of the familiarity Sacher-Masoch and, indeed, his readers would have had with the actual practice of slavery (xvii). Wolff goes even further and links Severin's fantasies of class inversion with the peasant struggle in Sacher-Masoch's native Galicia. Wolff is not alone in his reading of Sacher-Masoch. Wanda's cruelty is marked both by her ethnicity—her initiation into cruelty is signaled by her request for a whip that is "like those they use in Russia on disobedient slaves"—and her emotional coldness (183).

107. I. Gibson, *English Vice*.

108. Réage, *Story of O*, 138.

109. L. Sacher-Masoch, *Venus in Furs*, 232.

110. Ibid., 233.

111. Shapin, "Invisible Technicians," 558.

112. Spillers, "Interstices," 74.

113. Halberstam, *Female Masculinities*, 112.

114. Ibid., 133.

115. Réage, *Story of O*, 141.

116. Paulhan, "Happiness in Slavery," xxi.

117. Ibid., xxii.

118. Ibid., xxxvi.

119. Hammonds, "Black (W)holes," 131.

120. For an overview of the upheaval facing France during this time, see Agulhon, *French Republic*; Marceau, *Class and Status*; Kelly, *Cultural and Intellectual Rebuilding*.

121. For an analysis of how decolonization affected France identity politics, see Shepard, *Invention of Decolonization*, and Ross, *Fast Cars*.

122. Ross and Shepard make this argument in their respective books, *Fast Cars* and *Invention of Decolonization*.

123. Dean, "Productive Hypothesis," 287.

124. Stoler's *Race and the Education of Desire* reads the Foucauldian subject of *The History of Sexuality* against the colonial archive to argue that this subject's embeddedness in modernity must be considered against the colonial archive.

Notes to Chapter 4

1. Fanon, *Black Skin*, 165 [*Peau noire*, 134].

2. Ibid., 167 [*Peau noire*, 135].

3. "'Sale nègre!' ou simplement: 'Tiens, un nègre!'" Ibid., 109 [*Peau noire*, 88].

4. Ibid., 109, 112 [*Peau noire*, 88, 90].

5. Ibid., 113 [*Peau noire*, 91].

6. Ibid., 150 [*Peau noire*, 122].

7. Freud, "Mourning and Melancholia," 585.

8. Fanon, *Black Skin*, 112 [*Peau noire*, 90].

9. Ibid.

10. Fuss, *Identification Papers*, 40.

11. Sartre, *Being and Nothingness*, 631.

12. Fanon, *Black Skin*, 116 [*Peau noire*, 94].

13. Sedgwick, "Shame, Theatricality," 36.

14. Fanon, *Black Skin*, 113 [*Peau noire*, 91].

15. Ibid., 138 [*Peau noire*, 112].

16. Ibid. [*Peau noire*, 112].

17. In his examination of this, Bhabha argues that through mimicry this dialectic is problematized in many ways and that the master is also potentially imperiled by this nonrecognition (*Location of Culture*, 40–66).

18. The only way for the slave to act, however, is through negation, what we can identify as Kojève's historical motor. Negation hides the impossibility

of desire. The first act of negation is the slave's imagining of his work as for himself and not for the master, and the second act is his imagining of his existence as being more than simply a being-toward-death. This ability to imagine difference and enact change is attributed to negativity. As Nichols says, "This negativity is the key to radical freedom, through which a human being is not determined once and for all in all decisive respects by what is given in its initial being" (*Alexandre Kojève*, 29).

19. Fanon, *Black Skin*, 156 [*Peau noire*, 127].

20. Ibid., 63 [*Peau noire*, 51].

21. Bergner, "Who Is That Masked Woman?"

22. Chow, "Politics of Admittance."

23. Andrade, "Nigger of the Narcissist"; Sparrow, "Capécia, Condé"; Duffus, "When One Drop Isn't Enough."

24. Fanon, *Black Skin*, 42 [*Peau noire*, 34; "une énorme mystification"].

25. Ibid., 42 [*Peau noire*, 34; "Mayotte aime un Blanc dont elle accepte tout. C'est le seigneur. Elle ne réclame rien, n'exige rien, sinon un peu de blancheur dans sa vie"].

26. This is a reference to Pellegrini's discussion of Fanon and the infantilization of black women's desires (*Performance Anxieties*, 116–17).

27. Fanon, *Black Skin*, 47, 48 [*Peau noire*, 38].

28. Chow, "Politics of Admittance," 46.

29. Fanon, *Black Skin*, 7 [*Peau noire*, 5].

30. Ibid., 231 [*Peau noire*, 187; "Qu'il me soit permis de découvrir et de vouloir l'homme, où qu'il se trouve"].

31. Bhabha, "Foreword," vii–xlii: Gates, "Critical Fanonism."

32. Fanon, *Black Skin*, 109 [*Peau noire*, 88].

33. Ibid., 63 [*Peau noire*, 51].

34. Ibid., 81 [*Peau noire*, 66].

35. Ibid., 220 [*Peau noire*, 178].

36. Ibid., 221 [*Peau noire*, 179].

37. Ibid., 222 [*Peau noire*, 180].

38. Eng, *Feeling of Kinship*, and Puar, *Terrorist Assemblages*.

39. Brown, "Wounded Attachments," 400.

40. Ibid., 403.

41. Ibid.

42. Brown, "Desire," 55.

43. Ibid., 6. The parallels between Butler's subject and the masochist, specifically Deleuze's masochist, are numerous. Aside from the obvious linkage between subjection and submission, Butler's subject shares other similarities with the masochist Deleuze describes in "Coldness and Cruelty." In Butler, maintenance of subjectivity requires a "passionate attachment" to subordination because it preserves the illusion of coherence. Deleuze's masochist, on the

other hand, is attached to the performance of powerlessness, which he uses to shed the bonds of subjectivity (and coherence) and to permit the circulation of desire. Though these are opposing goals, they are both reached through the workings of disavowal, fantasy, and repetition. Disavowal, which Butler frames as passionate attachment, is central to the formation of the subject because it hides the debt owed to subordination. According to Butler, the subject is not merely constituted through subordination but "passionately attached" to this subordination, just as the masochist remains attached to his idea of subordination. This attachment allows the subject to maintain an illusion of coherence because it entails a disavowal of the process of subjection. Just as the masochistic subject depends on disavowal to maintain the fantasy of submission, Butler's subject uses disavowal to maintain the illusion of coherence and agency. In Deleuze's masochist, disavowal is framed by waiting and suspense, which simultaneously conceal and reveal the masochist's agency. In cloaking the masochist's agency, disavowal allows for submission. Repetition solidifies the work of disavowal and allows the fantasy (of agency in the case of the subject and powerlessness in the case of the masochist) to form. See Musser, "Masochism?"

44. Freud writes, "The real-life performances of masochistic perverts tally completely with these phantasies. . . . In both cases—for the performances are, after all, only a carrying-out of the phantasies in play—the manifest content is of being gagged, bound, painfully beaten, whipped, in some way maltreated, forced unto unconditional obedience, dirtied and debased." Freud's description of the perversion as one occurring primarily among men and concerning performances of pain and submission resonates strongly with Krafft-Ebing's descriptions of masochists. Freud, "Economic Problem," 162.

45. It should be noted that sadism could take the self as an object, but this resulted in secondary masochism, which amplified the existing erotogenic masochism.

46. Freud, "Economic Problem," 165.

47. Ibid.

48. Ibid., 167.

49. Ibid., 169–70.

50. Ibid., 170.

51. Ibid.

52. Farley, "Black Body," 475.

53. Ibid.

54. Ibid., 464.

55. Beauvoir, *Marquis de Sade*, 93.

56. Hartman, *Scenes of Subjection*, 18, 19.

57. Ibid., 19–20.

58. Halttunen, "Humanitarianism," 304.

59. Ibid.

60. Krafft-Ebing, *Psychopathia Sexualis: With Especial Reference* [trans. Klaf], 172.

61. Farley, "Black Body," 467.

62. Hartman, *Scenes of Subjection*, 52.

63. Somerville, "Queer Loving," 336.

64. Eng, *Feeling of Kinship*.

65. Rai, *Rule of Sympathy*, 163.

66. Blumrosen, "Twenty Years," quoted in Crenshaw, "Race, Reform," 1347.

67. Ellison, "Short History," 349.

68. Ibid., 350.

69. Ibid., 356.

70. Legal scholar Neil Gotanda articulates this white innocence with regard to *Brown v. Board of Education* and the evacuation of responsibility for the past harms of *Plessy v. Ferguson*. Gotanda writes, "I use 'innocence' in the sense that the Aha! Moment has, through the use of a 'new' beginning, cut off the moral, social, economic and political ties to the past. The 'innocence' is the innocence of a new beginning" ("Reflections on Korematsu," 673). See also Wiegman's "Whiteness Studies" for an analysis of the political ramifications of this ideology of innocence and color blindness.

71. Sedgwick, "Shame, Theatricality," 37.

72. In an interesting side note, one of the children studied by Freud in this work is his daughter Anna, who entered analysis with him in 1917. Young-Bruehl, *Anna Freud*.

73. Pellegrini, *Performance Anxieties*, 100.

74. Boyarin, "What Does the Jew Want?" 22.

75. Fanon, *Black Skin*, 183 [*Peau noire*, 148].

76. Pellegrini, *Performance Anxieties*, 120.

77. Ibid., 122.

78. Fanon, *Black Skin*, 115 [*Peau noire*, 93].

79. Ibid., 211 [*Peau noire*, 171].

80. Freud, "On the Universal Tendency," 190.

81. Fanon, *Black Skin*, 230 [*Peau noire*, 186].

82. Muñoz, *Cruising Utopia*, 1.

83. Beauvoir, *Second Sex*, 598 [*Deuxième sexe*, 2:307].

84. Edelman, "Part for the (W)hole," 43.

85. Fanon, *Black Skin*, 113 [*Peau noire*, 91].

86. Ibid., 197 [*Peau noire*, 159].

87. Ibid., 186 [*Peau noire*, 150].

88. Ibid., 217 [*Peau noire*, 176; "Mais l'ancien esclave veut *se faire reconnâitre*"].

89. Scott, *Extravagant Abjection*, 43.

90. Ibid., 5.

91. Ibid., 65–66.

92. Rothkopf, "Glenn Ligon," 26.

93. Glenn Ligon, "Glenn Ligon, *Untitled*."

94. In addition to essays by Okwui Enwezor, Saidiya Hartman, Bennett Simpson, Franklin Sirmans, and Hilton Als in *Glenn Ligon: America*, critical literature on these works includes Connor, *Imagining Grace*; English, "Painting Problems"; Meyer, "Glenn Ligon."

95. English, "Painting Problems," 212.

96. Rothkopf, "Glenn Ligon," 29.

97. English, "Painting Problems," 244.

98. Antonio Viego, *Dead Subjects*, 48.

99. Ibid., 108.

100. Ibid., 48.

101. Rothkopf, "Glenn Ligon," 26–27.

102. Freud, "Remembering, Repeating."

103. Ibid., 155.

104. English, "Painting Problems," 237.

105. Lorde, "Eye to Eye," 172.

106. Ibid.

107. In "Multiple Jeopardy," her historical review of the varying subject positions black women have inhabited vis-à-vis feminism and other social movements, King describes the theoretical invisibility produced by the race and gender analogy in which women's oppression is like the oppression of blacks but there is no space for overlap; the problematic discussion of "double jeopardy" in its elision of multiple spheres of oppression; the monism of movements for racial liberation; and the difficulty of considering movements solely based on socioeconomic class.

108. For more on the trope of the angry black woman, see Collins, *Black Feminist Thought*.

109. Lorde, "Eye to Eye," 145.

110. Ibid., 156.

111. Ibid., 152.

112. Ibid., 151.

113. Ibid.

114. Ibid.

115. Ahmed, *Promise of Happiness*, 67.

116. Here I am calling upon Ngai's discussion, in *Ugly Feelings*, of irritation with regard to Nella Larson's *Passing*.

117. Scott, *Extravagant Abjection*, 19.

Notes to Chapter 5

1. *Bob and Sheree's Contract*, from *Sick*.

2. Cooper, "Bob's Thing."

3. Kraus, introduction, 8.

4. Lorde, "Uses of Anger," 132.

5. Anderson, *So Much Wasted*, 38.

6. Ibid.

7. Ibid.

8. Ibid., 39.

9. I am referring here to conventional perceptions of S&M as an irrational desire for pain, which follows on the idea that masochists are behaving in ways counter to the norm in seeking out sadomasochistic relationships.

10. Bob Flanagan, "Bob Flanagan," 12.

11. *Sick*.

12. Foucault, *Discipline and Punish*, 23.

13. Ibid., 11.

14. Asad, *Formations of the Secular*.

15. Brintnall, *Ecce Homo*, 16.

16. Ibid., 36.

17. From this vantage point, we can see how Mansfield, in *Masochism*, and Silverman, in *Male Subjectivity*, have advanced arguments that masochism is a form of modern masculinity. Mansfield argues that it is emblematic of the postmodern concept of the divided (antagonistic) self, while Silverman argues that it describes a particularly pervasive form of masculinity that valorizes suffering and pain. Savran analyzes the rise of masochism as the dominant form of masculinity in late twentieth-century America in *Taking It Like a Man*.

18. *Sick*.

19. Ibid.

20. Asad, *Formations of the Secular*, 47.

21. Ibid., 69.

22. Ibid., 118.

23. Krafft-Ebing, *Psychopathia Sexualis, Translation*, 108.

24. Foucault, *Will to Knowledge*.

25. For more on this dynamic, see Musser, "Reading, Writing, and the Whip."

26. A large literature situates Jean Jacques Rousseau as one of the first to articulate a modern self. As Taylor writes in *Sources of the Self*, "Rousseau is at the origin point of a great deal of contemporary culture, of the philosophies of self-exploration, as well as of the creeds which make self-determining freedom the key to virtue. He is the starting point of a transformation in modern culture towards a deeper inwardness and a radical autonomy" (363).

27. E. Freeman, "(This Review Will Have Been)," 65.

28. Ibid., 69.

29. Sartre, *Being and Nothingness*, 335.

30. Ibid., 337.

31. Ibid., 333.

32. Svenaeus, "Phenomenology of Falling Ill," 53.

33. Flanagan, *Supermasochist*, 12.

34. For other articles on Flanagan and disability, pain, and pleasures, see Sandahl, "Bob Flanagan," and Kolářová, "Performing the Pain."

35. Flanagan, *Pain Journal*, 44.

36. Ibid., 112.

37. Ibid.

38. Ibid., 43.

39. Ibid., 98.

40. Flanagan, Rose, and Rugoff, "Visiting Hours," 66.

41. Ibid.

42. L. Hart, *Between the Body*, 134.

43. Ibid., 144.

44. Ibid., 145.

45. Ibid.

46. Ibid., 140.

47. Flanagan and Rose, "Rack Talk."

48. Jones, *Body Art*, 230.

49. Ibid.

50. Ibid., 235.

51. McRuer pursues this analysis of Flanagan to great effect in "Crip Eye."

52. Kauffman, "Bad Girls," 36.

53. Ibid., 41.

54. Deleuze, "Coldness and Cruelty."

55. Sheree Rose, interview in *Sick*.

56. Lorde, *Cancer Journals*, 25.

57. Ibid., 21.

58. Ibid., 10–11.

59. Ibid., 24.

60. Ibid., 30–31.

61. Ibid., 19–20.

62. Major, "Audre Lorde's *The Cancer Journals*."

63. Morris, "Audre Lorde," 168.

64. Alexander, "Coming Out Blackened," 696.

65. Ibid., 697.

66. Perreault, "That the Pain Not Be Wasted," 10.

67. Lorde, *Cancer Journals*, 22.

68. Ibid., 28–29.

69. Ibid., 33.

70. Ibid., 34–35.

71. Ibid., 35.
72. Alpern, *Amazons of Black Sparta*.
73. Lorde, *Cancer Journals*, 25–26.
74. Ibid., 40–41.
75. Spillers, "Mama's Baby," 74.
76. Lorde, *Cancer Journals*, 29–30.
77. Ibid., 42.
78. Ibid., 43.
79. Ibid., 44.
80. Ibid., 25.
81. Ibid., 12.
82. Ibid., 13.
83. Ibid., 20.
84. Ibid., 18.
85. Svenaeus, "Phenomenology of Falling Ill," 59.
86. Ibid.
87. For an in-depth analysis of Deleuze's health in relation to his theories of masochism, see Musser, "Reading, Writing, and Masochism."
88. Stivale, "M as in Maladie."
89. Ibid.
90. Ibid.
91. Stivale, "V as in Voyages."
92. MacCormack, *Cinesexuality*, 92.
93. Wendell, "Feminism, Disability."
94. Deleuze and Guattari, *Anti-Oedipus*.
95. Antoine Artaud, "Body Is the Body."
96. Deleuze and Guattari, "November 28, 1947," 150.
97. Ibid, 152.
98. Ibid, 159.
99. Ibid., 155.
100. Ibid.
101. Ibid., 156.
102. Deleuze, "Letter," 11.
103. Ibid.
104. Lorde, "Uses of the Erotic," 53.
105. Ibid., 58.
106. Ibid., 55.
107. Ibid., 54.
108. Ibid., 55.
109. Ibid., 56.
110. Ibid.
111. Ibid., 174.

112. Ibid., 54.
113. Ibid.
114. Ibid., 56.
115. Ibid., 58.
116. Ibid., 59.
117. Ibid., 58.
118. Ibid., 59.

Notes to the Conclusion

1. English, "New Context," 73–74.
2. Shaw, *Seeing the Unspeakable*, 38.
3. Ibid., 39.
4. Copjec, *Imagine There's No Woman*, 83.
5. Joselit, "Notes on Surface."
6. English, "New Context," 89.
7. Holland, *Erotic Life of Racism*, 66.
8. Combahee River Collective, "Black Feminist Statement," 13.
9. Nash, "Home Truths."
10. Ibid.
11. Holland, *Erotic Life of Racism*, 66.
12. Puar, "I Would Rather Be."
13. Holland, *Erotic Life of Racism*, 78.
14. Henderson, *Scarring the Black Body*.
15. Spillers, "Mama's Baby," 67.
16. Ibid.
17. Scott outlines the way these factors play into black masculinity in *Extravagant Abjection*.
18. Spillers, "Mama's Baby," 80.
19. Spillers, "Interstices," 76.
20. Ibid., 78.
21. Hammonds takes up the silence surrounding black female sexuality in her essay "Black (W)holes."
22. For a more complete analysis of black feminism's argument that representation is pernicious and "collectively presumes the meaning of the black female body in the visual field, assuming that representation is a site that necessarily injures black women," see Nash, *Black Body in Ecstasy*.
23. Collins, "Mammies, Matriarchs."
24. Nash, "Strange Bedfellows," 57.
25. Ibid.
26. Betty Saar, quoted in English, "New Context," 78.
27. Michael Harris, quoted in Dalton, "Past Is Prologue."

28. English, "New Context," 81.

29. Ibid.

30. Kara Walker, quoted in Saltz, "Kara Walker," 84.

31. English, "New Context," 84.

32. Ibid., 75.

33. Ibid., 87.

34. Walker, quoted in English, "New Context," 87.

35. Shaw, *Seeing the Unspeakable*, 43.

36. Ibid.

37. Ibid., 47.

38. Ibid.

39. Here we might think of Butler's discussion of agency in *Gender Trouble*.

40. Kara Walker, quoted in Copjec, *Imagine There's No Woman*, 98.

41. Sharpe, *Monstrous Intimacies*, 164.

42. Ibid., 157.

43. Ibid., 166.

44. Ibid., 168.

45. Scott, *Extravagant Abjection*, 155.

46. Ibid., 163.

47. Ibid., 165.

48. Ibid., 165–66.

49. Ibid., 167.

50. Ibid.

51. Ibid.

52. E. Freeman, *Time Binds*, 137.

53. Ibid., 144.

54. Ibid., 150.

55. Ibid. 144.

56. Ibid., 168.

57. Ibid.

58. W. Johnson, "Time and Revolution."

59. Sharpe, *Monstrous Intimacies*, 123.

60. Ibid., 117.

61. Ibid., 123.

62. Ibid., 121.

63. Ibid.

64. Scott, *Extravagant Abjection*, 155.

65. Ibid., 168.

66. Ibid., 171.

67. Walker, "Can This Sadomasochism Be Saved?," 207.

68. Ibid., 208.

69. Lorde, "Interview with Audre Lorde," 68.

70. Ibid.
71. Ibid., 70.
72. Williams, "Interview with the Perverted Negress."
73. In an interview with *racialicious*, a website dedicated to critical examinations of race, Williams describes the varieties of Race Play:

> We in the US like to think we have cornered the market on racial politics. So, obviously, people go for Antebellum South slavery stuff. But even there, there are many variations: you can have the White master/Black slave thing. You can have a "tables-turned" scenario, with a slave seducing the master, blackmailing them. The "Mandingo" black stud thing. And let us not forget we [Black folks] owned one another. And let us not forget the skin color caste system! "High yellow" versus dark skinned. . . .
>
> This expands to a lot of sins in this country: Whites [and] Native Americans; the internment camps where we packed up Japanese Americans.
>
> But it isn't just us. . . . How about a captured Iraqi prisoner tortured by Marines? Or a Sinn Féin extremist being interrogated by a rogue SIS agent? Or a dark skinned Indian person avenging themselves on a lighter-skinned higher-caste individual? North [and] South Koreans. Hutu [and] Tutsi. . . .
>
> The *only* limit is your imagination.
>
> This is part of the reason I boggle at the knee-jerk reaction people have. The fact that something is scary, dangerous, real: why does this mean you should *not* explore it? For fuck's sake, driving a car is dangerous. Falling in love is dangerous. Understanding that part of the draw, to me, of BDSM is that it tests my fortitude in this body and in this mind and with this heat is what keeps me doing it. How the fuck am I going to let something stop me because it is scary? (Ibid.)

74. Ibid.
75. Ibid.
76. Williams, "BDSM," 69.
77. Nash, "Strange Bedfellows," 64.
78. Ibid, 67.
79. Ibid., 68.
80. Ibid., 69.
81. Williams, "BDSM," 63.
82. Ibid., 66.
83. Ibid., 72.
84. Ibid., 70.
85. Muñoz, *Disidentifications*, 25.
86. Ibid., 8.

87. Ibid., 6.

88. Warner discusses the public life of marginalized subjects in "Mass Public."

89. Nash, "Strange Bedfellows," 57.

90. Weiss, *Techniques of Pleasure*, 189–90.

91. Ibid., 210.

92. Ibid., 211.

93. Ibid., 217.

94. Sharpe, *Monstrous Intimacies*, 176.

95. Reddy, *Freedom with Violence*, 89.

96. English, "New Context," 96.

97. Ibid.

98. Ibid., 101.

99. To a certain degree I see this project in conversation with José Esteban Muñoz's theorization of the brown commons.

100. Lorde, "Uses of the Erotic," 56.

101. Moten, *In the Break*, 26.

Bibliography

Agulhon, Maurice. *The French Republic, 1879–1992.* Oxford: B. Blackwell, 1993.

Ahmed, Sara. *The Promise of Happiness.* Durham, NC: Duke University Press, 2010.

Alexander, Elizabeth. "'Coming Out Blackened and Whole': Fragmentation and Reintegration in *Zami* and *The Cancer Journals.*" *American Literary History* 6, no. 4 (1994): 695–715.

Alpern, Stanley B. *Amazons of Black Sparta: The Women Warriors of Dahomey.* New York: New York University Press, 1999.

Anderson, Patrick. *So Much Wasted: Hunger, Performance, and the Morbidity of Resistance.* Durham, NC: Duke University Press, 2010.

Andrade, Susan Z. "The Nigger of the Narcissist: History, Sexuality, and Intertextuality in Maryse Condé's *Heremakhanon.*" *Callaloo* 16, no. 1 (1993): 213–26.

Appignanesi, Lisa. *Simone de Beauvoir.* London: Haus, 2005.

Artaud, Antoine. "The Body Is the Body." Translated by Roger Mckeon. *Semiotext(e)* 2, no. 3 (1997): 59. Originally published as "Le corps est le corps," from *Le théâtre de la cruauté,* in *Oeuvres completes,* vol. 13 (Paris: Gallimard, 1974), 287.

Asad, Talal. *Formations of the Secular.* Palo Alto, CA: Stanford University Press, 2003.

Barande, Ilse, and Robert Barande. *Histoire de la psychanalsye en France.* Paris: Regard, 1975.

Barthes, Roland. *Mythologies.* New York: Farrar, Straus and Giroux, 1972.

Bartky, Sandra Lee. "Foucault, Femininity, and the Modernization of Patriarchal Power." In *Femininity and Domination: Studies in the Phenomenology of Oppression,* 93–111. New York: Routledge, 1990.

Bauer, Heike. "'Not a Translation but a Mutilation': The Limits of Translation and the Discipline of Sexology." *Yale Journal of Criticism* 16, no. 2 (2003): 381–405.

Beauvoir, Simone de. *Le deuxième sexe.* 2 vols. Paris: Gallimard, 1949.

———. *The Marquis de Sade: An Essay by Simone de Beauvoir.* Translated by Annette Michelson. New York: Grove Press, 1996. Originally published as "Faut-il brûler Sade?" [Must We Burn Sade?] (Paris: Gallimard, 1955).

———. *The Second Sex.* Translated by H. M. Parshley. New York: Vintage Books, 1989.

Benjamin, Jessica. *The Bonds of Love: Psychoanalysis, Feminism and the Problem of Domination*. New York: Pantheon Books, 1988.

Bergner, Gwen. "Who Is That Masked Woman? Or, the Role of Gender in Fanon's *Black Skin, White Masks*." *PMLA* 110, no. 1 (1995): 75–88.

Bergoffen, Debra. *The Philosophy of Simone de Beauvoir Gendered Phenomenologies, Erotic Generosities*. New York: State University of New York Press, 1997.

Berlant, Lauren. *Cruel Optimism*. Durham, NC: Duke University Press, 2011.

———. "Neither Monstrous nor Pastoral, but Scary and Sweet: Some Thoughts on Sex and Emotional Performance in *Intimacies* and *What Do Gay Men Want?*" *Women and Performance: A Journal of Feminist Theory* 19, no. 2 (2009): 261–73.

Bersani, Leo. *The Freudian Body: Psychoanalysis and Art*. New York: Columbia University Press, 1986.

———. *Homos*. Cambridge, MA: Harvard University Press, 1995.

———. *Intimacies*. Chicago: University of Chicago Press, 2009.

———. "Is the Rectum a Grave?" *October* 43 (Winter 1987): 197–222.

Bhabha, Homi K. "Foreword: Framing Fanon." In *The Wretched of the Earth*, translated by Richard Philcox, vii–xlii. New York: Grove Press, 2004.

———. *The Location of Culture*. London: Routledge, 1994.

Blumrosen, Alfred. "Twenty Years of Title VII Law: An Overview." Unpublished manuscript, April 18, 1985, Harvard Law Library.

Boyarin, Daniel. *Unheroic Conduct: The Rise of Heterosexuality and the Invention of the Jewish Man*. Berkeley: University of California Press, 1997.

———. "What Does the Jew Want? Or the Political Meaning of the Phallus." *Discourses* 19 (1997): 21–52.

Bray, Abigail, and Claire Colebrook. "The Haunted Flesh: Corporeal Feminism and the Politics of Disembodiment." *Signs: Journal of Women and Culture* 24, no. 1 (1998): 35–67.

Brintnall, Kent L. *Ecce Homo: The Male-Body-In-Pain as Redemptive Figure*. Chicago: University of Chicago Press, 2011.

Brown, Wendy. "The Desire to Be Punished: Freud's 'A Child Is Being Beaten.'" In *Politics Out of History*, 45–62. Princeton, NJ: Princeton University Press, 2001.

———. "Wounded Attachments." *Political Theory* 21, no. 3 (1993): 390–410.

Butler, Judith. "Against Proper Objects." *differences: A Journal of Feminist Cultural Studies* 6, nos. 2/3 (1994): 1–26.

———. "Beauvoir on Sade: Making Sexuality into an Ethic." In *Cambridge Companion to Simone de Beauvoir*, edited by Claudia Card, 168–88. Cambridge: Cambridge University Press, 2003.

———. *Bodies That Matter: On the Discursive Limits of "Sex."* London: Routledge, 1993.

———. "Critically Queer." In *Bodies That Matter: On the Discursive Limits of "Sex."* New York: Routledge, 1993.

————. *Gender Trouble: Feminism and the Subversion of Identity*. London: Routledge, 1999.

————. "The Lesbian Phallus and the Morphological Imaginary." *differences: A Journal of Feminist Cultural Studies* 4, no. 1 (1993): 133–71.

————. *The Psychic Life of Power: Theories in Subjection*. Palo Alto, CA: Stanford University Press, 1997.

————. *Subjects of Desire: Hegelian Reflections in Twentieth-Century France*. New York: Columbia University Press, 1987.

Califia, Pat. "Among Us, against Us—The New Puritans." *Advocate* (San Francisco), April 17, 1980.

Caplan, Paula. *The Myth of Women's Masochism*. Toronto: University of Toronto Press, 1993.

Carron, Rene, and Raymon Lombes. *Guide de l'étudiant en psychologie*. Paris: Presses Universitaires de France, 1953.

Chafe, William Henry. *The Unfinished Journey: America since World War II*. Oxford: Oxford University Press, 2003.

Chaperon, Sylvie. "*Le deuxième sexe* en héritage." *Le Monde Diplomatique*, January 1999. www.monde-diplomatique.fr/1999/01/CHAPERON/11516.

Chemouni, Jacquy. *Histoire de la psychanalyse en France*. Que sais-je? series. Paris: Presses Universitaires de France, 1991.

Chen, Mel Y. *Animacies: Biopolitics, Racial Mattering, and Queer Affect*. Durham, NC: Duke University Press, 2012.

Cheng, Anne Anling. *The Melancholy of Race: Psychoanalysis, Assimilation, and Hidden Grief*. Oxford: Oxford University Press, 2001.

Chow, Rey. "The Politics of Admittance: Female Sexual Agency, Miscegenation, and the Formation of Community in Frantz Fanon." In *Frantz Fanon: Critical Perspectives*, edited by Anthony C. Alessandrini, 34–56. London: Routledge, 1999.

Cixous, Hélène, and Catherine Clément. *The Newly Born Woman*. Trans. Betsy Wing. Minneapolis: University of Minnesota Press, 1975.

Coalition for a Feminist Sexuality and against Sadomasochism. "Notes and Letters." *Feminist Studies* 9, no. 1 (1983): 180.

Cobb, W. Montague. "Surgery and the Negro Physician: Some Parallels in Background." *Journal of the National Medical Association* 43, no. 3 (1951): 145–52.

Colebrook, Claire. "How Queer Can You Go? Theory, Normality and Normativity." In *Queering the Non/Human*, edited by Noreen Giffney and Myra J. Hird, 17–34. Hampshire, UK: Ashgate, 2008.

————. *Understanding Deleuze*. New South Wales, Australia: Allen and Unwin, 2002.

Collins, Patricia Hill. *Black Feminist Thought: Knowledge, Consciousness, and the Politics of Empowerment*. 2nd ed. New York: Routledge, 1990.

————. "Mammies, Matriarchs, and Other Controlling Images." In *Feminist Phi-

losophies, 2nd ed., edited by Janet A. Kourany, James P. Sterba, and Rosemarie Tong, 142–52. Upper Saddle River, NJ: Prentice Hall, 1999.

Combahee River Collective. "A Black Feminist Statement." In *Capitalist Patriarchy and the Case for Socialist Feminism*, edited by Zillah R. Eisenstein. New York: Monthly Review Press, 1979.

Connor, Kimberly Rae. *Imagining Grace: Liberating Theologies in the Slave Narrative Tradition*. Chicago: University of Illinois Press, 2000.

Cooper, Dennis. "Bob's Thing." *ArtForum* 34, no. 8 (1996).

Copjec, Joan. *Imagine There's No Woman: Ethics and Sublimation*. Cambridge, MA: MIT University Press, 2002.

Cott, Nancy F. "Passionlessness: An Interpretation of Victorian Sexual Ideology, 1790–1950." *Signs* 4, no. 2 (1978): 219–36.

Crenshaw, Kimberle. "Mapping the Margins: Intersectionality, Identity Politics, and Violence against Women of Color." *Stanford Law Review* 43 (1991): 1241–99.

———. "Race, Reform, and Retrenchment: Transformation and Legitimation in Antidiscrimination Law." *Harvard Law Review* 101, no. 7 (1998): 1331–87.

Cvetkovich, Ann. *An Archive of Feelings: Trauma, Sexuality, and Lesbian Public Cultures*. Durham, NC: Duke University Press, 2003.

Dalton, Karen C. C. "The Past Is Prologue but Is Parody and Pastiche Progress? A Conversation." *IRAA* 14, no. 3 (1997): 25–27.

Dean, Carolyn. *The Frail Social Body: Pornography, Homosexuality, and Other Fantasies in Interwar France*. Berkeley: University of California Press, 2000.

———. "History, Pornography, and the Social Body." In *Surrealism: Desire Unbound*, edited by Jennifer Mundy, 227–44. Princeton, NJ: Princeton University Press, 2005.

———. "The Productive Hypothesis: Foucault, Gender and History of Sexuality." *History and Theory* 33 (1994): 271–96.

———. *The Self and Its Pleasures: Bataille, Lacan, and the History of the Decentered Subject*. Ithaca, NY: Cornell University Press, 1992.

Deleuze, Gilles. "Breaking Things Open, Breaking Words Open." Conversation with Robert Maggiori. *Libération* 2–3 (September 1986). In *Negotiations, 1972–1990*, 83–94. New York: Columbia University Press, 1995.

———. "Coldness and Cruelty." In *Masochism*. New York: Zone Books, 1991.

———. "Desire and Pleasure." Translated by Daniel W. Smith. In *Foucault and His Interlocutors*, edited by Arnold Davidson, 183–92. Chicago: University of Chicago Press, 1997.

———. *Foucault*. Translated by Seán Hand. Minneapolis: University of Minnesota Press, 1988.

———. *Francis Bacon: The Logic of Sensation*. Translated by Daniel W. Smith. Minneapolis: University of Minnesota Press, 2002.

———. "I Have Nothing to Admit." Translated by Janis Forman. *Semiotext(e)* 2 (1997): 110–17.

———. "Letter to a Harsh Critic." Translated by Martin Joughin. In *Negotiations, 1972–1990*, 3–12. New York: Columbia University Press, 1995.

———. "Mysticism and Masochism." In *Desert Islands and Other Texts, 1953–1974*, edited by David Lapoujade, translated by Michael Taormina, 131–35. Los Angeles: Semiotext(e), 2004.

———. *Nietzsche and Philosophy*. Translated by Hugh Tomlinson. New York: Columbia University Press, 2006.

———. "On Anti-Oedipus." Translated by Martin Joughin. In *Negotiations, 1972–1990*, 13–24. New York: Columbia University Press, 1995.

———. "On Philosophy." Translated by Martin Joughin. In *Negotiations, 1972–1990*, 135–56. New York: Columbia University Press, 1995.

———. "Preface for the Italian Edition of *A Thousand Plateaus*." In *Two Regimes of Madness: Texts and Interviews, 1975–1995*, edited by David Lapoujade, translated by Ames Hodes and Make Taormina, 309–10. Los Angeles: Semiotext(e), 2006.

———. "Re-presentation of Masoch." In *Essays Critical and Clinical*, translated by Daniel W. Smith and Michael A. Greco, 53–55. London: Verso, 1997.

Deleuze, Gilles, and Félix Guattari. *Anti-Oedipus: Capitalism and Schizophrenia*. Translated by Robert Hurley, Mark Seem, and Helen R. Lane. Minneapolis: University of Minnesota Press, 1983.

———. "November 28, 1947: How Do You Make Yourself a Body without Organs?" In *A Thousand Plateaus: Capitalism and Schizophrenia*, translated by Brian Massumi, 149–67. London: Athlone Press, 1988.

De Man, Paul. "Autobiography as De-Facement." *MLN* 94, no. 5 (1979): 919–30.

De St. Jorre, John. "The Unmasking of O." Life and Letters. *New Yorker*, August 1, 1994, 42.

Diamond, Elin. "The Violence of 'We': Politicizing Identification." In *Critical Theory and Performance Studies*, 403–12. Ann Arbor: University of Michigan Press, 2007.

Dijkstra, Bram. *Idols of Perversity: Fantasies of Feminine Evil in Fin-de-Siècle Culture*. Oxford: Oxford University Press, 1988.

Dinshaw, Carolyn. *Getting Medieval: Sexualities and Communities, Pre- and Post-modern*. Durham, NC: Duke University Press, 1999.

"Dominique Aury, 90; Wrote 'Story of O.'" *New York Times*, May 3, 1998.

Duffus, Cheryl. "When One Drop Isn't Enough: War as a Crucible of Racial Identity in the Novels of Mayotte Capécia." *Callaloo* 28 (4): 1091–1102.

Dworkin, Andrea. *Pornography*. New York: Perigee, 1981.

———. "Woman as Victim: Story of O." *Feminist Studies* 2, no. 1 (1974): 107–11.

Edelman, Lee. *No Future: Queer Theory and the Death Drive*. Durham, NC: Duke University Press, 2004.

———. "Part for the (W)hole." In *Homographesis: Essays in Gay Literary and Cultural Theory*, 42–78. New York: Routledge, 1994.

Ellison, Julie. "A Short History of Liberal Guilt." *Critical Inquiry* 22, no. 2 (1996): 344–71.

Eng, David. *The Feeling of Kinship: Queer Liberalism and the Racialization of Intimacy.* Durham, NC: Duke University Press, 2010.

English, Darby. "A New Context for Reconstruction: Some Crises of Landscape in Kara Walker's Silhouette Installations." In *How to See a Work of Art in Total Darkness,* 71–136. Cambridge, MA: MIT Press, 2007.

———. "Painting Problems." In *How to See a Work of Art in Total Darkness,* 201–54. Cambridge, MA: MIT Press, 2007.

Evans, Mary, and Jane Moore. "The Making and Remaking of Simone de Beauvoir." *Women: A Cultural Review* 6, no. 2 (1995): 249–55.

Fanon, Frantz. *Black Skin, White Masks.* Translated by Charles Lam Markmann. New York: Grove Press, 1967.

———. *Les damnés de la terre.* Paris: Éditions la découverte, 1985.

———. *Peau noire, masques blancs.* Paris: Éditions du Seuil, 1952.

———. *Wretched of the Earth.* Translated by Constance Farrington. New York: Grove Weidenfeld, 1991.

Farley, Anthony Paul. "The Black Body as Fetish Object." *Oregon Law Review* 76, no. 3 (1997): 457–535.

Ferguson, Roderick A. *Aberrations in Black: Toward a Queer of Color Critique.* Minneapolis: University of Minnesota Press, 2004.

Findlay, Heather. "Freud's 'Fetishism' and the Lesbian Dildo Debates." *Feminist Studies* 18, no. 3 (1992): 563–79.

Flanagan, Bob. "Bob Flanagan, Supermasochist." In *RE/Search People Series,* vol. 1, edited by Andrea Juno and V. Vale. San Francisco: RE/Search Publications, 1993.

———. *The Pain Journal.* New York: Semiotext(e), 2000.

Flanagan, Bob, and Sheree Rose. "Rack Talk: Deborah Drier Interviews Bob Flanagan and Sheree Rose." *ArtForum* 34, no. 8 (1996): 79–81.

Flanagan, Bob, Sheree Rose, and Ralph Rugoff. "Visiting Hours." *Grand Street,* no. 53, "Fetishes" (Summer 1995): 65–73.

Foucault, Michel. *Abnormal: Lectures at the College de France, 1974–1975.* Edited by Valerio Marchetti, Antonella Salomoni, and Arnold Davidson. Translated by Graham Burchell. New York: Picador, 2003.

———. *The Birth of the Clinic: An Archaeology of Medical Perception.* Translated by A. M. S. Smith. London: Routledge, 1989.

———. *The Care of the Self.* Vol. 3 of *The History of Sexuality.* Translated by Robert Hurley. London: Penguin Books, 1990.

———. *Discipline and Punish: The Birth of the Prison.* New York: Vintage, 1995.

———. "The Ethics of the Concern for Self as a Practice of Freedom." In *Ethics: Subjectivity and Truth Essential Works of Foucault, 1954–1984,* edited by Paul Rabinow, translated by Robert Hurley, 281–303. New York: New Press, 2001.

———. *History of Madness*. Translated by Jonathan Murphy. London: Routledge, 2006.

———. "Nietzsche, Genealogy, History." In *The Foucault Reader*, edited by Paul Rabinow, 76–100. New York: Pantheon Books, 1984.

———. *The Order of Things: An Archaeology of the Human Science*. New York: Vintage Books, 1994.

———. "Polemics, Politics and Problematizations." In *Ethics: Subjectivity and Truth*, vol. 1 of *Essential Works of Michel Foucault, 1954–1984*, edited by Paul Rabinow, translated by Robert Hurley, 111–20. New York: New Press, 2001.

———. Preface to *Anti-Oedipus: Capitalism and Schizophrenia*, translated by Robert Hurley, Mark Seem, and Helen R. Lane, x–xiv. Minneapolis: University of Minnesota Press, 1983.

———. *Psychiatric Power: Lectures at the College de France, 1973–1974*. Edited by Jacques Lagrange and Arnold Davidson. Translated by Graham Burchell. New York: Palgrave Macmillan, 2006.

———. "Sex, Power and the Politics of Identity." In *Ethics: Subjectivity and Truth*, vol. 1 of *Essential Works of Foucault, 1954–1984*, edited by Paul Rabinow, translated by Robert Hurley, 163–74. New York: New Press, 2001.

———. "Sexual Choice, Sexual Act." In *Ethics: Subjectivity and Truth*, vol. 1 of *Essential Works of Michel Foucault, 1954–1984*, edited by Paul Rabinow, translated by Robert Hurley, 141–56. New York: New Press, 2001. Reprint of interview by James O'Higgins, *Salmagundi* 58/59 (1982–83): 10–24.

———. *Society Must Be Defended: Lectures at the College de France, 1975–1976*. Edited by Mauro Bertani, Alessandro Fontana, Francois Ewald, David Macey. Translated by David Macey. New York: Macmillan, 2003.

———. "Technologies of the Self." In *Technologies of the Self: A Seminar with Michel Foucault*, edited by Luther Martin, 16–49. Amherst: University of Massachusetts Press, 1988.

———. *The Use of Pleasure*. Vol. 2 of *The History of Sexuality*. Translated by Robert Hurley. London: Penguin Books, 1992.

———. *The Will to Knowledge*. Vol. 1 of *The History of Sexuality*. Translated by Robert Hurley. New York: Vintage, 1990.

Foucault, Michel, and Gilles Deleuze. "Intellectuals and Power." In *Language, Counter-memory, Practice: Selected Essays and Interviews*, edited by Donald F. Bouchard, translated by Donald F. Bouchard and Sherry Simon, 205–17. New York: Cornell University Press, 1977. Reprinted from *L'Arc* 49 (n.d.): 3–10. Discussion recorded March 4, 1972.

Freeman, Elizabeth. "(This Review Will Have Been) Impossible to Write: Lesbian S/M Theory as Academic Practice." *GLQ* 5, no. 1 (1999): 63–72.

———. *Time Binds: Queer Temporalities, Queer Histories*. Durham, NC: Duke University Press, 2010.

Freeman, Ted. *Theaters of War: French Committed Theatre from the Second World War to the Cold War*. Exeter, UK: University of Exeter Press, 1998.

Freud, Sigmund. "Beyond the Pleasure Principle." Edited and translated by James Strachey. In *On Metapsychology: The Theory of Psychoanalysis: "Beyond the Pleasure Principle," "The Ego and the Id" and Other Works*, compiled and edited by Angela Richards. New York: Harmondsworth, UK: Penguin, 1984.

———. "A Child Is Being Beaten." In *The Standard Edition of the Complete Psychological Works of Sigmund Freud*, edited and translated by James Strachey, vol. 17, 175–204. London: Hogarth Press, 1957–74.

———. *Civilization and Its Discontents*. Translated by James Strachey. New York: W. W. Norton, 1989.

———. "Drei Abhandlungen zur Sexualtheorie." In *Gesammelte Werke: Chronologisch Geordnet*, vol. 5. Frankfurt: S. Fischer, 1968–78.

———. "The Economic Problem of Masochism." In *The Standard Edition of the Complete Psychological Works of Sigmund Freud*, edited and translated by James Strachey, vol. 19, 157–70. London: Hogarth Press, 1957–74.

———. *The Interpretation of Dreams*. Edited by James Strachey and translated by A. Strachey. New York: Allen and Unwin, 1971.

———. "'Ein Kind wird Geschlagen': Beitrag zur Kenntnis der Entstehung sexueller Perversionen." In *Gesammelte Werke: Chronologisch Geordnet*, vol. 12. Frankfurt: S. Fischer, 1968–78.

———. "Mourning and Melancholia." In *The Freud Reader*, edited by Peter Gay, 584–89. New York: W. W. Norton, 1995.

———. "On the Universal Tendency to Debasement in the Sphere of Love" (Contributions to the Psychology of Love II). In *(1910) Five Lectures on Psycho-Analysis, Leonardo da Vinci and Other Works*, vol. 11 of *The Standard Edition of the Complete Psychological Works of Sigmund Freud*, edited and translated by James Strachey, 177–90. London: Hogarth Press, 1957–74.

———. "Remembering, Repeating and Working-Through: Further Recommendations on the Technique of Psycho-Analysis II." In *1911–1913: The Case of Schreber, Papers on Technique and Other Works*, vol. 12 of *The Standard Edition of the Complete Psychological Works of Sigmund Freud*, edited and translated by James Strachey, 145–56. London: Hogarth Press, 1957–74.

———. *Three Essays on the Theory of Sexuality*. Edited and translated by James Strachey. New York: Basic Books, 2000.

Fullbrook, Kate, and Edward Fullbrook. *Simone de Beauvoir and Jean-Paul Sartre: The Remaking of a Twentieth-Century Legend*. Hemel Hempstead, UK: Harvester Wheatsheaf, 1993.

Fuss, Diana. *Identification Papers: Readings on Psychoanalysis, Sexuality, and Culture*. New York: Routledge, 1995.

Gates, Henry Louis. "Critical Fanonism." *Critical Inquiry* 17 (1992): 457–70.

Gearhart, Suzanne. "Foucault's Response to Freud: Sado-Masochism and the

Aestheticization of Power." *Style* 29, no. 3 (1995): 389–404.

Gerhard, Jane. *Desiring Revolution: Second-Wave Feminism and the Rewriting of American Sexual Thought, 1920 to 1982.* New York: Columbia University Press, 2001.

Gibson, Ian. *The English Vice: Beating, Sex, and Shame in Victorian England and After.* London: Duckworth, 1978.

Gibson, Margaret. "Clitoral Corruption: Body Metaphors and American Doctors' Constructions of Female Homosexuality." In *Science and Homosexualities,* edited by Vernon A. Rosario, 108–32. New York: Routledge, 1997.

Gilman, Sander L. *The Case of Sigmund Freud: Medicine and Identity at the Fin-de-Siècle.* Baltimore: Johns Hopkins University Press, 1994.

———. *Freud, Race, and Gender.* Princeton, NJ: Princeton University Press, 1995.

———. "The Jew's Body: Thoughts on Jewish Physical Difference." In *Too Jewish? Challenging Traditional Identities,* edited by N. Kleeblatt, 93–107. New Brunswick, NJ: Rutgers University Press, 1996.

Gladwell, Adèle Olivia, and James Havoc. "The Erogenous Disease." In *Blood and Roses: The Vampire in 19th Century Literature,* edited by Adèle Olivia Gladwell, 5–26. New York: Creation Books, 1992.

Gotanda, Neil. "Reflections on Korematsu, Brown and White Innocence." *Temple Political and Civil Rights Law Review* 13 (2004): 663–73.

Griffin, Susan. "Sadomasochism and the Erosion of Self: A Critical Reading of *Story of O.*" In *Against Sadomasochism: A Radical Feminist Analysis,* edited by R. R. Linden, 184–201. East Palo Alto, CA: Frog in the Well, 1982.

Grosz, Elizabeth. "Refiguring Lesbian Desire." In *The Lesbian Postmodern,* edited by Laura Doan, 67–84. New York: Columbia University Press, 1994.

Halberstam, Judith. "The Anti-social Turn in Queer Studies." *Graduate Journal of Social Science* 5 (2008): 140–56.

———. *Female Masculinity.* Durham, NC: Duke University Press, 1998.

———. *In a Queer Time and Place.* New York: New York University Press, 2005.

———. *The Queer Art of Failure.* Durham, NC: Duke University Press, 2011.

———. "The Unheroic Queer." Paper presented at "Rethinking Sex" conference, University of Pennsylvania, Philadelphia, March 4–6, 2009.

Hall, Stuart. "The After-Life of Frantz Fanon: Why Fanon? Why Now? Why Black Skin, White Masks?" In *The Fact of Blackness,* edited by Alan Read, 13–31. London: ICA, 1996.

Halttunen, Karen. "Humanitarianism and the Pornography of Pain in Anglo-American Culture." *American Historical Review* 100, no. 2 (1995): 303–34.

Hammonds, Evelynn. "Black (W)holes and the Geometry of Black Female Sexuality." *differences: A Journal of Feminist Cultural Studies* 6, nos. 2–3 (1994): 126–45.

Harris, Elizabeth. "Sadomasochism: A Personal Experience." In *Against Sadomasochism: A Radical Feminist Analysis,* 93–95. East Palo Alto, CA: Frog in the Well, 1982.

Hart, Francis R. "Notes for an Anatomy of Modern Autobiography." *New Literary History* 1, no. 3 (1970): 485–511.

Hart, Lynda. *Between the Body and the Flesh: Performing Sadomasochism*. New York: Columbia University Press, 1998.

———. "Doing It Anyway: Lesbian Sado-Masochism and Performance." *Women and Performance: A Journal of Feminist Theory* 13, no. 1 (2002): 89–105.

Hartman, Saidiya. *Scenes of Subjection: Terror, Slavery, and Self-Making in Nineteenth-Century America*. Oxford: Oxford University Press, 1997.

Henderson, Carol E. *Scarring the Black Body: Race and Representation in African American Literature*. Columbia: University of Missouri Press, 2002.

Higginbotham, Evelyn Brooks. "African-American Women's History and the Metalanguage of Race." *Signs: Journal of Women Culture and Society* 12, no. 2 (1992): 251–74.

Hoagland, Sarah Lucia. "Sadism, Masochism, and Lesbian-Feminism." In *Against Sadomasochism: A Radical Feminist Analysis*, 153–63. East Palo Alto, CA: Frog in the Well, 1982.

Holland, Sharon P. *The Erotic Life of Racism*. Durham: Duke University Press, 2012.

Hunt, Nan D. "Contextualizing the Sexuality Debate: A Chronology." In *Sex Wars: Sexual Dissent and Political Culture*, edited by Lisa Duggan and Nan Hunter, 16–29. New York: Routledge, 1995.

Imbert, Claude. "Simone de Beauvoir: A Woman Philosopher in the Context of Her Generation." Translated by Emily Grosholz. In *The Legacy of Simone de Beauvoir*, edited by Emily Grosholz, 3–21. Oxford: Oxford University Press, 2006.

Jagose, Annemarie. *Orgasmology*. Durham, NC: Duke University Press, 2012.

James, Susan. "Complicity and Slavery in *The Second Sex*." In *The Cambridge Companion to Simone de Beauvoir*, edited by Claudia Card, 149–67. Cambridge: Cambridge University Press, 2003.

Janos, Andrew. "The Politics of Backwardness in Hungary, 1825–1945." In *Balkan Economic History, 1550–1950: From Imperial Borderlands to Developing Nations*, edited by John R. Lampe and Marvin R. Jackson. Bloomington: Indiana University Press, 1982.

Jardine, Alice. "Woman in Limbo: Deleuze and His Br(others)." *Substance* 13 (1984): 46–60.

Jay, Karla, ed. *Out of the Closets: Voices of Gay Liberation*. New York: New York University Press, 1992.

Jay, Martin. *Downcast Eyes: The Denigration of Vision in Twentieth Century French Thought*. Berkeley: University of California Press, 1994.

Johnson, E. Patrick, ed. *Black Queer Studies*. Durham, NC: Duke University Press, 2005.

Johnson, Walter. "Time and Revolution in African America: Temporality and the

History of Atlantic Slavery." In *Rethinking American History in a Global Age*, edited by Thomas Bender, 148–67. Berkeley: University of California Press, 2002.

Jonel, Marissa. "Letter from a Former Masochist." In *Against Sadomasochism: A Radical Feminist Analysis*, 16–22. East Palo Alto, CA: Frog in the Well, 1982.

Jones, Amelia. *Body Art/Performing the Subject*. Minneapolis: University of Minnesota Press, 1998.

Joselit, David, "Notes on Surface: Towards a Genealogy of Flatness." *Art History* 23, no. 1 (2000): 19–34.

Judy, Ronald A. T. "Fanon's Body of Black Experience." In *Fanon: A Critical Reader*, edited by Lewis R. Gordon, T. Denean Sharpley-Whiting, and Renée T. White, 53–73. Oxford: Blackwell, 1996.

Kauffman, Linda S. "Bad Girls and Sick Boys: Inside the Body in Fiction, Film, and Performance Art." In *Getting a Life: The Everyday Uses of Autobiography in Postmodern America*, edited by Sidonie Smith and Julia Watson, 27–47. Minneapolis: University of Minnesota Press, 1996.

Keller, Richard C. "Clinician and Revolutionary: Frantz Fanon, Biography, and the History of Colonial Medicine." *Bulletin of the History of Medicine* 81 (2007): 141–47.

Kelly, Michael. *The Cultural and Intellectual Rebuilding of France after the Second World War*. London: Palgrave Macmillan, 2004.

King, Deborah K. "Multiple Jeopardy, Multiple Consciousness: The Context of a Black Feminist Ideology." *Signs* 14, no. 1 (1988): 42–72.

Kolářová, Kateřina. "Performing the Pain: Opening the (Crip) Body for (Queer) Pleasures." *Review of Disability Studies: An Interdisciplinary Journal* 6, no. 3 (2010): 44–52.

Krafft-Ebing, Richard von. *Neue Forschungen auf dem Gebiet der Psychopathia Sexualis: Eine medicinisch-psychologische Studie*. Stuttgart: F. Enke, 1890.

———. *Psychopathia Sexualis: A Medico-Forensic Study*. Translated by Dr. Harry E. Wedeck. New York: G. P. Putnam's Sons, 1965.

———. *Psychopathia Sexualis, mit besonderer Berücksichtigung der conträren Sexualempfindung: Eine klinisch-forensiche Studie*. 5th ed., partially revised. Stuttgart: F. Enke, 1890.

———. *Psychopathia Sexualis: Mit besonderer Berücksichtigung der conträren Sexualempfindung: Eine klinisch-forensische Studie*. 7th ed. Stuttgart: F. Enke, 1892.

———. *Psychopathia Sexualis, Translation of the Seventh German Edition*. Translated by Charles Chaddock. Philadelphia: F. A. Davis, 1908.

———. *Psychopathia Sexualis with Especial Reference to Antipathic Sexual Instinct: A Medico-Forensic Study, the Only Authorized English Translation of the Tenth German Edition*. Translated by F. J. Rebman. Chicago: W. T. Keener, 1901.

———. *Psychopathia Sexualis: With Especial Reference to the Antipathic Sexual Instinct: A Medico-Forensic Study, Complete English Language*. Translated by Franklin S. Klaf. New York: Arcade, 1998.

Kraus, Chris. Introduction to *The Pain Journal*, by Bob Flanagan. New York: Semiotext(e), 2000.

Kruks, Sonia. *Situation and Human Existence: Freedom, Subjectivity and Society.* London: Unwin Hyman, 1990.

Lamos, Colleen. "The Postmodern Lesbian Position: *On Our Backs.*" In *The Lesbian Postmodern*, edited by Laura Doan, 85–103. New York: Columbia University Press, 1994.

Laqueur, Thomas. *Solitary Sex: A Cultural History of Masturbation.* New York: Zone Books, 2003.

Lauretis, Teresa de. "Difference Embodied: Reflections on *Black Skin, White Masks.*" *Parallax* 23, no. 2 (2002): 54–68.

Lederer, Laura. *Take Back the Night.* New York: William Morrow, 1980.

Lieberson, Stanley. *A Matter of Taste: How Names, Fashions, and Culture Change.* New Haven, CT: Yale University Press, 2000.

Ligon, Glenn. *Glenn Ligon: America.* New Haven, CT: Yale University Press, 2011.

———. "Glenn Ligon, *Untitled (I Feel Most Colored When I Am Thrown against a Sharp White Background)*, 1990." Watch and Listen Audio Guide Stop. Whitney Museum of American Art, 2013, http://whitney.org/WatchAndListen/Artists?context=Artist&context_id=3425&play_id=372.

Linden, Robin Ruth. "Introduction: Against Sadomasochism." In *Against Sadomasochism: A Radical Feminist Analysis*, 1–15. East Palo Alto, CA: Frog in the Well, 1982.

Lorde, Audre. *The Cancer Journals.* Argyle, NY: Spinsters Ink, 1980.

———. "Eye to Eye." In *Sister Outsider: Essays and Speeches*, 145–75. New York: Random House, 2007.

———. "Interview with Audre Lorde." By Susan Leigh Star. In *Against Sadomasochism: A Radical Feminist Analysis*, 66–71. East Palo Alto, CA: Frog in the Well, 1982.

———. Uses of Anger: Women Responding to Racism." In *Sister Outsider*, 124–33. 1984. Reprint, New York: Ten Speed Press, 2007.

———. "Uses of the Erotic: The Erotic as Power." In *Sister Outsider*, 53–59. 1984. Reprint, Berkeley, CA: Crossing Press, 2007.

———. *Zami, A New Spelling of My Name—A Biomythography.* Freedom, CA: Crossing Press, 1982.

Love, Heather. *Feeling Backward: Loss and the Politics of Queer History.* Cambridge, MA: Harvard University Press, 2007.

Lundgren-Gothlin, Eva. "Simone de Beauvoir's Notions of Appeal, Desire, and Ambiguity and Their Relationship to Jean Paul Sartre's Notions of Appeal and Desire." *Hypatia* 14, no. 4 (1999): 83–95.

MacCormack, Patricia. *Cinesexuality.* London: Ashgate, 2008.

Macey, David. *Frantz Fanon: A Biography.* New York: Picador USA, 2001.

MacKinnon, Catharine. "Francis Biddle's Sister: Pornography, Civil Rights, and

Speech." In *Feminism Unmodified: Discourses on Life and Law*, 163–97. Cambridge, MA: Harvard University Press, 1987.

Major, William. "Audre Lorde's *The Cancer Journals*: Autopathography as Resistance." *Mosaic: A Journal for the Interdisciplinary Study of Literature* 35, no. 2 (2002): 39–57.

Mansfield, Nick. *Masochism: Art of Power*. Westport, CT: Praeger, 1997.

Marceau, Jane. *Class and Status in France: Economic Change and Social Immobility, 1945–1975*. Oxford: Oxford University Press, 1977.

McNally, Raymond T. *In Search of Dracula: The History of Dracula and Vampires*. Boston: Houghton, 1964.

McRuer, Robert. "Crip Eye for the Normate Guy: Queer Theory and the Disciplining of Disability Studies." Special Cluster on "Disability Studies and the University." *PMLA* 120, no. 2 (2005): 586–92.

Metz, Christian. "The Imaginary Signifier." *Screen* 16, no. 2 (1975): 14–76.

Meyer, Richard. "Glenn Ligon and the Force of Language." In *Glenn Ligon: Unbecoming*, edited by Judith Tannenbaum, 13–36. Philadelphia: Institute of Contemporary Art, University of Pennsylvania, 1997.

Mirzoeff, Nicholas. "The Right to Look." *Critical Inquiry* 37, no. 3 (2011): 473–96.

Modleski, Tania. *Feminism without Women: Culture and Criticism in a Postfeminist Age*. New York: Routledge, 1991.

Moi, Toril. "Ambiguity and Alienation in *The Second Sex*." *Boundary* 19 (1992): 96–112.

———. "Existentialism and Feminism: The Rhetoric of Biology in *The Second Sex*." *Oxford Literary Review* 8 (1986): 88–95.

———. "Politics and the Intellectual Woman: Clichés and Commonplaces in the Reception of Simone de Beauvoir." In *Simone de Beauvoir: The Making of an Intellectual Woman*, 73–92. London: Wiley-Blackwell, 1993.

———. *What Is a Woman?* Oxford: Oxford University Press, 1999.

———. "While We Wait: Notes on the English Translation of *The Second Sex*." In *The Legacy of Simone de Beauvoir*, edited by Emily Grosholz, 37–68. Oxford: Oxford University Press, 2006.

Moore, Alison. "Frigidity, Gender and Power in French Cultural History: From Jean Fauconne to Marie Bonaparte." *French Cultural Studies* 20 (2009): 331–49.

Mordier, Jean-Pierre. *Les debuts de la psychanalyse en France, 1895–1926*. Paris: Librairie Francois Maspero, 1981.

Morgan, Robin. "The Politics of Sado-Masochistic Fantasies." In *Against Sadomasochism: A Radical Feminist Analysis*, 109–23. East Palo Alto, CA: Frog in the Well, 1982.

Morris, Margaret Kissam. "Audre Lorde: Textual Authority and the Embodied Self." *Frontiers* 23, no. 1 (2002): 168–88.

Moten, Fred. *In the Break: The Aesthetics of The Black Radical Tradition*. Minneapolis: University of Minnesota Press, 2003.

Mulvey, Laura. "Visual Pleasure and Narrative Cinema." *Screen* 16, no. 3 (1975): 6–18.

Muñoz, José Esteban. *Cruising Utopia: The Then and There of Queer Futurity*. New York: New York University Press, 2009.

———. *Disidentifications*. Minneapolis: University of Minnesota Press, 1999.

Murphy, Ann V. "Between Generosity and Violence: Toward a Revolutionary Politics in the Philosophy of Simone de Beauvoir." In *The Philosophy of Simone de Beauvoir*, edited by Margaret A. Simons, 262–75. Bloomington: Indiana University Press, 2006.

Musser, Amber Jamilla. "Masochism: A Queer Subjectivity?" *Rhizomes* 11/12 (2005–6). www.rhizomes.net/issue11/musser.html.

———. "Reading, Writing, and Masochism: The Arts of Becoming." *differences: A Journal of Feminist Cultural Studies* 23, no. 1 (2012): 131–50.

———. "Reading, Writing, and the Whip." *Literature and Medicine* 27, no. 2 (2009): 204–22.

Nash, Jennifer C. *The Black Body in Ecstasy*. Durham, NC: Duke University Press, 2014.

———. "'Home Truths,' on Intersectionality." *Yale Journal of Law and Feminism* 23, no. 2 (2011): 445–70.

———. "Re-thinking Intersectionality." *Feminist Review* 89, no. 1 (2008): 1–15. www.palgrave-journals.com.offcampus.lib.washington.edu/fr/journal/v89/n1/full/fr20084a.html.

———. "Strange Bedfellows: Black Feminism and Antipornography Feminism." *Social Text* 26, no. 4 (2008): 51–76.

Ngai, Sianne. *Ugly Feelings*. Cambridge, MA: Harvard University Press, 2005.

Nichols, James H. *Alexandre Kojève: Wisdom at the End of History*. New York: Rowman and Littlefield, 2007.

Noyes, John. *The Mastery of Submission: Inventions of Masochism*. Ithaca, NY: Cornell University Press, 1997.

Oosterhuis, Harry. *Stepchildren of Nature: Krafft-Ebing, Psychiatry, and the Making of Sexual Identity*. Chicago: University of Chicago Press, 2000.

Paras, Eric. *Foucault 2.0: Beyond Power and Knowledge*. New York: Other Press, 2006.

Paulhan, Jean. "Happiness in Slavery." Preface to *The Story of O*, by Pauline Réage. New York: Grove Press, 1965.

Pellegrini, Ann. *Performance Anxieties: Staging Psychoanalysis, Staging Race*. New York: Routledge, 1996.

Perreault, Jeanne. "That the Pain Not Be Wasted: Audre Lorde and the Written Self." *A/B: Auto/Biography Studies* 4, no. 1 (1988): 1–16.

Person, Ethel Spector, ed. *On Freud's "A Child Is Being Beaten."* New Haven, CT: Yale University Press, 1997.

Puar, Jasbir. "I Would Rather Be a Cyborg Than a Goddess . . ." EIPCP. January 2011. http://eipcp.net/transversal/0811/puar/en.

———. *Terrorist Assemblages: Homonationalism in Queer Times*. Durham, NC: Duke University Press, 2007.

Rai, Amit. *The Rule of Sympathy: Sentiment, Race, and Power, 1750–1850*. New York: Palgrave, 2002.

Réage, Pauline. *The Story of O*. New York: Ballantine Books, 1981.

Reddy, Chandan. *Freedom with Violence: Race, Sexuality, and the US State*. Durham, NC: Duke University Press, 2011.

Rich, Adrienne. "Compulsory Heterosexuality and Lesbian Existence." *Signs* 5, no. 4 (1980): 631–60.

———. "The Meaning of Our Love for Women Is What We Have to Constantly Expand." In *On Lies, Secrets and Silence: Selected Prose, 1966–1978*, 223–30. New York: W. W. Norton, 1979.

Rosario, Vernon. "Phantastical Pollutions: The Public Threat of Private Vice in France." In *Solitary Pleasures: The Historical, Literary, and Artistic Discourses of Autoeroticism*, edited by Vernon Rosario, 101–32. New York: Routledge, 1995.

Ross, Kristin. *Fast Cars, Clean Bodies: Decolonization and the Reordering of French Culture*. Cambridge, MA: MIT Press, 1995.

Roth, Michael S. *Knowing and History: Appropriations of Hegel in Twentieth-Century France*. Ithaca, NY: Cornell University Press, 1988.

Rothkopf, Scott. "Glenn Ligon: America." In *Glenn Ligon: America*, 15–49. New Haven, CT: Yale University Press, 2011.

Roudinesco, Elisabeth. *Jacques Lacan & Co.: A History of Psychoanalysis in France, 1925–1985*. Translated by Jeffrey Mehlman. Chicago: University of Chicago Press, 1990.

———. *Philosophy in Turbulent Times: Canguilhem, Sartre, Foucault, Althusser, Deleuze, Derrida*. Translated by William McCuaig. New York: Columbia University Press, 2008.

Rousseau, Jean-Jacques. *Confessions*. Translated by Angela Scholar. Oxford: Oxford University Press, 2000.

Rubin, Gayle. "The Leather Menace: Comments on Politics and S/M." In *Coming to Power: Writings and Graphics on Lesbian S/M*, 194–229. Boston: Alyson, 1981.

———. "Leather Times." *Samois* 21 (2004): 3–7.

———. "The Miracle Mile: South of Market and Gay Male Leather, 1962–1997." In *Reclaiming San Francisco: History, Politics, Culture*, 247–72. San Francisco: City Light Books, 1998.

———. "Sexual Traffic." Interview by Judith Butler. *differences: A Journal of Feminist Cultural Studies* 6 (1994): 73–75.

———. "Sites, Settlements, and Urban Sex: Archaeology and the Study of Gay Leathermen in San Francisco, 1955–1995." In *Archaeologies of Sexuality*, edited by Robert Schmidt and Barbara Voss, 62–88. London: Routledge, 2000.

———. "Thinking Sex: Notes for a Radical Theory of the Politics of Sexuality." In *The Lesbian and Gay Studies Reader,* edited by Harry Abelove, 3–44. New York: Routledge, 1993.

———. "The Traffic in Women: Notes on the 'Political Economy' of Sex." In *Toward an Anthropology of Women,* edited by Rayna Reiter, 157–210. New York: Monthly Review Press, 1975.

Sacher-Masoch, Leopold von. *Venus in Furs.* In *Masochism.* New York: Zone Books, 1991.

Sacher-Masoch, Wanda von. *The Confessions of Wanda von Sacher-Masoch.* San Francisco: Re/Search Publication, 1990.

Salberg, Jill. "Hidden in Plain Sight: Freud's Jewish Identity Revisited." *Psychoanalytic Dialogues* 17, no. 2 (2010): 197–217.

Saltz, Jerry. "Kara Walker: Ill-Will and Desire." *Flash Art* 29 (November/December 1996): 82–86.

Sánchez-Eppler, Karen. *Dependent States: The Child's Part in Nineteenth-Century America.* Chicago: University of Chicago Press, 2005.

Sandahl, Carrie. "Bob Flanagan: Taking It Like a Man." *Journal of Dramatic Theory and Criticism* 15, no. 1 (2000): 97–103.

Sartre, Jean Paul. *Being and Nothingness: An Essay on Phenomenological Ontology.* Translated by Hazel E. Barnes. New York: Philosophical Library, 1969.

Savran, David. *Taking It Like a Man: White Masculinity, Masochism, and Contemporary American Culture.* Princeton, NJ: Princeton University Press, 1998.

Scott, Darieck. *Extravagant Abjection: Blackness, Power, and Sexuality in the African American Literary Imagination.* New York: New York University Press, 2010.

Sedgwick, Eve Kosofsky. "Shame, Theatricality, Queer Performance." In *Touching Feeling: Affect, Pedagogy, Performativity.* Durham, NC: Duke University Press, 2003.

Seidman, Steven. "AIDS and the Discursive Construction of Homosexuality." In *Sexualities in History,* edited by Kim M. Philips and Barry Reay, 375–85. New York: Routledge, 2002.

Shainess, Natalie. *Sweet Suffering: Woman as Victim.* Indianapolis: Bobbs-Merrill, 1984.

Shapin, Steven. "Invisible Technicians." *American Scientist* 77 (1989): 554–62.

Sharpe, Christina. *Monstrous Intimacies: Making Post-Slavery Subjects.* Durham, NC: Duke University Press, 2010.

Shaw, Gwendolyn DuBois. *Seeing the Unspeakable: The Art of Kara Walker.* Durham, NC: Duke University Press, 2004.

Shepard, Todd. *The Invention of Decolonization: The Algerian War and the Remaking of France.* Ithaca, NY: Cornell University Press, 2006.

Sick: The Life and Times of Bob Flanagan, Supermasochist. Directed by Kirby Dick with footage by Sheree Rose. Lions Gate, DVC, 1997.

Silverman, Kaja. *Male Subjectivity at the Margins*. New York: Routledge, 1992.

Simons, Margaret A. *Beauvoir and the Second Sex: Feminism, Race, and the Origins of Existentialism*. Lanham, MD: Rowman and Littlefield, 1999.

———. "The Silencing of Simone de Beauvoir: Guess What's Missing from *The Second Sex.*" *Women's Studies International Forum* 6, no. 5 (1983): 559–64.

Smith, Pamela. *The Body of the Artisan: Art and Experience in the Scientific Revolution*. Chicago: University of Chicago Press, 2004.

Somerville, Siobhan. *Queering the Colorline: Race and the Invention of Homosexuality in American Culture*. Durham, NC: Duke University Press, 1999.

———. "Queer Loving." *GLQ* 33, no. 2 (2005): 335–70.

Sontag, Susan. "The Pornographic Imagination." In *Styles of Radical Will*, 35–73. New York: Macmillan, 2002.

Sparrow, Jennifer. "Capécia, Condé, and the Antillean Woman's Identity Quest." *MaComère* 1 (1998): 179–87.

Spillers, Hortense. "Interstices: A Small Drama of Words." In *Pleasure and Danger: Exploring Female Sexuality*, edited by Carole Vance, 73–100. London: Pandora, 1989.

———. "Mama's Baby, Papa's Maybe: An American Grammar Book." *Diacritics* 17, no. 2 (1987): 64–81.

Stanley, Adam C. "Hearth, Home, and Steering Wheel: Gender and Modernity in France after the Great War." *Historian* 66, no. 2 (2004): 233–53.

Steintrager, James A. "Liberating Sade." *Yale Journal of Criticism* 18, no. 2 (2005): 351–79.

Stewart, Suzanne. *Sublime Surrender: Male Masochism at the Fin-de-Siecle*. Ithaca, NY: Cornell University Press, 1998.

Stivale, Charles. "M as in Maladie/Illness." In "Overview of Gilles Deleuze's ABC Primer, with Claire Parnet." July 28, 2011. www.langlab.wayne.edu/CStivale/D-G/ABC2.html#anchor770565.

———. "V as in Voyages." In "Overview of Gilles Deleuze's ABC Primer, with Claire Parnet." July 28, 2011. www.langlab.wayne.edu/CStivale/D-G/ABC2.html#anchor770565.

Stockton, Kathryn. *Beautiful Bottom, Beautiful Shame: Where "Black" Meets "Queer."* Durham, NC: Duke University Press, 2006.

Stoler, Ann Laura. *Race and the Education of Desire: Foucault's History of Sexuality and the Colonial Order of Things*. Durham, NC: Duke University Press, 1995.

Stowe, Steven. *Doctoring the South: Southern Physicians and Everyday Medicine in the Mid-Nineteenth Century*. Chapel Hill: University of North Carolina Press, 2004.

Sulloway, Frank J. *Freud, Biologist of the Mind: Beyond the Psychoanalytic Legend*. New York: Basic Books, 1979.

Svenaeus, Fredrik. "The Phenomenology of Falling Ill: An Explication, Critique and Improvement of Sartre's Theory of Embodiment and Alienation." *Human Studies* 32 (2009): 53–66.

Taylor, Charles. *Sources of the Self: The Making of Modern Identity*. Cambridge, MA: Harvard University Press, 1989.

Terry, Jennifer. *An American Obsession: Science, Medicine, and Homosexuality in Modern Society*. Chicago: University of Chicago Press, 1999.

Treichler, Paula. *How to Have Theory in an Epidemic: Cultural Chronicles of AIDS*. Durham, NC: Duke University Press, 1999.

Turkle, Sherry. *Psychoanalytic Politics: Jacques Lacan and Freud's French Revolution*. London: Free Association Books; New York: Guilford Press, 1992.

Twitchell, James B. *The Living Dead: A Study of the Vampire in Romantic Literature*. Durham, NC: Duke University Press, 1981.

Viego, Antonio. *Dead Subjects: Toward a Politics of Loss in Latino Studies*. Durham, NC: Duke University Press, 2007.

Vintges, Karen. *Philosophy as Passion: The Thinking of Simone de Beauvoir*. Bloomington: Indiana University Press, 1996.

Walker, Alice. "A Letter of the Times, or Can This Sado-Masochism Be Saved?" In *Against Sadomasochism: A Radical Feminist Analysis*, 205–8. East Palo Alto, CA: Frog in the Well, 1982.

Warner, Michael. "The Mass Public and the Mass Subject." In *Publics and Counterpublics*, 159–86. New York: Zone Books, 2005.

Weiss, Margot. *Techniques of Pleasure: BDSM and the Circuits of Sexuality*. Durham, NC: Duke University Press, 2011.

Wendell, Susan. "Feminism, Disability and Transcendence of the Body." In *Feminist Theory and the Body*, edited by Janet Price and Margrit Shildrick, 324–34. London: Taylor and Francis, 1999.

Whitaker, Stephen. "A Case Study in Southern Justice: The Murder and Trial of Emmett Till." *Rhetoric and Public Affairs* 8, no. 2 (2005): 189–224.

Whitehead, Gwendolyn. "The Vampire in Nineteenth-Century Literature." *University of Mississippi Studies in English* 8 (1990): 243–48.

Wiegman, Robyn. "Whiteness Studies and the Paradox of Particularity." *Boundary 2* 26, no. 3 (1999): 115–50.

Williams, Mollena. "BDSM and Playing with Race." In *Best Sex Writing 2010*, edited by Rachel Kramer Bussel, 60–79. San Francisco: Cleis Press, 2010.

———. "Interview with the Perverted Negress." Interview by Andrea Plaid, July 9, 2009. www.racialicious.com/2009/07/10/interview-with-the-perverted-negress/.

Wilson, Elizabeth. "The Context of *Between Pleasure and Danger*." *Feminist Review* 13 (1983): 35–41.

Wolff, Larry. Introduction to *Venus in Furs*, by Leopold von Sacher-Masoch, vii–xxviii. New York: Penguin, 2000.

Wright, D. G. "Rousseau's Confessions: The Tragedy of Teleology." *Journal of Social and Political Thought* 1, no. 4 (2003). www.yorku.ca/jspot/4/rousseau. html.

Young-Bruehl, Elisabeth. *Anna Freud: A Biography*. New York: Summit Books, 1988.

Index

113–115; recognition in context of, 90, 93–95, 106–107, 116–117; *ressentiment* in context of violent revolution and, 96; sensations in context of, 29, *112*, 113–116; sexuality and, 88–89, 93–94, 93–95; shame in context of, 91–92, 107–108; subjectivity in context of revolutionary nationalism and, 95–96, 109; subjectivity of black women in context of, 116, 203n107; suffering in context of temporality and, 115; temporality in context of, 103–104, *112*, 113–116; white guilt and, 29; whiteness in context of sexuality and, 93–95. *See also* becoming-black; blackness

becoming-black: abjection and, 20, 109–110, 165–166; black body and, 89, 108; flesh in context of black body and, 108; history in context of blackness and, 108–109; identity formation in modernity and, 96–98; laboring black men's body in context of whiteness and, 93–96; liberal subject as motivated by white guilt and, 29, 47–48, 97, 98–100; pain in context of black body and, 89; recognition linkage to blackness and, 108–109; *ressentiment* in context of identity and, 96–97; sensations in context of temporality and, 108; shame in relation to identity and, 91–92; stickiness sensations in context of historical modes of racialization and, 29, 89, 111, 114–115; suffering and, 29, 89–93, 99–100; sympathy and empathy in context of, 99–100; tense black bodies in context of embodiment of temporality and, 109–110, 117. *See*

also becoming-biological linkage to blackness

Benjamin, Jessica, 28, 60, 77–79, 82, 86

Bergoffen, Debra, 67

Berlant, Lauren, 28

Bersani, Leo, 14–16, 188n38

Bhabha, Homi K., 95, 199n17

biology: blackness linkage to, 88–89; women's body and, 68–69, 195n46. *See also* becoming-biological linkage to blackness

black body: becoming-biological in context of, 29, 88–89, 100, 107–108, 114–115; becoming-black in context of, 89, 108; depersonalization in relation to othering of, 89; as flesh, 19–20, 107–108; othering of, 27, 53, 89, 101; in pain, 29, 89, 100, 114–115; power of, 114–115; as tense, 109–110, 117; white subjectivity production in context of othering, 89, 101; wound/woundedness of, 20. *See also* laboring black body

black butch, 54–57, 85

black female body: flesh in context of, 30, 155, 156–161, 176; sensations in context of, 83–85; wound/woundedness and, 20, 155, 157–161, 173. *See also* black women

black female masochism: agency of, 30, 173, 178, 180–181; BDSM in context of race play and, 172–178, 209n73; black butch and, 54–57; blackness in context of race play and, 175, 177; cultural difference in context of race play and, 174–175, 177; disidentification in context of race play and, 175–176; historical play in context of, 167; interracial relations in context

desubjectification: eroticism in
context of, 30, 146, 156, 181,
194n33; illness and pain in context
of, 29–30, 146–149; masochism
as practice of, 2, 29–30, 141,
143–146, 148, 180, 197n81,
200n43; politics of, 29–30, 149;
sensations in context of colonial
racism and, 46–48; subversive
mode of masochism and, 2. *See
also* subjectivity
Deutsch, Hélène, 48
Diamond, Elin, 25, 189n64
difference: agency in context of, 18,
30; black women in context of
sexuality and, 160–161; colonial
racism and, 53; embodiment of,
1–2; empathetic reading and,
19, 22–24; masochism and, 2, 3,
18–19; power and, 18–19, 33–35;
sensations in context of, 1, 3,
22–24; sexuality in context of, 30;
subversion in context of power
and, 12, 18–19
Dijikstra, Bram, 73–75
dildo debates, 31, 40–43, 191n55
Dinshaw, Carolyn, 24
Diop, David, 51
disidentification, 175–176
distance: colonial racism in context
of, 32, 46, 53–54; patriarchy in
context of, 27, 31–33, 35–39, 53
dominance: colonial racism, 32,
46, 48–53, 191n55, 192n71;
as compromised in context
of masochism, 119, 123, 131;
distance in context of radical
feminism and, 27, 53; masochism
in context of institutionalization
of, 171; objectification in context
of feminine, 60; patriarchy and, 27,
31, 33–34, 36–41, 39, 44–45, 53,

55–57; power in context of, 172;
radical feminism in context of, 27,
33, 38, 43–45, 53, 191n40. *See also*
power
Dreier, Deborah, 131
Duffus, Cheryl, 94
Dworkin, Andrea, 35–36

Edelman, Lee, 17, 18, 108
empathetic reading: affect and, 20,
21–24; corporeality of reading
and, 20, 21, 24–25; difference
and, 19, 22–24; embodied
knowledge production and, 21,
189n55; flesh and, 19, 21, 24;
intensive reading practice and,
20, 23–24; lived experiences and,
21–23, 25; multiplicity in context
of, 19, 21, 24–25, 153, 189n64;
pain and, 24; sensations and,
20–24, 189n53
empathy and sympathy: becoming-
biological in context of, 101–102,
117; becoming-black in context of,
99–100; black women in context
of histories and, 166; masochism
in context of, 106, 130, 170–171;
miscegenation analogy in context
of, 100–101; race in context of, 29,
100–102
End of Uncle Tom . . . , The (Walker),
151–152, *153*, 154, 162–163,
177–179
Eng, David, 96, 101
English, Darby, 111, 113, 152, 154–
155, 161–163, 179
equality, 39, 47, 68, 90, 92, 101–102
erotic, the, and Lorde, 30, 139–141,
146–148, 156, 181, 194n33
eroticism: authentic emotions or
relations and, 67–68, 82, 195n40;
confession in context of, 123–125,

inability to act as masochist and, 105–106; masochism as, 5–8, 73, 186n13, 196n63; subjectivity and, 28; submission and, 7–8, 78

Farley, Anthony Paul, 99, 100, 102

fear, of black men, 46, 48–49, 51, 54

feelings, and sensation, 23, 25, 39, 149

femininity: illness and pain in context of, 133, 136, 140; in radical feminism, 26, 31–34, 39–40, 54–55, 190n22; recognition in context of blackness and, 95; submission linkage to, 4, 27–28, 60, 64–69, 65, 185n3

feminism and radical feminism. *See* radical feminism and feminism

Ferguson, Roderick A., 29

Findlay, Heather, 41

Flanagan, Bob, and topics discussed: overview of sadomasochistic performance art, 29, 118–119, 120, 132–133; agency in context of chronic illness, 119, 121; agency in context of masochism, 121, 123, 133; *Bob and Sheree's Contract* (film), 118–119, 120, 127; body as flesh in context of chronic illness, 126, 129–130, 132; body as object in context of chronic illness, 128–130; Christianity in context of masochism, 123; coldness in context of masochism, 128, 132–133; corporeal intimacy and survival in context of masochism, 121, 130–133, 141; dominance as compromised in context of masochism, 119, 123, 131; empathy and sympathy in context of sadomasochist performances, 130; gender in context of transformation through masochism, 132–133; maternity in

context of masochism, 128, 132–133; objectification in context of chronic illness, 123, 129–130; pain in context of chronic illness, 119, 127–128; *Pain Journal,* 119; pain of masochism, 119, 121, 123, 130–133, 204n9; pain performance, 120–125, 131; phallus in context of masochism, 128, 131; physical vulnerability of white masculinity in context of masochism, 119, 131; posthumanism in context of chronic illness, 127, 132, 141; queer white masculinity in context of masochism, 130–131; realism in context of masochism, 130–131; self-knowledge in context of masochism, 121, 126, 129; shame in context of masochism, 128, 130; Sheree, Rose as collaborator in masochism, 118–119, 120, 131, 132–133; *Sick* (documentary), 118, 121; subjectivity in context of chronic illness, 119; subversion in context of masochism, 121, 127, 204n9; suffering in context of chronic illness, 122–123, 131–132; *Visible Man* (installation), 123; *Visiting Hours* (installation), 129–130; white masculinity in context of chronic illness, 128–129; white masculinity in context of masochism, 118–121, 123, 125, 130–131, 133; women's agency in context of masochism, 132–133; wound/woundedness in context of white masculinity, 118, 120

flesh: overview of, 19–20, 30; agency as absent and, 20; black body as, 19–20, 107–108; blackness linkage to, 20; empathetic reading and, 19, 21, 24; in feminism, 20;

About the Author

AMBER JAMILLA MUSSER is Assistant Professor of Women, Gender, and Sexuality Studies at Washington University in St. Louis.

Printed in the USA
CPSIA information can be obtained
at www.ICGtesting.com
JSHW021509270824
68858JS00001B/1